TO KYLE

THANK YOU

To Peter Workman: I knew you were the
   right one. That's why I pestered you for
   10 years.
To Sally Kovalchick, Lynn Strong
   and Julie Hansen, for remaining
   happy throughout the manuscript's
   many iterations.

And to my son Kyle. There is no greater
   happiness than you.

This book represents 20 years of recording all the little things that make me happy. Beginning in the sixth grade with a tiny spiral notebook, I graduated to larger notebooks and finally to a personal computer that today contains more than a million bytes' worth of word-pictures. Words, and the images they create, can be a great source of pleasure and inspiration. Sometimes, on a gray day, I flip through this collection to cheer myself up; often I use it to get ideas about what to cook for dinner or something fun to do with my son on the weekend.

As you read through these pages, give yourself time to conjure up your own images—to reminisce, wish, and dream. I hope you will find, as I did, that happiness comes from noticing and enjoying the little things in life.

A stream-of-consciousness list
pajamas at breakfast
reed-fringed lagoons
seeing the moon rise
the feel of a rug under bare feet
sweet fresh corn and tender baby green
    lima beans, drenched with cream
the "snuggle right in" feeling
a lake catching the last flecks of sunlight
    coming in over the pines
the position of your head as you bite into
    a taco
shadows cast by shutters against shiny
    white walls

a small music box that plays *The Blue
    Danube* and a tune from *La Traviata*
moderation
starting to make things happen
a baby's first tooth
teakettles
sweet-potato soufflé with miniature
    marshmallows and raisins
brass-decorated cash registers
clam-strewn sandbars
headphones
a baseball game going into extra innings
the groan of ice on a lake when the
    temperature has flirted with zero all
    week
babies who never cry
orchestras
a boat tour to see picturesque little ocher-
    and-red villages
brand-new notebooks
pachyderms
Staffordshire calico dinnerware
braiding gimp at camp
picnic-cooler colors
a rich spiced chocolate drink
the eastern seaboard
declawing the canary
medallions béarnaise
old-time radio shows
red-carpet treatment

toddlers' vocabulary
French playing cards
French toast, butter, and powdered sugar
open-weave
the cinema
leaves to sniff: pennyroyal, dill,
    bergamot, sage, geranium
fruits to smell: early apples,
    fresh strawberries
Italian cheese toast
peach/banana/cream, yellow/pink/gray/
    sand color combinations
yankee ingenuity
roast boneless duckling flambé
roast pork
ties the width of lobster bibs
uneven parallel bars
viewing everyday surroundings with a
    tourist's eye
the delicious smell of cooking food and
    the hustle and bustle of the
    preparation
the ketchup that collects at the lip of the
    bottle
Welcome Back, Kotter (TV show)
an eat-in-the-rough restaurant
cherry tomatoes stuffed with deviled ham
driving under an overpass during a storm
chew face or smash mouth = kiss
fresh ginger muffins

coffee steeped with cinnamon sticks and
   cloves and then iced
regional offerings on the menu
bags of magic tricks
eight hours of sleep
lying on your back in a snowy field;
   making an angel by moving your
   arms in arcs
paintboxes
building a bed frame
spinach and sour-cream omelets
an idyllic quiet broken only by the ripple
   of the stirring water, the splash of
   fish rising to flying insects, and the
   crackle of a driftwood campfire
stickpins
thick slices of radish, pepper, and sweet
   butter on sliced French baguette
using large scallop shells to serve
   coquilles St. Jacques, salmon
   mousse, marinated scallops,
   or shrimp cocktail
white cupcakes with multicolor sprinkles
stilt-legged wharves
writing a screenplay
aging a stew or soup
animals and toys for a nursery
the Florida Keys
Amish buggies
briefcases

hollow-stemmed Pilsner glasses

building a model car

dainty dishes of strawberries, plum
    cakes, cheesecakes, a tray of melons,
    baskets of fruit, cream, and a surprise
    salad

doing your own thing

flickering gaslights

a 10-gallon jug of fruit salad

lakeside roads with farm stands offering
    apples, pumpkins, pears, and other
    fruits and vegetables

making friends with the police

poking holes in church bulletins and
    passing notes

"skit night" at camp

jellyrolls

flipping the record-selection flaps on the
    jukebox until told to stop

nylon tennis panties

splendid "dunkers" with coffee

allowances

collecting beer cans

halcyon = calm, peaceful, happy, golden,
    prosperous, affluent

rosemary = remembrance

semi-boned duckling with plum sauce
    and fried rice

competence

hymn-sings

dim, low-hanging factory lamps
a dimly lit room with candles flickering
    in red jars
hemming your clothes
smooth, muscular arms
snorkeling
homemade cider jelly
long hands
miniature artichokes
pink butcher's paper
Montego Bay, Jamaica
10¢ ferry rides
window spray de-icer
winter as a master miniaturist
candy-stripe shirts, unironed
cinnamon coffeecake
snow outlining the elements of trees'
    architecture
dinner with laughter
funny toes
knowing there will be many surprises in
    the future
stuffing a phone booth with people
rooms with polished pine floorboards and
    doorjambs that tilt and slant and
    extra touches like silk flowers and
    current issues of antique and wildlife
    magazines
snow-white carpeting
sports-art galleries

stopping being a perfectionist

wall storage systems

Rhode Island: Newport, mansions, breakers, yachts, Block Island

tropical fruits: cherimoya, Chinese grapefruit, kiwi, mango, and papaya

two-handed backhands

Heinz tomato ketchup

an old Welsh dresser

broiled fish topped by slices of lemon and cut-up parsley, with browned butter around it

cloudy days and sunny thoughts

pipe tongs

a portable aluminum camp grill

crocheted bedspreads

floating poinsettias

working better in dull weather

food gifts

frosted-glass ceilings and pink-capped chandeliers

ghost stories and marshmallows by a fire

paper logs

apple beer

apple squares with cream cheese

Copenhagen

happy feelings emanating from the kitchen

parallel and crisscross styles of lacing sneakers

personality profiles
Marshall Field's store, Chicago
strawberry-peach pie
throwing the corsage
a wire basket filled with leafy green ferns
and eggs
working on a project
across-the-breast watch chains
Bart Starr, football player
attic junk
chrome-banded tables
curling up on a chaise longe with the
London *Times* crossword puzzle
the first week of school
for November chills: thick chili, loaves of
crusty bread, and crunchy crudités
"in the red"
horse-show ribbons on the wall
insulated food totes
moss-laden terra-cotta pots of geraniums
watching others play
mushrooms stuffed with spinach, capers,
and cheese
pasta with prosciutto and peas
test tubes
washing the car mats
a shrug of the shoulder when things don't
get done
hot peppers threaded on a long string in a
kitchen

a suit made to order
50s music
designing billboards
fish fries
"Out to din-din" signs
putting on the sound track of a favorite
    Broadway show and singing in the
    shower
Saturday lunch for leaf-rakers
watch fobs
watching the winning touchdown
waterfront properties in Maine
trammel = adjustable, two-piece pothook
after-shower cologne
children's toy ovens
"It's better to ask twice than lose your
    way once"
butter-crumbled eggs
cotton-velour terry wrap robes
eating all your snack bar items before the
    movie even starts
sauntering
getting carried away
hot sauce "chugging"
the pounding of a hammer
slumberousness
true, lasting values
spun glass
blue for delphiniums, inky dark lobelia,
    the sea, and sky

church bells pealing, lights going on, and
    a festival beginning
the poem "June" by James Russell
    Lowell
giving others ample opportunity to speak
a new canvas
Bob Greene, newspaper columnist
New Haven and Waterbury clocks
a white-gold sunrise
textile laboratories
waxed-cotton jackets
Exodus (movie, song)
BLTs at the corner coffee shop
learn-a-language playing cards
an Italian coffee press
shatterproof bottles
a slatted wooden mat for sauna or bath
    use
"not worth a red cent"
small packages wrapped with foil papers,
    bits of calico, embroidered ribbons,
    lace, and tiny flowers
toasting and buttering a little delicacy
an alarm clock that would tell you when
    to wake up—and why
"Fancy Colours" by Chicago
an apothecary jar with multicolor,
    different-shape shells
beating people at crazy eights
braking for rainbows

glass canisters with brass-handled copper
lids and copper bands around the
bases
glassed-in cupboards
pocket fishing poles
gramophones
feeling heady with optimism and warmth
Nebraska: midpoint between the Atlantic
and Pacific oceans; cowboys,
Herefords, cornfields, Arbor Day
ruby = contented mind
embossers that stamp "The Library of"
in books
incubators
kicking off your shoes and splashing your
feet in a fountain
packing cookies in popped corn
rice-basket planters
secret love notes and candy hearts hidden
all over
succulence
picking out a card and sending it to
someone who would never expect it
a cardinal's brilliance against the snow
cheering influences
archaeology buffs
decorating magazines
Coca-Cola dispensers
encouraging your children to be creative
Indian cotton shirts

weathered docks on tall stilts

modern art

old-fashioned cake tester: a bundle of
straws with shiny metal bands
around them

red velvet

spending the morning in bed, watching
old movies, collaborating on the
crossword puzzle, making popcorn,
napping, exchanging long stories of
childhood, ordering in pizza, and just
being lazy

wide pants

a cathedral of trees

jeep trips

Greek salad dressing

knee socks

oven-baked biscuits, generous amounts of
strawberries, and freshly whipped
cream

pie wedges

seeing happy parents

the D.A.R.

spending a quarter on old-favorite
"penny" candies

steaks with A-1 sauce and salt

a "winged" hairstyle after wearing
a baseball cap

the National Register of Historic Places

the best information

olive wood music boxes
cheddar-topped eggplant casserole
the brisk dusk of a late October
    evening
the cool underside of a pillow
the return of plain white Keds, the yo-yo,
    clove chewing gum
a field mouse scritch-scratching in the
    wall
Lake Michigan's shoreline
the stone pier of an old railroad bridge
The Dictionary Store, New York City
trees' preparations for winter
remembering when life moved at a more
    leisurely pace
"Never mind!"
breadfruit
cherry-vanilla fudge
the Chemical Man exhibit at Science and
    Industry Museum, Chicago
elegant tea services
feelings of security
greenbacks
light beer
tiger-stripe cats
getting home, turning off the telephone,
    turning on the radio, and hopping
    into a scent-filled tub for one hour
eight-ball
highly polished parquet floors

"The Country Store," which carries
    monogrammed sweaters, Skyr
    turtlenecks, and little gold turtle-
    buckled belts
obi sashes
princesses
spinach dip stuffed into cherry tomatoes
    and sugar snap peas or with cut-up
    fresh vegetables
swimming a quarter-mile being equal to
    running a mile
egg plates
swingsets
unimprovable culinary combos like
    champagne and caviar, milk and
    graham crackers
whispering
being sorority social chairman
building a birdhouse
chicken-filled tacos
emerald suede jackets
Chinese fern baskets
taking a short stroll before deciding on
    new shoes
crisp cotton dresses
sun-dried tomatoes, steamed shrimp,
    and sauce
going up to the attic and trying to throw
    away 10 things bigger than a
    breadbox

chilled orange juice
making new bookstore friends
taking a walk when the world is too much
island-made hammocks
polished-stone heart necklaces
chinchilla
panoramic murals
Rolex-watch copycats
television broadcasts from space
    satellites
walking a country lane on a cool morning
"Do not disturb" signs
wild roses over a cottage door
bold, exciting looks
cellophane
tree houses
custom cowboy boots, gingham dresses,
    and Smithfield ham
golfing with fathers
lemon sherbet atop a tall glass of apple
    cubes and minced berries
numerology
simple, satisfying tasks like sharpening
    pencils or straightening the clutter
    on your desk
older, atmospheric bars
game birds
candle sconces with reflectors
gymnastics
sending your spirits soaring

long light glowing on a crusted meadow
cheese-stuffed manicotti
pan-roasted potatoes
running down a beach
sunrise at 5 A.M.
tangy mint
10¢ phone calls
tender-textured yellow muffins
candles hooded with red parchment
    shades
penthouses
tuna salad
candy-stripe smocks
men's ties
minarets
January: carnation or snowdrop
repairing a lamp
cinnamony applesauce
confectioners' sugar
dentists who expect you to carry on a
    conversation with a mouthful of
    novocaine and their fingers in your
    mouth
Coney Island hot dogs
hand-operated clothes wringers
knot-tying
looking back on the past with as much
    pleasure as you get from looking
    forward to the future
Ivory soap

people knowing where they stand
    with you
shoehorns
candy-cane haystacks
two-handed solitaire
whole baked tomatoes
an old musket hanging over the fireplace
broccoli with sour-cream sauce
third markdowns
cool lakes
frozen white chocolate mousse with
    raspberry sauce
paper campaign plates, cups, and
    napkins
ripe peaches on a summer's eve
Capistrano
exploring, taking chances, being
    adventurous and spontaneous
the Hawaiian Islands
a pure silk plaid robe
spray cologne in your sneakers
coolers of cold cola
turning a plush bath sheet into a sarong
an old-fashioned wooden trencher (plate)
block-party potlucks
yard sales
a raisin sauce for baked ham bubbling on
    the stove
across-the-tub trays
barstools

sleeping gerbils
Christmas ball ornaments that open to
    reveal smaller balls
ballroom dancing
garlands draped over banisters
nosegays of silk violets, tied with lilac
    and silver ribbons
suspenders
a silly bubble of anticipation
TV studios
tossed salad with cheese cubes
washed-red color
burnishing your own philosophy
carrying cups of coffee out to the porch to
    enjoy the morning sunshine
lemon = zest
dreaming on the riverbank
a small candle in a wineglass
designer jeans and cowboy hats
easeful days, dreamless nights
washing the car while barefoot
late roses
not-fit-for-man-nor-beast February nights
putting out baskets and bowls of fresh
    cranberries, bright red apples,
    lemons studded with cloves, nuts in
    their shells, potpourri, pomegranates,
    or fresh holly
nuthatches
setting up an office

watch caps with rolled-up brims
automobile brochures
a sauce bowl and ladle
wet babies
feeling witty, confident, devastatingly
    feminine
antique or old childhood books
butter of the peanut
catamarans
getting catalogs in the mail
hot, perfumed freshen-up towels
round dice
squirrels with question-mark tails,
    burying dogwood berries in the lawn
study-hall escapades
butterscotch sundaes
stuffed pork chops, roast turkey,
    whipped potatoes, coleslaw, and
    homemade pies
touch football games
gathering around the piano in the lounge
Currier & Ives winter scenes
"Thursday's child has far to go"
aluminum pie weights
fluorescent-bright food stores
houseboats
love light
buttered maple syrup
the reverberation of a school bell
woven bags

Challah bread
new cheers
O'Hare Airport and Pancake Shop,
    Chicago
a wish box
Mexican sand dollars
sexy music
boxed cake
laying in a supply of paper plates and
    taking a week's vacation from
    dishwashing
paying attention to how different kinds of
    music affect you
designs reminiscent of Renaissance
    paintings
any refund
buying a set of postcards at a museum to
    bring the museum home with you
long phone calls
10- or 20-pound bags of apples
McDonald's hot caramel sundaes
near-perfect weather
S.W.A.K.B.A.L.W.S. = sealed with a kiss
    because a lick won't stick
on a weekend night, setting the alarm for
    2 A.M. to bake oatmeal cookies and
    read, write, or do whatever
plain cottage cheese
reaching for the sky
baby floodlights

sea-captains' houses
stationery embossers
teatime meringues, sweet and
    lightweight
slaw with celery-seed dressing
the weathered shingles of fishermen's
    shacks
an all-night vigil of pleasure
apartments
chafing dishes and skimmers of brass and
    copper reflecting kitchen firelight in
    their cheerful disks
avalanches that are harmless
beachfront vacations
brandied cranberries
challenging yourself with a jigsaw puzzle
    or electronic game
crazy kids
Mazda cars
fraternity rush week
glass cheese keepers
Scottish oatcakes
a bookcase end table
being as cute as a bug
fabric patterns: check, cord, dapple,
    diamond, dot, floral, geometric,
    herringbone, pin-check, plaid,
    polychromatic, print, rib, solid,
    speckle, stripe, swirl, windowpane
incumbents

microfiche
uncirculated pennies
handmade afghans
medallions au poivre
cranberry-honey barbecue sauce
old pharmacy-table shell lamps
old-pine Sheraton Period country kitchen
    furniture
pedometers
needlepoint planters
"When I'm good, I'm very good; but when
    I'm bad, I'm better" (Mae West)
scented shoe pillows
seeing interesting people in an elevator
floppy felt hats
steaks with mushroom sauce, peeled
    baked potatoes, and salad
western sundowns
the "horse-cow" game
fresh chunky strawberry spread
the biggest smile in the world
Elmer's Glue-All
the kind of chocolate cake that
    automatically suggests a glass of
    milk
freezing bread dough
origins of words
the quick flash of deer startled by the
    orchard's windfall
street musicians

the rhythms of speech, the blend of deep
and shrill voices, the medley of
laughs
theatrical spotlights with amber filters
Tretorn Dynamixx aerobic shoes
weekend bicyclists who collect jacket
patches the way gourmet cooks
collect recipes
when friends drop in
anesthesia
a work/sewing room
cream cheese with chives, minced parsley,
and chopped red pepper, spread on
toasted rye cocktail bread
when tulip bulbs start appearing in
grocery stores
deep-dish apple pie
feeling like a child who thinks he's
mastered the art of shoe-tying
the moon on the snow
sleeping with a jacket over you
the soft feel of cotton sheets
pineapple slices wrapped in bacon and
broiled, a warm croissant, hot
chocolate with marshmallows, and
orange juice
Life Savers
"off the beaten track"
having your luck suddenly change for the
better

raiding the refrigerator

waffles with berries and fresh fruit: peaches, nectarines, apricots, and bananas

daffodils dancing on fresh clean breezes

Difficult, Tennessee

leg of lamb and cheesecake with fresh strawberries

ragged rain clouds scudding over Long Island Sound

an edging of pansies in front of an inn

high-banked, one-car-wide lanes that lead to picture-postcard thatched villages

Anne Frank's *The Diary of a Young Girl*

wild cherry orchards

the corner of the bed that's impossible to reach when putting on new sheets

Neiman-Marcus stores

switching places in bed with your spouse

thick fur on the bottom of rabbits' feet

trim jeans

white chocolate that comes gratis after a meal

writing your memoirs

brilliance

things that fortify the spirit

Palm Beach tan color

bringing a sense of adventure to a children's birthday party

children running in and out of narrow
    streets like swallows in their chaotic
    evening flight patterns
yachting blazers
sandboxes
chilled orange or tomato juice
china blue and mushroom colors
friendship
going where there's still room
the greatest truths being the simplest
making a new bed in the spring
baked potato jackets
Goldilocks
biking around campus
Illinois: trains, Lake Michigan, wheat,
    stockyards
old tree decorations
nasturtium = splendor
village church bells
wallpaper decorated with roses
onion buns
making an apple-picking ladder
wild roses, blush-pink and spicily
    fragrant in the cool of the evening
Walt Whitman, author
All Quiet on the Western Front (book and
    movie)
calzone = pizza dough turnovers with
    cheese filling
Milford, Connecticut

wine decanted into a mason jar
celebrating the imperfections of your
    relationship
gold teeth
Filofax agenda books
helping a child find unexpected ways of
    playing with household objects
holly logs
mammoth dictionaries
pumpkin in pies, cakes, pancakes,
    muffins, quick breads, ice creams,
    cheesecakes
rumpusing around on rainy days
some really special and fitting words at
    Thanksgiving dinner
campfire parties in the desert
lanes that lead to the sea and the
    rockbound coast
wind-whistling days of January
long winter weekends
pantry shelves loaded with jars of fruit
Monticello
sandpipers
tandem snow-shoveling projects
sandwiches that taste like picnic food,
    flavored by a coal fire, with a tasty
    charred surface
community leadership
juicy hamburgers
pinstripes

tangy scent of wax and varnish
wanting to gain some perspective on your
    life, finding answers to unsolved
    dilemmas, and contemplating future
    directions
the panic button
Bonwit Teller stores
Danish oil
looking irresistible
people zooming on hang gliders
production
snow-capped volcanoes
Indian wrestling
the hum of a freezer
sponge or color-blot paintings
stockiness
two-inch-thick golden brown French toast
booths plying sweet corn, sausages, and
    draft beer
brown eggs, cauliflower, and white onions
    in a pale straw basket with a few
    bronze daisies
chocolate pound cake
the coolest/hottest/wildest colors
floats and fireworks
food that means love
maple-pecan scones with marmalade,
    butter, and jam
ripe plums
upper New York State

"spirit sticks" at pep rallies
department store fashion shows
"happy legs"
marinated vegetables
perfect balance on the subway without
    using the straps
spring collections of clothing
striking while the iron is hot
the Hamm's beer bear
flower-decked floats
Worcestershire sauce
workworkworkworkwork
a room that overlooks the high fields at
    the rear of an inn or resort
après-ski atmosphere
barbecued baby spareribs with a very
    special sauce
birch bark
carrots growing deep
cartwheels
harp seals
inspecting big caldrons bubbling with
    apple butter
kosher butcher shops
ecology
P's and Q's = pints and quarts
washing the car windows
    on the inside
a small dish of Venetian
    glass "candies"

baskets filled with fake fruit

Barbra Streisand, actress/singer

lettuce green, pearly cottage cheese,
sunny pineapple, tawny peanut, icy
white milk colors

not getting lost in a new town

osteopathy

potato skins with dip and cold roasted
green beans

sitting down and reading all your old love
letters

watching people eat corn chips

a tapestry-and-hardwood Victorian rocker

Easter basket treats

interior bay windows

a Technicolor sunset

afternoons

batter-dipped chicken topped with bacon
and covered with melted cheese

butcher-block tables

keeping the same baby-sitter for years

butter on every bite

Happy Days (TV show)

cathedrals

cats jumping down and walking away
calmly after being knocked off laps

date bread

extra rest

extremely tiny pancakes formed from the
batter that fell off the ladle

getting the guts to go jogging
hot-chocolate cups and saucers
laughing at yourself
someone laughing
saucepot and fresh vegetables
blue-jeaned students
double-pack pinochle
circuit breakers
fruit hats
vivid paisley cotton velveteen
a view of sailboats skimming the horizon
giving snakes the right of way
sea angling
lawn-cutting, garden-tending, house-
    tidying chores
a wheelbarrow for joyful rides
a wish for adventure
having lots of candles burning
boxer shorts and jockey shorts
laying out patterns or the Sunday paper
    on the kitchen table
saying yes
60 Minutes (TV show)
a Danish waffle iron
construction paper
learning a headstand
leaves becoming a restless golden drift,
    a wine-red flurry in the wind
neatly pressed pants
places where you can lunch in a swimsuit

roads winding through orchards
Noah's Ark
slam-dunks
stargazing
coatracks
Magnum Force (movie)
tabulators
"Babalu" by Desi Arnaz
seven varieties of fruit salad
a basket of balloons
cable-knit cardigans
packing lunches for the whole week
    ahead
record-platter cakes
rich and fluffy unsugared whipped cream
a cat chirping when it's happy
archaeological sites
escaping from an overwhelming
    department store and buying an
    armful of daffodils from the vendor on
    the corner
Rice Krispies cereal
the indentations on the side of a
    dictionary
judo belts
Indiana specialties: chicken and
    dumplings, roast pork with dressing,
    ham and beans, and pocketbook
    rolls—flour-dusted foldover Parker
    House rolls

"Barbara Ann" by the Beach Boys
weathered towers on high hills
blackberry ice cream
old-fashioned hot fudge sundaes
red flares
having your coffee in the park
body slips
cider jugs
Greenwich, Connecticut: "The Gateway
    to New England"
one fantastic lover in college
pretty floral-patterned plates
sheer sleeves in the glow of candlelight
sledding on the lawn
the spooky "Mary, I'm on one stair" game
strombolis
the competing claims of nature
dramatic shadows of the stooping sun
the glow of a potbellied stove
stealing a few minutes to watch the
    clouds drift by your window and the
    leaves wafting in the breeze
snowfields
the marvelous lighting effects created by
    skies, sun, clouds, and moon
evergreens
the patter of dozens of feet on pavement
the system whereby one dog can quickly
    establish an entire neighborhood
    network of barking

log cabins
baby beads
the thin red string
    you pull to
    uncover a Band-Aid
exchanging restaurant recommendations
    at breakfast
treasures within a windowpane
learning the art of compromise
tree farms
Tretorn rubber boots
used bikes
hearts warming when friends meet
American flag decals
breaking hay in half
being clear-eyed
cream-soda lollipops
deepest raisin color
everything
freshly threshed wheat, oats, and barley
refinishing a flea-market find
soft, slender skirts
daffodils dancing on fresh ocean breezes
chocolate aromas
small dinner parties
church bells chiming as a millstream
    gurgles
different card games
blueberry = ingenuous simplicity
the bulge of athletes' muscles

digital thermometers

The Electric Company (TV show)

school of spring: where little winds go to
 learn how to blow

"The Long and Winding Road" by the
 Beatles

rainstorms

Phillips screwdrivers

spicy-hot enchiladas

switching to whole-wheat bread

whirlpools

white-painted bamboo

making your house look welcoming on
 the outside

taking a bowl of berries or thick, fruity
 yogurt out to the patio or front stoop

wringer from a washing machine

writing a letter to the editor

Ali MacGraw, actress

chicken fried steak, peas, mashed
 potatoes, cornbread and butter, and a
 quart of cold milk

doing everything with flair and a sense of
 fantasy

fireplace bursts

going to sleep with a line through every
 item on the things-to-do list

hailstones

enjoying morning coffee on the terrace of
 your hotel room

preparing English-style tea with a
    teapot, your favorite loose tea and
    lemon slices
secret passages
making stained glass
taking a food-and-drink dictionary to a
    restaurant
learning to play a musical instrument
milkweed pods ripening and freeing their
    seeds to sail away on fluffy
    parachutes
Milky Way candy bars
salad served with a chilled fork
talking to reporters
volunteers
wallpaper that simulates hammered
    copper
soft music
balconies overlooking a brook and forest
balls of real butter
motels
gold topaz
Jamaica, Bermuda, or clamdigger shorts
going-out-of-business sales and auctions
Jimmy Carter, former president
pumpkin muffins with cream cheese or
    cottage cheese and ginger orange
    marmalade
golf books
lemon swizzle sticks

summer-weight slacks
time to open the windows and let the
    street sounds mingle with our own
camel's-hair jackets
completing a project while still in your
    robe and feeling productive all day
hamburgers called wimpies
inn rooms equipped with terry-cloth robes
Hank Aaron, baseball player
length, width, depth, and time
pine-clad peninsulas
sand, soft underfoot
taking the cat along to a drive-in movie
singing to your favorite music
sunbonnets
wind-surfing regattas
sunscreens
tank drums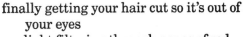
nurses' caps
wind songs
band rings
bone china
finally getting your hair cut so it's out of
    your eyes
sunlight filtering through panes of red,
    blue, and yellow leaded glass
hand-painted fireplace bellows
promenades
scones and honey and marmalade
"Colour My World" by Chicago

those lines and markings on a gym floor
    that have no purpose
a wooden Pepsi bottle case as a spice rack
"No problem!"
avoiding people who make you feel guilty
broad purple pools of shadow lying in
    every hollow
clover waking and rising in the morning
    in a slow, unfaltering stretch
windowpane-checked towels, tablecloths,
    and napkins
sipping vintage wine while a crimson fire
    crackles
crocheted snowflakes
frolicking
big hunk Chunky candy bars
puppy love
supper dances
serving French toast with hot raspberry
    sauce and chilled Bloody Marys
taping hockey sticks
vintage cooking gear
marinating
pork tenderloin dinner with French fries
dewberries
stretching out on the carpet with games
    and puzzles
strong French-roasted coffee and hot milk
    poured at the same time into large
    breakfast cups

experience
being surrounded by a grove of maple and
    sweet gum trees
Gothic lettering
antler hat racks
getting silly on two glasses of wine
the shortest day of winter
torrential downpours
vermicelli
warm-from-the-oven pastries that start
    off the day
sandwich glass knobs
work shoes
turntables
a rising middle moon
walking barefoot in the park
Barbie Doll weddings
burying the hatchet with an old friend
    with whom you had a falling out
carousels with music
tavern firelight and playing parlor games
"You name it"
six-ounce Coke bottles
fireplaces
gardening in bottles
hard, young tomatoes
horoscopes
a sailboat passing within 50 yards of
    where you're sunning yourself
seeing red

a silver George III meat skewer used as a
    letter opener
basketball
not paying attention to stupid questions
dust bowls
fishponds
lettuce-edged skirts
antique pop-up books
lots of water paints
testing a "wet paint" sign for yourself
nothing making more sense in the
    summer than forgetting to be
    sensible
watering your garden
a three-year-old's imagination
astronauts
marquetry floors
cats making velvet semicircles of
    contentment on the pillows
date-nut sauce over apple, pear, or
    pumpkin pie or ice cream
eating over at someone's house
extroverts
plumber's copper-pipe pot rack
rough wood
watching Shirley Temple movies
Paul Revere's silver
stuffed toy lambs with babies snapped on
unusual toilet seats
counting your change

country house hotels
David Brinkley and Chet Huntley,
    newsmen
giving thanks for what we have
having a picnic on the living room floor
eating Oreo cookies and then looking at
    your teeth
power-steering fluid
strawberry champagne
luxuriating in an unhurried morning
    bath
trying to wash stuffed animals
dry toast and buttered toast, muffins and
    crumpets, hot bread and cold bread,
    white bread and brown bread,
    homemade bread and baker's bread,
    wheaten bread and oaten bread
putting a flower on someone's pillow
T.T.F.W. = too tacky for words
a Western Civ. class
learning a new dance
learning to say no
Italian salad dressing shaken in a cruet
plastic bags for wet swimsuits
a sunken living room
playhouses
boys who get hoarse yelling at games
standard black dial telephones
chairs with sidearm tables
tracking mud through the house

a brainchild
a draftsman's tool kit
flat tires
boys' giant sweaters
a bathroom with mirrored walls, scented
    soaps, and great fluffy towels
a butter-churn dasher
the fresh green of spring's young shoots
embroidering a jock for a jock
lacquered basket-weave coasters
"I can't give you anything but love, baby"
the lawn of an old English country house
rock caves
tucking something special, like a little
    note, into a lunch box, briefcase,
    pocket, or purse
the hand movements of the hula
a candlelight parade
kids and video games
the vibrant colors of a Haitian painting
kids who think bath is spelled y-e-c-c-h
riding bikes and jogging along a seawall
    promenade
ice-cream pops, Eskimo pies, Good
    Humors
artistic license
keeping a few little pots of herb butter in
    the refrigerator
the clear northern Vermont air
meeting someone at the airport

open ocean, snug harbors, picturesque
     fishing boats, and gorgeous rocks
oven-fresh buttermilk biscuits
pieces of willowware
sketching in a field
the Brooklyn Dodgers
sweatsuits
sweet wine
tweedy faculty types
crowds
the attuned eye/ear/mind finding
     "tongues in trees, books in the
     running brooks, sermons in stones"
keeping busy at your highest natural
     level
the bottom of the Grand Canyon
the icicle hanging at the eave
when the February sky is gun-barrel gray
the person at theaters who tears tickets
used china
the small piece of lid that the electric can
     opener always passes over
chameleons
the subtle flavor of honey, carrots, and
     dates mingling in moist, golden
     muffins
being kind to the child in you
an extended vacation
the place where one sock in every
     laundry load disappears to

biergartens
cleaning rings with toothpaste
feeding large groups
the windows in envelopes that never line
    up with the printed return address
theater-curtain advertisements
fresh asparagus soup garnished with
    slivers of ham
greasing and dusting cake pans
starting a savings account
refrigerators filled with soda
coffeepots
log fires and feasts
night football games
dogs at field hockey practice
Edgar Bergen with Charlie McCarthy
    and Mortimer Snerd
written-on notebooks
English sling chairs
green beans spiced with dillweed and
    curry powder
high notes of an opera soprano
jailhouses
white-collar workers
being cool
philosophy
thin Swedish roll-up pancakes served
    with lingonberries or blueberries
third-grade teachers
bright yellow lemons

lining a mushroom or berry basket with a
    lace handkerchief and trimming with
    a twisted tartan ribbon
using a kite as a wall hanging
whipped cream and strawberries
The Wizard of Oz (movie)
being all spruced up
childhoods
the smell of the sea
dairy cows
doing something that will put a smile on
    your face
collapsing in bed and cuddling
going to three movies in one day
enjoying popcorn, songs, and campfire
    camaraderies
Dijon mustard and freshly ground pepper
    to add spice to life
giving a briefcase to someone who really
    needs one
bake shops
oak blocks
baked beans and home fries for breakfast
ankh rings
building a dictionary database
would-be artists
milk money
rollaway beds
split swinging doors
cold hands

hollyhocks
colored cotton balls
jumping over the widest puddle
birthday banners
remembering when kids used to want to
     be President
shivering in your stadium seat
skinny Pepsi bottles
complexion scrubbers
dimestore key chains
family-style all-you-can-eat restaurants
homemade pasta dough
the inner city
kindliness
lengthened lifespans
many small, worn Oriental rugs
pinecones
Bermuda's pink beaches
"Monday's child is fair of face"
ranch life
sun visors
winter twilight like moonlight reflected
     from a clear-iced lake, or fireglow
     seen through the frosted window
summer school breaks
campfires, campsites
sunflower, country rose, buttermilk soap
large scrapbooks
chocolate milkshakes
windows looking out on acres of woodland

announcers

banquettes of burgundy velvet, cushy as
the fur of a fat cat

remembering when there were no
McDonald's

wonderful tiny restaurants in old houses
with slanted floors

a bench at the foot of the bed that rolls on
casters for dining and writing in bed

conversing in many languages and
accents

dining by the window

Connecticut: saltboxes, church spires,
village greens, postcard towns

wearing real jewelry

finding each other being only the
beginning

honey and wheat germ

springing along a sidewalk

George Washington's cure for a cold:
eating a toasted onion before bed

an old Bordeaux wine

an overnight at a nice hotel in the city

cooking for people all weekend

tiny books to hang on the tree: *The
Nutcracker, The Night Before
Christmas,* and *A Treasury of
Christmas Carols*

crocheting

the crowing of a rooster

suntan oil

flopping in the hammock for a snooze
 before dinner

frolicking in a pile of leaves

goodnights

maple seeds whirling away on single-
 bladed helicopters

the rip-p-p of a zipper

Superball toys

a plum-pudding crock

copper-bottomed pans

hip pleats

Girl Scout Handbooks

remembering when all soda came in
 bottles and had sugar in it

fresh pineapple slices marinated in rum

maple-sugar men, spiles, and sap buckets

porcelain melon jars

Morse code

screwballs

being told you're dazzling

Paris Match magazine

stretching

thrilling to parades

firm, moist, and crusty rye and
 pumpernickel bread

turquoise umbrellas shading white
 ironwork tables and chairs

warming winter meals

a rainbow of ribbons

apricots to zucchini
burgers on homemade dilly buns
carved ivory spheres
paperback guidebooks
curling up
farmwives unbuttoning peas on the porch
hard-working waiters
in summer, bayberry and eel grass
    brushed with sun
forgetting to turn the oven on
angelica = inspiration
listening to your silent voice
massed molten colors
music by Bobby Short
visiting the playgrounds that hold special
    meaning
washing your hair in rainwater
a scrawny pup with a high-frequency tail
a sideboard set with cold meats and pies
natural wild mustard
a slippery firehouse pole
snappy comebacks to "Shut up"
a summer hamlet where cottages and
    picket fences crawl with wild roses
the certain way you smile at each other
    as soon as your eyes meet
hot-air balloons
living each day for itself
designing a brochure
St. Louis, Missouri: Gateway to the West

natural Swiss cheese
on the beach at dusk
petits pois in cream and butter
putting perfume on your bike, in your
    hair, on your neck
setting up your first aquarium
"Saturday's child works hard for a
    living"
watching TV with a bowl of ice and a fan
watermelon
a trip to the old neighborhood
alternating between reading a novel and
    looking at the hilltop skyline
antique bisque dolls
Dutch butter cookies
routines for soothing the soul
stuffed calico yo-yos
courtrooms
not being known as grouchy or mean—
    just quiet sometimes
reversible place mats
antifreeze
breathing deeply
a wedge of fresh lime to turn a glass of
    mineral water into a cocktail
six-course gastronomic dinners
trying to play the harmonica
when anyone can look at the two of
    you and tell you are head-over-heels
    in love

peach, pear, raisin, and rum cheesecakes
buying a new mascara
the buzz of a bumblebee
an English arboretum
a May wine party with crackers and
    bland cheese
khaki walking shorts
meandering
peaceful countryside
roasting the corn, hurrying it to the
    table, buttering it well, salting
    judicially
tea and a basket of assorted breads with a
    plate of sausage and cheese slices,
    and pots of honey and marmalade
planting by the moon
tear-stained pillows reminding you that
    times always get better
traveling beach mats
wearing an old necklace clasp on a chain
Chanel No. 5 cologne
the crackle of new money
a blaze of color
feasting on crisp green salads
flat trees
glasses that don't pinch your ear or nose
lobster salad on split wiener buns
ribbons as bookmarks
hot dogs called tube steak
locating the fountain of youth

the real importances: the fundamentals
  with which you have to live
pockets crammed with treasures
Wedgwood mint dish with cover
finally getting off the ground
yacht supply stations
decathlons
overlooking the ocean from a candlelit
  terrace
decorating
that excited birthday-party feeling
indicating with a long-pronged fork that
  one of the steaks on the charcoal fire
  is "yours"
Kodak photo supplies
old suitcases as coffee tables
padre hats
plexiglass
soda fountain treats
Sadie Hawkins dances
reciprocity
lemon blossom = fidelity in love
ice-cream sandwiches
riding your bike to the local farm store
driving along country roads through
  woodland valleys that smell of the
  earth; hearing leaves whipping in
  the wind
Joe Namath, football player
seeing with new eyes

the blissfully splendid smell of mustard
    at the game
shell-framed mirrors
Burger King Whoppers
sketching trees in the backyard or in
    nearby woods
the little things in life that really make
    your day go right
sweet, hot summer days when terraces
    were porches and air conditioning
    was a pitcherful of lemonade
climbing on rainbows
life after 60
the essence of humor
white beggar's cloth
the promise of a small package
adequate preparation
an extension sifter to fit any size bowl
a handful of raisins
the sweet air of spring inspiring a
    different sort of hunger
beer signs
the times when you feel you're the only
    two people in the world
bread-and-butter pickles in blue-tinted
    mason jars
tiered jewelry boxes
breakers of the fast
the gentle dip of a paddle
coed dorms

breakfast cooked over an outdoor fire
electric typewriters
green candles sitting on a bed of leaves
French hybrid grapes
life moving in mysterious ways
soft, buttery things
cleaning windshields
Ruffles potato chips
unfinished furniture
buffet table setting
cartoons from *The New Yorker*
megaphones
vegetable dressing of crunchy mustard
    seeds in thick, creamy sauce, honey,
    brown sugar, horseradish, olive oil,
    and eggs
huge dunes
"Shaving Cream" (song)
priorities
raisin bread pudding
egg tosses
shiny hair
sticky fingers after eating cotton candy
"Dirty Harry" movies
thinking happy summer thoughts
coffee, tea, or milk
triplexes
tying shirts up high
using a paint roller
white sand

bringing home brush for cooking fires,
    shed roofing, and the cow's bed
building a dollhouse
genealogy charts
the Maine wilderness
making your own quotation book
attending a concert after work
baked beans cooked in maple syrup and
    liquid smoke
hanging in there
millionaire's pie: coconut flakes,
    chocolate chips, pecans in an amber
    filling
sale racks
tall ships on blue-and-white porcelain tea
    jar, cups, teapot, and warmer
walking the dog and he won't do
    anything
"all the tea in China"
color film
exploring a city at a browser's pace
golf clubs
"American Pie" by Don McLean
lemon to keep vegetables from turning
    brown
something to kick you out of
    unproductive doldrums
James Taylor, singer
summer school dances
miniature tea cups and saucers

running over a piece of lint a dozen times
while vacuuming, continuing to give
the vacuum a "chance"
summertime
Tom Sawyer
being camera-shy
complimentary appetizers of barbecued
meatballs and cheese spread served
with garlic toast
inner tubes
lengthening your jeans
snow-white color
long-stemmed glasses
mini-meals
sand cats of the Sahara Desert
sunflowers
tiny cartons of milk
wine lists
bench saws
winter vacation kits
boned chicken breast in a sour-cream
sauce accented with sweet Hungarian
paprika
cinnamon and slate-blue satins
showing a child how much fun life can be
congratulatory notes
fine snow in the air
gentle head and shoulder rolls
isosceles trapezoids
looking at each tabletop as a still life

mood lighting
moonlit dances on paddlewheel
    steamboats
acting goofy
scones served with butter, jam, and
    Devonshire whipped cream
two friendly chicken appliqués on a
    plump cotton toss pillow
"moo" cows
an oversize mohair sweater and new
    tapestry flats
Avon books
Bloody Mary mix in a Tropicana orange
    juice jar
chocolate buttercream frosting
collecting kindling with a child on a crisp
    autumn afternoon
tip sheets
perpetuation
copperware
experiencing the thrill and sweat of a
    locker room
turquoise = success, prosperity
nurturing creativity
curveballs
good broth
corn-seed road signs
corned beef spiced with ginger
Dior gowns
cloud-high trees

perfect leaf lettuce and tiny onion rings
    with a wonderful vinaigrette
scrap yarn
gizmos
serving food at a fraternity dinner
throat-parching days
curling up in a ball
throwing orange or lemon peel twists into
    the fire for scent and color
worm = spiral part of corkscrew
arrowheads
the feeling of satin
Carson Pirie Scott & Company
first buds
Chris-Craft foul-weather boots
horseradish sneaking up on you
poster-bright colors
research fellowships
designing a calendar
a summer screen house
Slo-Poke, 3 Musketeers, Nestle's Crunch,
    Chunky, Heath, and Skor candy bars
wearing truly bag-out clothes
discovering your own quiet joy
gasoline-pump globes
dustcloths
attempted feedings of children
gaslights
interludes
little wool cap-hats

nuts, pinecones, seed pods, cinnamon
    sticks, plastic apples
playing patty-cake
pot roast/mashed potato meals
the peal of an organ
lingering over coffee and buttered
    muffins
watching river barges negotiate the lock
watermelon à la mode
"It's key"
situation comedies
a towel warmer in the bathroom
"as thick as oats in a feed bag"
bateau-necked shirts
saving almost everything, even Cracker
    Jack prizes
cats basking on the windowsill
ditty bags
butterscotch-striped swimsuits
getting along well with others
journalism
giving your hands cold-weather first aid
mountains of produce
plump floor cushions
stuttering when nervous
butcher-wrap dresses
houses built of butter-colored limestone
a whisper impossible to resist
having a few sugar maples near the
    house

never dramatizing a difficulty
roving photographers
get-away-from-it-all-and-relax times
having someone to come home to
newspaper stylebooks
New England pen-and-ink prints
a wonderfully desolate beach in
    November
at water's edge, empty shells that
    whisper when summer waves turn
    them
lexicology
trying a new sleeping schedule
buying something outrageous and then
    something very practical to feel
    vindicated
cozy rooms with pretty details
repositioning the Christmas tree lights so
    no two of the same color are together
40-hanger coatracks
go-getters
100 acres of mountaintop with saltbox
    house in New Hampshire
Lacoste luggage and portfolios
a January night that engraves itself on
    the senses
"Open" signs
a Twelfth Night cake
learning a new sport
Heath ice-cream bars

wearing safety glasses outside lab class
orange tea doughnuts
plain old bad habits
platters of good things to eat
reading outside on a blanket wearing a
    big sweater in the autumn sun
soaking up some extra memories
pinning your hat on
dozing
Thanksgiving dinners
traveling by bicycle
wearing white cotton
an aging flowerpot
black tin bread pans
brandy Alexander pie
chamois-cloth shirts
planning trips to country inns
chasing evil spirits
Chanel quilted purses with chain straps
one-person kayaks for rent
enamelware
teaching one another
the flat wooden "spoons" that come with
    ice-cream cups
graduation
learning to like yourself better
heavy pots
a birdwatchers' path
wide-wale corduroy shirts
naming your baby

liberating your husband from a
traditional male task now and then
and watching the benefits that come
your way
baby shoes
kick lines
Jack Frost

nocturnal drinking expeditions
picking flowers for your room at the inn
a picnic at the office for lunch
children racing headlong into the water,
joy splashing up around them
receptions
steel drums and street dancing
recreation department meetings
sack races
a chance to sleep in
kid gloves
medics' scrub pants or dresses
old calfskin wallets
the device at intersections marked "push
to cross"
the trumpet of a train passing
old mechanical banks
red brick Federalist buildings
riding a bicycle long distances
TV dinners
French onion soup, Caesar salad, and
baked bananas
ice-cream dispensers

solving problems
never forgetting the creation of a special
    moment
opening milk cartons
steamed clams, salad, and French bread
    as a light summer dinner
the Rangeley knot on moccasins
old-fashioned straw dispensers
the best things said coming last
sweatbands
cherry pie à la mode
the village telephone operator
when the worst does not happen
bread sliced slim as a leaf
cheeks all aglow with the outdoors
breaking out of an old routine
cheap thrills and satisfying
    extravagances
free books
Chevrolets
Fleet Street, London
hieroglyphics
soft, crushy leather
unfinished kindergarten blocks
big Christmas lights on trees outside a
    restaurant
defendants
fresh corn, partially husked, with sprays
    of wheat on a low straw tray
suit coats

dogs leaning against your legs
usherettes
iridescence
Irish coffee glasses
quill pens
spice-brown corduroy
spine-tingling views
trimming your own hair
using a pumice stone
white lies
an individual sconce to illuminate an
    eating booth
spiced tea
electric sanders
chicken and noodles and spaghetti served
    at the local school
chip 'n dip servers
flimflam = nonsense
ham houses
feeding ducks on the river
enjoying a glass of iced tea under the
    grape arbor
lake fish, boiled potatoes, homemade
    coleslaw, fresh-baked bread, and
    cherry pie
thin cocktail straws
skating parties
tie-dyeing
hand-cut full-lead crystal decanters
scudding clouds of spring

take-a-number stores
the ability of parents to guide their small
    children around by the tops of their
    heads
falling asleep to the sound of foghorns
miles of toilet paper in trees
multi-hued vineyards
Li'l Abner
roller skating on the sidewalk
salad with extra bowls of goodies around
homographs
walking around a swimming pool
milk paint
getting warm by a fire or in his arms
    with something to eat or drink after
    you've been in the rain or snow
yellow and red roses for Valentine's Day
"hunky-dory"
balloonmen
homemade egg noodles
collections from everyday life
making colored chalk drawings on the
    sidewalk
columnists
dill butter for corn
a gold-plated megaphone charm dangling
    from a dainty chain
half-baked people
lemon chicken, buttered peas, and stuffed
    tomatoes

men who eat cheese and drink wine
    rather than cook
tam-o'-shanters
humble pie
long socks
miniature tins of tea, jams, or jellies, or
    blended coffees for a treat
gold button earrings
getting chills when new dictionaries are
    published
hot chocolate sauce of a deep, cocoa-like
    strength
penicillin
candlelight and wine
pine-paneled lounges
singing waiters and waitresses
winter bringing long, silent nights to
    dream on
boneless breast of chicken topped with
    blue cheese
a candelabra of hand-crafted tin
cinnamon apple waffles with maple or
    cane syrup, pepper bacon, fresh fruit,
    coffee, and freshly squeezed juice
dining out
finding a newspaper someone left on
    the train when you were too cheap
    to buy one
fine-wale corduroy tent jumper
containers

funnel cakes, deep-fried to a golden
brown and served hot with a coating
of powdered sugar
hand-painted Chinese silk
hand-blown posy vases
burning an orange peel to cover bad
cooking smells
those who are up and outdoors while the
day is young and damp with dew
toolsheds
an old-fashioned slumber party with junk
food, AM hit singles, and ghost
stories
being apologetic
letting the flavors of aromatic brandy and
dark chocolate mingle on your tongue
book clubs
broiled bacon-wrapped tomatoes
clothes-drying racks
wooden chicken coops
an old American appliqué quilt folded at
the foot of the bed
cooking a quick company dinner
frosted walnut cakes
suppertime
beating the heat
apple, cranberry, or blueberry festivals
the hearth broom
using your time to cultivate gardens
hopsacking

our lives being what our thoughts make
   them
personalized wallets
listening to a child
portfolios
strange bugle sounds at basketball games
turkey cooked over a wood fire
very colorful and cleverly lit oil paintings
   and watercolors
the warbling of a canary
working too hard and getting paid for it
worn brick paths with moss-filled cracks
a river trip on a stern-wheeler
aerobatics
bare bricks and lantern lights
birds' nests
air hockey
proudly wearing a wedding band
smoking-hot biscuits
corn silk
creamy white English pitchers
ferries to New England islands
formal dance garters
garage sale antiques
inspiring yourself by self-encouragement
luscious peach chaises and floor pillows
postprandial drinks
researching a business venture
a screened-in gazebo
a singing vendor

soda water

a snowfall of powdered sugar and a sprinkling of colored sugar crystals, white icing, and tiny candles

pitching tents, setting the campfire blazing, and serving spaghetti with meatballs and tossed salad

a standing clipboard

baskets made of woven strips of construction paper, tied with ribbons and filled with sugar cookies

designing a race car

dishwasher detergent

kite-flying contests

letters from close friends in far places

mattresses

not resisting truth and beauty

outdoor thermometers

potato pancakes, sausages, and homemade applesauce

sitting in a rocker, listening to the silence and reflecting

untangling something

traditional French onion soup topped with croutons and melted cheese

treating yourself to orchestra seats for one performance

antimacassars or tidies

Astroturf on porches

buttercream frosting

cats darting through alleyways
detectives
Dots candy
hot-dogging
square-wool scarves
Southern fried chicken with hush
    puppies
touching toes in bed
vaudeville
double-decker Fifth Avenue buses
gourmet relishes for fish, beef, poultry,
    and hors d'oeuvres
investing your money
November clouds, high, gray, and passing
waving out the car's back window
advertisements with beautiful pictures of
    food, water droplets, something
    caught in motion
kiwi fruit
the smell of bathroom soap
saying "Nice doggie"
scanning a star-filled sky on a still winter
    night
anything houndstooth
Boy Scouts
a Nantucket oil lamp
leaf tours
buttering toast generously and
    immediately so that the butter melts
    and sinks in

antique irons, cameras, radios
leather hiking boots
buying a bunch of anything that is useful
    and nice
peanut-butter makers
reading a lot of strange books
snacks after a movie
plaid cotton flannel
soap balls
tea towels
wrap coats
baseballs signed by famous players
"Want him to be more of a man? Try
    being more of a woman"
    (advertisement)
an adventure such as a hike, ice skating,
    or a football game
Aladdin and his Wonderful Lamp
crackly-skinned all-beef kosher hot dogs
a glass hors d'oeuvre server with a spot
    for the dip
grapefruit, sliced bananas, berries,
    cornflakes, and poached eggs for
    breakfast
hearing a brooklet gurgling and making
    bewitching sounds under the snow as
    it goes to join the waters of the pond
hearthside
lab smocks
rubber or plastic door runners

lobster tails baked individually in pastry
    with mushrooms and butter and
    served with wild rice and a vegetable
baling hay
a bake sale with apple butter, apple
    dumplings, sausage, scrapple, cider,
    and funnel cakes
a cemetery from the 1700–1800s
dachshunds
enchiladas
hickory-grilled duck
midnight phone calls
old wicker chairs with floral fabric-
    covered seats
red candles wrapped with ribbon and lace
The Old Farmer's Almanac
soda jerks
a cat running 30 mph
when suddenly TV dinners didn't come in
    aluminum trays, popsicles didn't
    have two sticks, and everything was
    made for the microwave
children singing
wide-swinging skirts
"I don't go that route"
friendship cards
icehouses
over-the-coals herbs
seeing someone famous at a baseball
    game

omelet pans
sherbet fruit splits
special art exhibits
ambling across fields with a sketchbook
     or camera
wickerwork
special stationery for a child
steak au poivre vert
piggy banks
the chug-chug of fishing boats
spending a great deal of time walking the
     boards of your porch
the freshest of ingredients, the optimum
     in color, texture, and flavor
"the gangster of love"
melting snow making streams along the
     roadside
falling asleep on the lawn
the quintessential carrot cake
the fireplace as a combination of
     sentiment, emotion, and vague
     memories
white football shoes
being a night person
the smell of onions and Italian sausages
being the happiest in our lives
the sweet bass accompaniment of
     burbling spaghetti
Boeing 727s and 747s
the season of the harvest moon

Jesus Christ Superstar (movie)
cream cheese and jam
dressing for business
feeling the heat of the sun while sitting
    in a car
pink eye shadow
freshly delivered French bread
defending your beliefs
steel tennis rackets
rug-making
Raggedy Ann and Andy
the whine of the September air
The New York Times Book Review
sugarless bubble gum
angel hair
ice-eaters
English muffin rings
high-spired churches
being an "anti-plastic" person
"the big cheese" and "the second
    banana"
painter's pants, Lacostes, and Top-Siders
painting pictures of your garden flowers
"Silver Bells" (carol)
slipcovers
thick carpets in red, orange, and yellow
Swiss chocolate cake
thinking of the day, of your home, of
    your family, of things past, of things
    to come

waistbands
white carved statues
being able to hold a glass to your mouth
    by sheer lung power
building a fireplace
sailing slickers
chilliness
getting what you want and what you
    need at the same time
fried egg in a frame
grilled cheese club sandwiches
making toast with homemade bread
poster beds, hooked rugs, hand-stitched
    quilts, wide pine floorboards,
    stenciled wallpaper, wing chairs
taking lots of notes
baked ziti
Cokes drawn from a classic bomb-shaped
    dispenser
jelly jars
molasses sweet bread
being happy together
nylon crushed velour
fresh fruit pancakes
the reliability of restaurant food
roller skating with a pillow strapped on
telephones
"Camp Granada" by Allan Sherman
wild mushrooms, dried and arranged in a
    wooden bowl

wall desks
tabby cats
billboards
collegiate functions
cultured gray and white pearls
falling crazily, I'd-kill-or-be-killed-for-
    that-man in love
holiday petits-fours
lamb's wool and angora
memories of garden parties and weekends
    by the sea
samovars = urns with a spigot
simmering herbs and spices for good
    holiday smells
time cards
coming up with ideas
toast turning the required shade of gold
femininity
ham and Swiss cheese
miniature gingerbread cottages
Junior Miss pageants
A & W rootbeer mugs
pine-scented forests
pink Lady Baltimore layer cake
a rendezvous
a ring around the moon
sending the sheets out to the laundry for
    wrinkle-free bliss
Pennsylvania Dutch chicken-and-corn
    soup

sunny yellow napkins
vine-covered trellises
windjammer vacations
candy tins
pinked-apricot color
canisters with scoops attached
contributing something uniquely yours to
    the world
finding a place for yourself
generosity
knowing popular notions are always
    wrong
loose-leaf notebooks
moon tides
shorelines
moors covered with bayberry, wild roses,
    brambles, and cranberry vines
photocopying rare and/or expensive books
fig tree = profuseness
smoky eyes
souvenirs on the road: snowshakers,
    beaded belts, ashtrays, scene-viewers,
    pens with figures that move, bumper
    stickers, refrigerator magnets, pins,
    hats, patches, mugs, pennants
"Those who have . . . get"
sitting in a special position before a
    shocking scene in a movie
cable knit
hand-hammered dishes

lap eating

something hand-painted with tiger lilies

cardinals, quail, and robins flitting about
the rhododendron and mountain
laurel

working as an umpire

chopping fresh herbs

cool chopped tomatoes, crisp scallions,
cucumbers, green peppers, brown
olives, feta cheese, and hard-cooked
eggs

doodlebugs

"Love Grows Where My Rosemary Goes"
(song)

frosty-weather lunch or brunch

lipstick in tiny plastic tubes

napping in a hammock

papier-mâché piñatas

a potbellied-stove kind of day

apple berries, apple wines, apple country,
autumn apple color

experimental theater

margaritas

a pride of lions

Stradivarius violins

pure beeswax candles

sprigs of parsley or slivers of red pepper
highlighting monochromatic
vegetables

barbecuing

strawberry dressing for salads
crossing something dreaded off a list of
      things to do
turkey dumpling soup
turn-of-the-century type cases
warehouses
working toward goals
a reflective turn of mind and a special
      spirit of enjoyment found in New
      England
air hose = loafers without socks
barhopping
sprinklers
burning calories while resting
apple rings fried in bacon or ham
      drippings, covered with a little sugar
      glaze and served with bacon
carrying 10 books home from the library
herb-roasted chicken
musclemen
mushrooming, whether you end up with a
      bushel basketful or none
post-prom breakfast, a walk on the beach
sash windows that look out on the street
wassail = a punch made of cider,
      lemonade, orange juice, brown sugar,
      spices, and baked apples, served in a
      large bowl
a scarecrow that does not work
a sunny place set up for lunch

Casablanca (movie)
lit-from-within glow
Introverts Anonymous
not waiting too long
nut stores
a single bird making a graceful descent
    and perfectly timed splashdown
a sudden glimpse of a lit-up Christmas
    tree through a window
rotisseries: Ferris wheels for chickens
satin-paper ribbon curled into crisp
    flower shapes
watching a craftsman whip up a
    straw hat
water polo
a troop of kangaroos
buttery Danish dough
gatehouses
mountains: a canvas for clouds
sluiceways
"Soup's on!"
tough feet
blue topaz
counted cross-stitch
double mattresses on the floor
wondering why things look the way they
    look, feel the way they feel; how
    they're used and why
Doubleday bookstores
squirrels gathering nuts early

lovingness
new babies
a well-crafted chair
fawn and deer
psychology

having a sense of your own space
Edward Bear: Winnie-the-Pooh's real
    name
a yummy gourmet shop
buying an I-feel-good hat and wearing it
    on your better days
puzzles: acrostics, anagrams, charades,
    conundrums, crosswords,
    cryptograms, enigmas, mazes,
    palindromes, tongue twisters
peninsulas
FUBAR = Fouled Up Beyond All
    Recognition
sharp kids
H.M.S. Pinafore (movie)
inability to leave the theater because
    your date insists on watching the
    credits
leaves snuggled around the foundations
    of old country houses
plant food
hiking
playing in a closet as a child
snacks in the pantry
staying home on New Year's Eve

tea wagons
track-and-field days
wrap robes
an air of expectancy
beach gear
planting raspberries
brass whiskey chests
changing handwriting
"Last Train to Clarksville" by the
    Monkees
cracker baskets in restaurants
fixing gourmet meals
crayons without their "papers"
dial tones
standing next to someone you love
dwarf iris
frajitas: a sizzling platter of charbroiled
    meat served with soft flour tortillas,
    cheese, tomato, lettuce, sour cream,
    and guacamole
grapes, berries, pears in wine
heavy farm doughnuts
a blanket of vapor on a still summer day
pick-up sticks
the Morton Salt girl
picking handfuls of big purple violets,
    dogtooth violets, and anemones
the Indianapolis 500
a cascade of foliage
bicycle shoes with crepe soles

the smell of Nair hair remover

Sting, actor/singer

individual baskets with freshly squeezed
    orange juice, fresh-ground coffee,
    homemade yeast breads with sweet-
    butter jam

over-the-head shirts

kidding around with your child

a clapboard house stained Indian red
    with black and white trim

the quintessential lumberjack's
    breakfast, piled high, glistening with
    melted butter, dripping with maple
    syrup, and partnered with a few
    choice strips of bacon or plump
    sausages

old fire alarm posts

stone-washed jeans

the morning waitress

red ivory, desert mauve colors

keeping your secrets

the smell of flowers through the screens

ouzo

breakfast in bed with something good to
    read: one of the most blissful escapes

steaming cups of Darjeeling or Earl Grey

oven fries

pierced-tin lanterns

the spirit of the American man

poetry in everything

prepleated ruffling
the World Football League flop
shells and postcards
spending a lunch hour in a beautifully
    planted, air-conditioned atrium
the PTA
deep leather couches
the best-kept romantic secrets
electric hot-doggers
the last crumpled leaf quivering on
    the oak
the rising of the sun on a misty morning
washing a car to make it rain
the wild blue yonder
treating yourself to a massage
when the maples turn
an early-evening cookout with barbecued
    chicken and new corn
cleaning off your desk
the container on the side of a cash
    register into which your change
    slides
fresh and tangy lime
the fragrance and happy flavor of butter
    and almonds, cinnamon, brown sugar,
    apricots, honey, and cream
important trivia
fresh-cut hay, seasoning in the June sun
great ways
French fruit candles

cuff links
bagels for Christmas breakfast
dog dishes that say "Good Dog"
high shoes
The Graduate (movie)
"the hots"
paisley scarves from the Provence region
    of France
quilting hoop on a floor stand
raising glasses of choice wine
making something new
Prince Edward Island wool caps
being so proud you could burst
things turning out best for the people
    who make the best of the way things
    turn out
triple sheets and show pillows
whipped-cream makeup
jonquils
being a novice hiker
chicken-dinner halls
drinking juice out of a can with a straw
going barefoot in grass cropped close as
    fine baby's hair
chickadees
taking a chicken picnic and the cat for a
    lunch on the green
thick slices of buttered sourdough toast
being taken to the zoo
tyke bikes

Hollywood love lives
male chauvinist pigs
silo vanes
milkshakes
salad bars
split-second thrills
telephoning overseas
all-butter pound cake, ice cream, and
    strawberries
Belgian endive and breadsticks for
    scooping cheese
bulldozers
collared sweatshirts
Dull Center, Wyoming
golf links
lame ducks
Memorial Day parties
pumpernickel-cheddar triangles
cold or hot lemonade
tumbling children on the beach
atmosphere
complimenting a total stranger
gym shirts
hem facing
miniskirts
penny-pitching games
tomato and round steak on skewers
lining closet shelves with scented paper
sandwich-type, pressed-glass candlesticks
sending a fan letter

home brews
sun reflecting the cove waters
sunny-chestnut color
tiny deep-fat fryers
windjammers cruising
bandstands
story hour
Bancroft and Bata tennis goods
candy-cane icicles hanging from rooftops
snow forts
cinnamon-brown birds
concerts in the park
Danish Brie, Camembert, Havarti, and
    Samsoë cheese
finding two good reasons to do something
fondue bourguignonne
honeymoons
loosening-up motions with the wrist
    before writing
people in jeans, T-shirts, and sweaters
    who are happy munching fried
    chicken and sipping Italian red
shooting a whole roll of film in one day
short-sheeting a bed
wrought-iron barrel birdcages
an old Regina music box with metal disks
booty bags
stone-ground wheat cakes and maple
    syrup
a rustic bench in a sequestered spot

maple keys
peppermint
applejack
containers and tubs of cascading flowers
Appomattox
that irresistible, clean-baby smell
remembering when jeans were only for
    play
merriment, delightful conversation,
    toasts, speeches, sharing, kinship
par-3 golf
Norwegian open-faced sandwiches
wrought-iron lighting fixtures from the
    turn of the century
Vermont's atmosphere
warranties
acrobatics
strawberry ice-cream shortcake
air-brush hair dryers
carnation = pure and deep love
the corners of your mind
Christmas trees from all lands
a showoff
a small act of grace
earthworms
farm-style picnics featuring chicken,
    turkey, beef, fresh garden salads and
    vegetables, homemade cakes and
    pies, relishes, and potato salads
farmhouses

tattersall
foraging for hickory nuts, apples, and
    crab apples
kissy-face
misty mountain paths
positive daydreaming
a salad of miniature marshmallows,
    pineapple chunks, pecans, and
    American cheese
a shake-shingle roof
waterfront buildings
fishermen early in the morning
gas stoves
not eating when you're not hungry
interviews with coaches
lots of books, a good bed lamp, vases of
    flowers in the room
notetaking
patchwork bench pads
antiperspirant tests
putting a pumpkin on the porch and a
    wreath of dried flowers on the door
sitting in bed watching the sun rise over
    the park
tetherball
watching the sunset and the world
    turning backward
antedating
a thoughtful thought
a toast to the bride

water beds
mental alertness
cat food commercials
making a fire on the beach and staying
    warm while the winter night works
    its way on the water of the lake
eating after brushing your teeth
Dutch-looking dishes
hot eggnog
a tribe of goldfish flicking their tails
playfulness
sour-cream doughnuts
coupons that would self-destruct after
    their expiration date
fruit salad with mint dressing
lovemaking
peach Bavarian cream
revelers in satin and taffeta
wavy old glass panes
giving yourself a mind massage
"It will rain if cows are lying down in the
    pasture"
low-bush blueberries
newsstands
Army-Navy stores
town halls
maximizing the positive things
trying to figure out the theme of a
    conversation in a foreign language
buying fresh flowers

50s desks
do-gooders
Mr. Wizard, science explicator
Dr. J. (Julius Erving), basketball player
3-D movies
loaves of tine bread for tea
boccie balls
peach Melba with whipped cream
pharmacy floor lamps
city parks
practicing first aid
scalloped coastlines
sharpening your vision
trapdoors
veal Oscar
an analytic approach
sea otters
an apartment cook-in
boathouses
chairlift up a slope
spare ribs cooked in pineapple juice,
    garden corn on the cob dripping with
    butter, and fluffy mashed potatoes
    with lumps
chalk-white walls and floors of red tile
Brahms on the stereo
the boarding up of graceful Victorian
    summer homes in winter
the celebration of being alive
crazy New York taxis

flames for boiling and baking, coals for
    broiling and frying
framed antimacassars
glass bowls and an ice-cream certificate
hearing church bells
rebuilding an engine
pure white pants
fabulous garlic salad dressing
licorice-flavored anise hyssop
Jack Sprat
absorbent cotton
secret civilizations
socks folded in matching pairs
bacon tasting like salt, honey, brown
    sugar, or maple syrup; or like hickory,
    mahogany, apple wood, or oak smoke
encouraging a child to collect something
sweet faces and hands to wash up before
    supper and kiss before bedtime
the fragrance of a summer rose
scarecrows
the last glow of the fireplace
jade-colored lagoons
kiddy cars
old-fashioned glass snow domes
padded bicycle seats
oven mitts
seeking out uncrowded stretches of beach
area codes
coffee-mill planters

Oregon red raspberry, sun-ripened
    strawberry, Oregon black raspberry,
    wild Maine blueberry, and Michigan
    red tart cherry preserves
sweet shrimp, lobster, and squid in an
    intensely garlicked vinaigrette
the hundred voices of a January wind
the warm feeling of waking up on a cold
    morning and discovering you have
    another 20 minutes to sleep
beech leaves delicate as a fluff of silk
the year of Our Lord
breakfast as a generous, help-yourself
    affair with fresh-baked breads,
    granola, eggs, juices, steaming coffee
    and tea
creative photography
dreaming nice dreams
red-tile roofs and rolling Pacific waves
exercising
street merchants
freedom of the press
Limoges boxes
office file cabinets
the mesmerizing flames of a roaring fire
the soothing winter wind in the hemlocks
forgiving someone
stretching your legs and arms, yawning,
    and visualizing an ideal day before
    getting out of bed in the morning

Bugs Bunny
dog tricks
an hour of lonely communion with your
     coffee cup before communion with
     fellow human beings
joining several linguistics and language
     societies
swim meets
olive orchards that slope down to fields
     punctuated with clumps of cypress
     trees
blowing bubble gum bubbles
paint-by-number kits
stone fireplaces
Skippy peanut butter
white-water canoeing
Amish Acres, Indiana
beige-and-cream checked shirts
making banana splits
chicken sautéed in butter with brandy
     and apricots
editorials
flipping coins into a fountain
calm tempos
frivolous cakes
going tramping, getting outdoors and
     basking, or just gloating and being
     content
adjustable hairbands
Pikes Peak

waking up with a cat
milk toast
"Mowing the carpet; painting the baby;
    shaving the kitty" (Lily Tomlin)
rolling hill country
salad days
tall beeswax candles
being softly propped up in bed
telescopes
velvety lemon mousse
volleyball
cold cream
uproarious laughter that must be forcibly
    squelched due to its
    inappropriateness in a situation
the delights of finding first spring flowers
full green vineyards
humorous phone calls
jump shots
lemon balm
Memorial Day picnics
remembered tales beside a fire
symphonies
atmosphere drenched in history
gymnasiums
ham smothered with brown sugar,
    cinnamon, onion, milk-soaked bread
    crumbs, and ground cloves
alley cats
hamburger-stand hats

home, where we tie one end of the thread
     of life
pen wipers
sandwiches
single-strand pearls
Pennsylvania Station
vinegar for sunburns
Winn-Dixie stores
banging screen doors

Canada geese returning in long, dark
     distant lines
controlling the largest empire on a
     Monopoly board
fancy combs for hair
busy times
funny get-well cards
ivory-colored ribbon
herds of black-and-white cows drinking
     their reflections
ordering the mind, replenishing the
     heart, finding ourselves again
"Who loves you, baby?"
stained-wood buttons
"You'll Never Walk Alone" (song)
blouses with Peter Pan collars
brown sugar melting over fresh pineapple
answering the phone with "Joe's Pool
     Hall, who in the hall do you want?"
elopements
woven straw mats

Florida: gleaming, whitewashed hotels,
    sponges, alligators, glass-bottomed
    boats
pipe racks
ripe fruit
a press party in New York City
waiting for the school bus
Cape Cod cranberries
empty crab shells on the beach
explaining computers
irrigation
a maraschino cherry and orange slice
    stuck through a toothpick
Marlon Brando, actor
rare birds
throw rugs
working at the polls
a rag rug in tones of rose and aubergine
bar lights
discount tickets
birdhouses
cardsharps
unplugging the phone
curried drawn butter
gargantuan slabs of roast beef
lush trees
having an unfortunate knack for
    approaching a set of double doors and
    always pushing the locked one
wash lines

mulberry tree = wisdom

a seersucker robe with frills and puffed
     shoulders

a single flower floating in a small brandy
     snifter

ensuring there will be at least one slice of
     banana for every spoonful of cereal

basking in the spring sunshine

cesspools

displaying paintings on easels

fasting on warm milk and sweet bread
     the night before turkey

the be-all and end-all

little boys' spiraled curls ruffling up

not signing anything

American English

potatoes Anna: a crisp hunk of potato
     heaven served with sour cream and
     chives

watch caps

wet T-shirt contests

a thousand fantasies

a tweed cape and matching hat

bath wraps

buttermilk

rain at night, if you're safe in bed

getting "thrown out"

getting a sliver out

lounging on the deck

pound cake

Mount Baldy, Indiana Dunes: a living
     dune, moving southward about four
     feet a year
Naugahyde
sculpturing ribbons to ornament
     packages or hang on the tree
an unexpected letter
blue-and-yellow-trimmed dishes
blueprints
Hullabaloo (TV show)
brushing the dew from sneakers
reviving an old plan
the business of the day falling into
     manageable perspective
envisioning a scene out of the movie *The
     Way We Were*
having orange juice and champagne
     while wearing silk pajamas
lawn bowls
town houses
a well-worth-it wait
blowing the wrapper off a straw
Edwardian sideboards
layers of sweatering
buying and painting unfinished furniture
flying in crosswinds
fuzzy rugs
H2 = hot and heavy
W.C. Fields, actor
a June morning, the color of purest honey

BLTs and potato salad
a Victorian bay window, big four-poster
    bed with a blue-and white quilt
koala bears
learning how to polka
playing foreign-language tapes in the car
blue inlets and crystal creeks
playing in the brick barbecue in the snow
reaching a compromise
snare drums
track meets
wraparound sunglasses
brake fluid
chafing-dish creations such as veal
    Madeira, steak Stroganoff
charcoal-gray mirrors
travel mugs
a clawfoot adjustable piano stool
crabmeat-filled mushrooms
crawling out of a tent on a frosty morning
framed calico appliqué pictures
guarantees that don't run out the day
    before something needs fixing
table ideas
umbrella'd tables set out on a sunny pier
a baby-powder back rub
a bag of buttery yellow muffins
cobblestone streets
once-a-year headaches
picture-book villages

rice-pattern tea sets
a cashmere sweatshirt
escorts offering their arm
Dick and Jane's cat Puff
the intimacy of humor
indulging in the rich self-pity of
    believing that nobody can possibly
    understand you
Indian corn
Coca-Cola commercials
flashlights that work
the courthouse square
old friends to help us grow old
saddle soap
a bowl of tiny mandarin oranges
the best fruit market
the vegetable gardener secretly wishing
    for a frost
a breeze tiptoeing into the room, afraid to
    intrude
sod growers
Timbuktu
Greek pizza
opening stuck windows
adding a symbol to your
    signature (star, heart, flower, etc.)
the appropriate wine for dinner
smelling corncob-smoked bacon sizzling,
    maple-scented muffins, and pancakes
    on the griddle

steam rising from a tureen of hearty
  vegetable soup
the Statue of Liberty
cream cheese potatoes
the fragrance of cookies baking
steak fries
tie racks used for playing "elevator" in
  the closet
breadboxes
cream satin furniture
the splendor of fall
updating clothes
deep-set windowsills
dueling if challenged
electric morning coffee-starter
the twang of banjo and whir of cotton gin
every seventh wave being a big one
feeling deliciously invisible while you
  watch the world go by
fresh blueberry sauce to serve over peach
  or another favorite ice cream
the pleasure of water
the return of curls, ponytails, crew cuts
fresh strawberry pie made on a graham
  cracker crust
green jello
TV football
V-formations of migrating geese
puffed heart pendants
lighthouses and piers

French doughnuts called croquignoles, corn oysters, marble cakes, buffalo stew, hickory-smoked chicken, apple butter, corn cakes, pies, cider, and sassafras tea

sightseers in all types of garb

"Roger, Wilco"

Unger yarns

vegetable sauces: butter, hollandaise, Mornay, polonaise, sour cream/mustard, vinaigrette, white or cream

wiggling your flip-flops over the edge of the porch

dog-walking

engagement rings worn above wedding rings

English pedlar dolls

school figures and free skating

knit ribbing on cuffs

freshly made hot biscuits filled with ham

old report cards

shining, smiling, sweetly peanut-buttered faces

sliding back and forth in the bathtub in order to mix the too-hot water with the cooler water

multicolor rag rugs

sliced ham with mustard pickles

Swiss steak sandwich with butter and salt

thinking with someone
light verse
using a supercomputer
an introductory offer
being especially partial to book-lined
    dining rooms
chipped ham with dried apricots
birthstone rings
doing something every year so that it
    becomes traditional
tinsel
frizzled hot dogs, split and fried in oil
making an "I wish" list and then taking
    action so the wishes come true
waking up Christmas morning and
    drinking hot eggnog
Arkansas strawberries
slices of rare roast beef, green peas, and
    baked potato with everything
bike radios
"Old Kentucky Rain" by Elvis
kilt skirts
malt-makers
milk-can salt shakers
taking a federal exam
living-room oil lamps
political discussions on breaks and at
    lunch
flying kites
absolute revelations

oil wells
yellow bug lights
bells pealing out the good news
Belgian lace curtains
falling in love again
hills covered with almond trees
holding your tummy in
jumping frog contests
lumberyards
singing songs around a campfire
mimosa of sparkling wine and orange
    juice
bamboo packing crates
gambrel-roofed houses
home movies
sandglasses
sending a love letter
homemade bread and peach butter
lunch money
miniature jellybeans
a vast wonderland of soaring, snow-
    capped peaks, turquoise lakes,
    glittering glaciers, and tumbling
    waterfalls—all framed by dense green
    forests
King Leonardo
being as warm as toast
rent-a-cars
singing all the hymns in church
sun burning off the morning fog

sun-touched shoulders
a tiny plant in a little clay pot
wandering the fairgrounds, watching
   demonstrations of making soap,
   Christmas ornaments, and apple
   fritters
candle lighting, turkey stuffing,
   mistletoe hanging
wind heard at the chimney and around
   the corners of the house, swishing
   and roaring through the naked
   woodland and sighing among the
   pines and hemlocks
windshield wipers on eyeglasses
bongo drums
candles glowing in the entryway
Bunker Hill
conflicts with an umbrella on a
   windy day
"In My Life" by the Beatles
fondue sets
Dunes State Park, Chesterton, Indiana
   (especially the sunset)
sunshine filtering through hanging
   plants
gentle, warm afternoons created for
   tennis parties and games of croquet
people who understand there's a lot
   to you
shoe freaks

wanting your teddy bear
slow curves
brownies with no nuts
Brooklyn banana splits
news conferences
snowy beaches and billowy palms
spoon dolls
Prophetstown, Indiana
"You're never too old for Koolaid"
brown bread
the call of the coyote
chocolate-dipped butter cookies
hooves on cobblestone
maple oatmeal muffins
sap buckets
supernatural delights
a place to stretch out on the sand, to
    beachcomb for unusual driftwood
    formations
apples and cheddar cheese cubes
navy blue cable-knit socks
narrow columns of type, meant to be read
    quickly
porcupines scratching
yawning being good for you
rare-book collecting
strolling troubadours
air castles
"April Fool-ing is to end at noon, anyone
    who tries it later is the fool"

barn houses
coral-colored cottons
earth tones
garlanding a banister
kiss timers
a steak over charcoal
a sunset with someone
cashew wood
Easter eggs
lithographed cardboard soldiers
little brass pitchers
miter boxes
air pistols
not smoking
potholders
potpourris of dried flower petals, herbs,
    and aromatic spices
watching a yacht race
buttermilk bath salts
Waterford crystal salt and pepper shakers
a sled and team of horses for gathering
    the sap, which is taken to the sugar
    house for boiling down to syrup
a 12-quart covered stockpot
dahlias, marigolds, asters big as saucers
bathinettes
batik dyeing
a small boy running into his mother's
    hug
butterscotch streusel

cats: Abyssinian, alley, Angora, Burmese,
     calico, Cheshire, domestic shorthair,
     Manx, Himalayan, Persian, seal
     point, Siamese, tortoiseshell
data hounds
eating the right food
gathering a list of people's ideas of cheap
     thrills
squeezed cherries with a scoop of vanilla
     ice cream
gloriously satisfying extravagances
stuffed pizza, descendant of Chicago's
     famous deep-dish pizza
getting sunburned on a sailboat
your own private slice of beach
aqua and toast colors
azure skies
counting the seconds between lightning
     and thunder and dividing by five to
     tell where the lightning is
Flutephones
Leve fit quod bene fertur onus =
     "That load becomes light which is
     cheerfully borne"
advertising in the Yellow Pages
having the cleanest car in town
New England
feeling satisfied with the rightness of the
     world
Twinkles the elephant

a wooden apple basket
track shoes
always wanting to be a kid when you
    grew up
saying something nice
Toyota cars
days of ripened fruit
a "bad egg"
the reassurance of being petted a little,
    praised a little, appreciated a little
1930s and '40s white wooden kitchen
    cabinets with fruit decals
a Subway sandwich run
plant-encrusted walls
platform-deck rockers
a tropical fish tank
seaweed tapestries woven with shells,
    fish bones, feathers, sponge bits
team tennis
tranquillity
planning an audition for a community
    play
traveling your own road
wearing a man's watch
bean lovers
braided treads on the staircase
a bag of chocolate-chip cookies
a basket filled with strawberries,
    cherries, and green grapes
twirling a baton

chautauquas

class books

flamingo coral, sunny red, sunflower
  pink, pink orchid colors

framed maps

spinning pennies

brandy snifters with colored water and oil
  for a burning wick

heart-shaped bathtubs

the hearty taste, rich aroma of fresh
  yeast and golden brown crust of bread

Robert Redford, actor

a basket of towels in each room

a belief that caution often deserves to be
  thrown to the winds

bubbling cool springs

Jack and Jill sundaes

recipes found in grocery stores

rocking chairs, more evocative than
  almost any other piece of furniture

tic-tac-toe

Victorian knickknacks

a campus-like atmosphere of maples,
  dogwoods, and walnut trees

a cast-iron farm bell

the purr of a kitten

panel quiz shows

old-fashioned English steak-and-onion pie

a 1930s hot dog stand

WIN buttons

old country inns to get lost in
a book wall
the silence of close friendship
old pewter wine pots from China
paddleballs
Madison Square Garden
red lettuce
red plaid lunch boxes
Old Town, Wells Street, Chicago
wedding gown fittings
hodgepodges
meeting men
steering-wheel covers
needlepoint ornaments
opening a bottle of wine just for yourself
    and cooking a good dinner for one to
    go with it
sleepyheads
speeding through caution lights
the bottom of the sundae glass that you
    can't quite reach with your spoon
press boxes
the smell of aerosol hair spray
the beach in the fall
the expressive faces of pansies
gulls swooping and scolding
the hotel coffee shop
beef kabobs
the name "Kyle Brian"
watching football practice

the purple, bell-like flowers of the false
    foxglove
tweed hacking jackets
where berries lie in hidden clusters, the
    scent of leaves and ripened fruit
    filling the air
an elegant stone terrace where guests
    drop by for croissants and coffee
an epic diary entry, detailing love life,
    career, friendships
beer gardens at fairs
the catch of the day
"Hey Baby, They're Playing Our Song"
    (song)
the smell of fresh-cut greens
clear Lucite flatware
mittens in a basket by the back door
the detector in an aspirin that tells it
    exactly what part of the body to go to
the twirling-fork-in-bowl-of-spoon school
    of spaghetti eating
crescent salad and relish trays
diet guides
one perfect rose
informing TV characters of impending
    danger, thinking that they can hear
    you
official scorekeepers
magic shows
nightclubs

pogo sticks
vegetables boiled in a huge kettle over an
    open hardwood fire
high chairs
johnnycakes
steam rooms
knit shirts
nail glazes
the spicy odor of lasagna
things that don't cost a bundle
whipping up a casserole
shearling fleece
white doves restlessly circling a château
animals at their watering troughs
beige denim
daisy = innocence
flirtatiousness
going someplace you've never been
gristmills
hair towels
adjusting the car and yourself for good
    night vision
oak spiral staircases
biding your time
golden retrievers
multicolor ski hats
rolling lawns and tennis courts
salads in restaurants
collecting colorful wine labels
balconied wood houses

balloons, banners, hats, noisemakers,
    special invitations, place cards, crepe-
    paper twists, nut cups, and confetti
"I love it"
celebrating the harvest moon by taking a
    long stroll with someone special after
    dinner or heading to the beach with
    warm blankets and wine
collaging a cigar box
helpfulness
colorful shopping bags loaded to the brim
falling asleep on someone's lap
fillet of beef served with sauce béarnaise
the Gulf Stream
"Half a loaf is better than none"
drivers yielding to other drivers
lemon-sesame sauce for grilled vegetables
Memphis pork barbecue
pumpkins heaped on the roadside
romantic declarations written in the sand
bumper pool
combining cocktails and a fresh box of
    Crayolas for everybody
dime novels
a backless sundress
homemade shadow boxes
kindergarten drawings
landscaping
linen toweling sold by the yard
Pogo comic strip

miniature bottles of liqueur to pour over
    ice cream
pine needles soft as kitten fur
rent-a-wreck, hire-a-heap, or lease-a-
    lemon to view the foliage or drive to a
    football game
sandwiches called Tex-Mex, Smørrebrød,
    Muffuletta
tin-lined copper pans
Tinkertoys
Venetian blinds hanging in big plate-
    glass windows
wind meters
sweet-smelling pine on the fire
Winnie-the-Pooh TV shows, books
bonbon pink
sinking your teeth into fresh peaches,
    plums, watermelons, and apricots
the sun shining through a blue haze
cinch belts
handed-down Christmas ornaments
finishing the last freezing and canning
    for the winter supply
Dunkin' Donuts stores
ginger jars
hanging clean, dry towels in your
    bathroom
the honking of auto horns
progressive relaxation: tightening and
    then loosening various muscles

"Your cake will brown slowly in the oven
and rise like a perfect sun"
blood tests
photography
booths plying hot dogs, Polish sausage,
Italian beef, and frozen custard
a rolltop desk
croissants with country jam and
crumpets with honey
good things coming your way
brown bread sandwiches of anchovies,
butter, herbs, and spices in a paste, or
generous slices of good pink ham
spread with a skimming of hot
mustard
groundhogs
imparting an aura of passion, childlike
innocence, or serenity
telephone booths
paper mills
popcorn at the circus
bookcases in kitchens
facing the truth
hope chests
liquid silver jewelry
perky pea-green color
blow-dryers
personalized compacts
rural roadside stands
snow-capped mountains

scrub pants
tester beds
strawberries and powdered sugar
stripes and terries on the beach
a record that teaches you the sounds of
	the instruments in an orchestra
airy eggnog
barefoot beachcombing
curry color
farmers' winter boots
listening to classical music during lunch
sling pumps
wishing for a new car
a soft summer's night
a street full of bookstores and galleries
cashing in your chips
discovering only twin beds on a
	honeymoon
dusky colors for fall
interesting wooden house siding
jet streams
little girls frolicking in furs
putting all your senses to work
satin Christmas balls
antique Chinese porcelain oil pots with
	wooden lids
butterflies lighting on the rim of the milk
	pitcher
attic rooms
cutting your own hair

art techniques: airbrushing, collage,
    engraving, etching, finger painting,
    line drawing, melt-and-color, oil
    painting, pencil drawing, relief
    rubbing, scrimshaw, spatter painting,
    wash drawing, watercoloring, wood
    carving
city council meetings
eating three slices of pizza and the next
    morning finding you're a pound
    lighter
getting sunburned on lunch hour
hot to-go coffee and sandwiches
laughing at someone's attempt at
    watermelon growing
laundering your money
mousse cups
plus-fours golf pants
snuffboxes
boutique candy stores
double beds
being lovey-dovey
movie stars
a very soft, old-fashioned teddy bear with
    plaid paws, ears, and ribbon
covering the walls with sheets that match
    the bed's
having an advantage over every other
    girl
buying your first expensive dress

lawn swings

new posters

New Jersey: crossroads of the Revolution,
Miss America, wild orchids, pixie
moss, Atlantic City

sewing cards for kids

a windsock

down quilts

joys and vicissitudes

Hayley Mills, actress

buying yourself a toy

cryptograms

flying kites in March

pizza sauce

a "belt-busting" meal

no-curl bacon cookers

a Victorian wicker sewing stand

leaving fresh cookies for Santa

meat broiled in the fireplace by holding it
over a bed of hot coals on the end of a
long, sturdy fork

Italian red wine and sticks of sesame seeds,
cornmeal, and flour

peach crème

playing hide-and-seek in the park

having a dictionary by the bed

slam of a screen door

thawing out hamburger

autumncades

traveling and viewing

a brass and black-enameled steel piano
    lamp
clambering over rocks
diapers and baby food
snap purses
starflowers
fearing that everyone thinks you
    picked the awful tune coming from
    the jukebox
grand slams
heart-shaped ottomans
classic oxblood pumps
public transportation
tablecloths
a baked-out-back cake
baby cereal
open-faced sandwiches
Bob Hope, Bing Crosby, and Dorothy
    Lamour in the "Road" pictures
picking out landmarks
rice-strewn suitcases
corn = riches
Rice Krispie Marshmallow Treats
a champagne breakfast
backpacking
old-time roller towels
cider in a jug and bourbon in a hip flask
French vanilla sheets
one-piece bowl and sandwich plate for
    soup/sandwich

an archaeological dig
opening a nearby window to let in sounds
    and smells of spring
preventive medicine
see-through disks of cucumber sprinkled
    with vinegar and salt
rosy cheeks
the book that made a difference
overdue library books
the collar never folded down on a cotton
    turtleneck
the natural path that clings to the cliffs
    high above the sea
red-checked shoelaces
bad dining hall meals
the pinch marks on the ends of hot dogs
the sound of the wind
when mellow days turn into brisk
    evenings
the upper peninsula of Michigan
trees: the quick-change artists of fall
when the cattle stomp and chew and
    swish their tails as if to keep warm
an epiphany
Brentano's bookstores
cheap Hawaiian shirts
when someone throws you a curve
checking out new grocery stores
the cool, shimmering mist that fishermen
    know on inland lakes

the midnight hungries
clear, cool alpine breezes blowing on
      steep, snowy mountains
dress shoes
dressing up
freshly prepared soup
library research
coffee mugs
the habit of checking for change in every
      coin return you pass
light-giving flecks of diamonds
peg-leg jeans, penny loafers, bobby socks,
      sloppy joe sweater
soft, puffy, foot-long bread sticks with
      Italian tomato sauce
pigeonholes
making a beeline
Angora cats
engagements
high diving
nail polish
neither scurrying nor haste at an
      early hour
olive-green velveteen
painting the town red
things that are quiet and old and simple
      and ordinary and very real
rain lovers
shimmering blue lakes
sliced leftover roast lamb and mint jelly

poinsettias
slit shorts
Slinkies
white porcelain cups and saucers
    sprinkled with delicate confetti dots
"His bell has been rung"
chinos
climbing a tall white pine tree
driving up to the lake and having a picnic
    with the squirrels
fairgrounds
two people listening to each other
a drive-up, drive-in mailbox
Renoir
getting an early start
flight bags
quiet times
liking the people you work with
old rail fences wearily climbing the hill
solid black walnut and hard rock maple
    chessboards
playing Clue
a Calvin Klein jean skirt worn with a
    gold snake belt
homecomings
cold vegetable salads
delivering compassion
lemon Cokes
finding the new *People* magazine at the
    hairdressers

half chili and half Boston baked beans,
  both hot and sweet and great with
  tortillas or corn bread
rum raisin flavor
someone who says you're beautiful
alma maters
everyone jumping up and down at
  midnight to "Help Me, Rhonda"
after-hours use of computer room
  equipment for a gambling network or
  figuring a stock market takeover
homemade soap bubbling in an iron pot
  on the hearth
a mini-print cotton foulard dress
miniature bowling games in bowling
  alleys
Sunday puttering
munching marshmallows
penny candy
sand, sea, and sunset
tennis, Bloodies, backgammon, Bloodies,
  and sailing
Sunday loaf bread filled and topped with
  raspberry or strawberry jam or
  preserves
ventriloquists' dummies
wandering into an antique furniture
  store
wind shirts
handshaking

candles of different heights on terra-cotta
    saucers
confronting
dance halls
hand-painted Limoges tea warmer
people leaning on the counter, reading
    the newspaper
short socks
stoneware and breakfast fixings
candymaking
wrought-iron lanterns
"You are the banana of my tree; you are
    the peanut of my shell"
avoiding lunatics by sitting in the middle
    of the bus
bookmobiles
short-order talk
clotted cream the rich color of yellow
    garden roses
cookie-cutter'd jello
doors that open amiably to dumb dogs
    shambling home
gooseneck floor lamps
paper-white gardenias
popcorn at the movies
rope tricks
the Poppin' Fresh doughboy, Flapjack the
    dog, Popper, Poppie Fresh, Biscuit the
    cat, Bun Bun the baby, Granmommer,
    Granpopper

pipsqueaks
typing a cryptic message on the
    department store demonstrator
butterflies migrating
apples and sweet potatoes with pork
    chops
liquidation companies
Raquel Welch, actress
German fried potatoes
three essentials for happiness: something
    to do, someone to love, something to
    hope for
atrocious prices of movie eats
bars of late afternoon sunshine
car washing
watching Christmas lights twinkling on
    a cabin home
circle pins
fire screen with duck in flight
for blue dye: blueberries, elderberries,
    indigo plant, larkspur flowers
European-style yogurt
hard sauce over plum pudding,
    gingerbread, Indian pudding, or
    apple pie
Miss Muffet
reserving your own quiet corner
casual Friday dinners
flounced awning-stripe cushions
Filofax horoscope inserts

disco music
not sulking
out-of-reach cabinets
petal vases
pitchers on the porch
Notre Dame University
Saturday night dances
water's shiny surface
waterwheels
a pond right in front of a home
eating Milky Way bars at room
    temperature
fat jewelry
getting caught singing to Muzak when
    taken off "hold"
hot whipped chocolate
Paul McCartney, singer/composer
acupuncture
chubby and skinny Santa Clauses
court-green color
never being short on confidence
a vandyked grapefruit
give-and-take in a relationship
low, burl wood tables
sexy people
ivy-planted hillsides
toy doctor/nurse kits
buying socks that fit
a Black Russian drink
leather Keds sneakers

orange-and-marshmallow ambrosia
sea breezes
stamped tin
pear butter
planting tulips at Thanksgiving
country cottage lamps
playing holiday music
overcoming scaredness
rear-window defoggers
scatter-straw baskets
swag lights
teakwood wine goblets
"What is essential is invisible to the eye"
amaretto cake: light yellow confection
    accented by almond liqueur and
    toasted almond slivers
black pants
crackle glaze ceramic
drawbridges
flaky and nicely browned pastry
graceful sofas with slightly faded covers
a binge day
tear sheets
a broiler that cooks both sides of a steak
    at once in an oven
amber music
baby powder
microphones
rocks dashed with sea
a box of Lincoln logs

the tradition of drinking toasts, from the
　　old custom of floating toasted bread
　　in punch
orderliness
soda fountain parties
French-cut lamb chops
iceboating
iced tea with mint sprigs in wineglasses
Greece travel folders
jack-in-the-box music
"prepmobiles"
seeing the twinkling lights of town in the
　　distance
speaking loudly to foreigners as if
　　somehow it makes you easier to
　　understand
open-hearth baked ham
pledge pins
something spellbinding
steak sauce and meat tenderizer
a sweet tooth
the clatter of cross-country skis being
　　stacked in the corner
the day slipping away
people demonstrating organs and pianos
　　in shopping malls
the length of icicles
sweetbreads
the rye bread recipe a grandmother
　　hoards for years

a thermos of water or fruit juice
the setting sun splashing a pink tinge
    over fleecy clouds
voicing your opinion where no one can
    hear you
Viennese coffee, ground each morning,
    filtered into a thermos pot and
    garnished with a cinnamon stick
beer on tap
bread ovens
electric toothbrushes
fresh flowers at work
fresh pink tablecloths and huge pink
    cotton napkins
great human happiness
healthy exercise or a swim at the Y
French "filoche" shopping bags
oxford cloth curtains
raffia sun hats
being soft-spoken
wafer mints
sugar cubes
"egg in snow" with smoked bacon
big changes
eight-packs
English rose potpourri in a jar
mahogany book presses
things best done alone: poetry,
    performing, exercising, wallowing
joining a flying club

knit tights
quilted gold-and-silver glitter place mats
raisin racks for drying California grapes
pull-out writing boards on desks
Quincy Market, Boston
thick woolen blankets
impatiently popping toast up and down in
    the toaster
toilet kits
amino acids
side saddles and horse tack
chive butter for corn
climbing a tree to do some constructive
    daydreaming
"killer mud" = overboiled, reheated java
crisp fritters dipped in warm maple syrup
crisp, batter-coated vegetables
making love on a secluded beach
taking a cooking class together
miles of dense virgin forest, laced with
    lakes and waterfalls
jelly beans
panty raids
multicolors
ski mittens
self-reliance, strength, pride,
    and a romantic vision of life
Don Maynard, football player
telling a letter "Have a good trip" as it
    goes in the mailbox

tall glass hurricane lamps with natural
    woven bamboo shades on tall bamboo
    stakes
baking your own bread
wildflowers alongside a highway
Will and Ariel Durant's *The Story of
    Civilization*
Bolla wines
celebrating this special moment
a colonial wood desktop organizer
colorful trays for lap-snacking
"Come outdoors with me"
filibusters
filling a vase with red and blue anemones
halter tops
memory lane
remembering being awakened and
    carried outside on your father's
    shoulders to watch a satellite
    overhead
semitropical foliage
summer dinner out in the garden
coming home to a crackling fire
family time
games with jump ropes
home weather stations
homemade caramel corn
langoustines
Henley-style Fair Isle sweaters
piney woods

consumerism

pink tinge on the clouds created by the setting sun

a candle burning under a vegetable grater

Monday night football

senior year

sunlight streaming through the trees

tending to your knitting

Sunday naps

the tinkle of glass at a door entry

tiny ice-cream stores

anniversary telegrams

candlelit supper under the stars: glazed Cornish hens with pineapple-almond stuffing, sesame asparagus stir-fry, watermelon, brandied coffee, champagne

cinnamon raisin rolls

the whimsy of kittens

gingered melon wedges

conciseness

gentle gray, heather plum, teak brown, jungle green, silver smoke, polar white, peach moonstone, rice-powder white colors

hanging lace curtains for an airy, open-window look

George Harrison and Ringo Starr of the Beatles

Finnish crystal martini glasses
a shish kebab of herbs on charred meat,
    alternated with slices of blackened
    onion
lion taming
shorty skis
a ride on a hay wagon drawn by a pair of
    Belgian draft horses
a smoke-blackened brick fireplace
cookies made in stoneware molds
floaty, filmy clothes
growing citrus fruits
a pond so placid it mirrors a willow tree
apple trees
pastel love
making decisions
expositions and fairs
happiness being the atmosphere in which
    all good affections grow
large backgammon sets
parcel post
the old American custom of serving coffee
    on New Year's Day
street maps of Boston
turning cartwheels, doing headstands or
    somersaults
Worcestershire sauce, scallions, and
    mustard blended with beef on a bun
a rainbow of relishes
airy peach-pink color

United Nations gift stores
carrying heavy things
a sense of competence
a serenading minstrel
corncob-smoked ham from Vermont plus
    cob-smoked bacon and aged cheddar
early-returning birds
"bats in the belfry"
harvest baskets lined with pine needles
    or bright cloth napkins, filled with
    tangerines, apples, nuts, shoots of
    dried wheat, and tied with a ribbon
inspiration
working out a problem
spring dinner parties
instant poker parties
misting indoor plants
music boxes
passion purple, fire engine red
Mesopotamia
rustic-look furniture
visiting a farm to see all the newborn
    baby animals
a slightly stale doughnut, split, sprinkled
    with water, then toasted and buttered
"I scream, you scream, we all scream for
    ice cream"
cos (romaine) lettuce
custard pies
gaslights illuminating tree-lined streets

kitchen garden prints

little candle sconces

motorcycles

a small sheepskin rug

a storm sheathing every cable of
Mackinac Bridge in glittering ice,
making it a silver harp playing the
music of the wind

someone who wants to take you dancing

putting up the storm sashes, checking the
woodpile, and making sure the oil
tank is full

"Steamboat Willie" starring Mickey
Mouse in 1928

setting up the bath as a cul-de-sac: a tub
tray, bookrest, inflatable bath pillow

a treat for the house

the early mixing tool called a twirler

anticipation being the greater joy

butterscotch-colored straw hats

cutting out a pattern

a trip to the library

sitting on the shelves of a closet when you
were a kid

eating what you like and letting the food
fight it out inside

Dutch apple pie, made of the thinnest
apple slivers with a topping of butter
crumbs

hitchhiking

"hotsy-totsy"
Mountain Dew soda pop
round pancake turners
the Qantas koala bear
squaw bread
setting the scene, arranging the props,
and inviting your wittiest, chattiest
acquaintances
young robins trailing their mothers on a
search for worms
houseguests
inventing a new dance
inviting your best friend over and giving
each other manicures and new
hairstyles
loving freely, purely
saved money
wave-splashed beaches
having small picture books, magazines,
quick reads for guests
New England cookbooks
a wicked jacks player
a window close to the floor
layer cakes
Ray Charles, musician
trying something you haven't before:
an artichoke or pomegranate
a yard of hair ribbon
boys' bikes
frying eggs

bizarre fireplace tools whose function no
    one knows
R & I = radical and intense; heavy, great
4-H ribbons
a Scottish thistle-design shortbread mold
khaki pants
leaving notes on cars
meat carving into beautiful slices and the
    fluffy mashed potatoes awaiting
    abundant, flavorsome gravy
orange skin "baskets"
olive = peace
planning a purse sale
planting a windowbox
roadside displays of wild aster and
    fringed gentian
sea fishing
a team coming through a paper hoop at
    the game
toasting marshmallows
an almost full moon emerging from
    behind the clouds
crayons for kids at restaurants
flaky powdered-sugar pastry squares
    called beignets
Make a Wish (TV show)
glasses of cream sherry or port
small lidded baskets
starting a collection
glazed sweet potatoes

library reading rooms

your book-of-the-moment

tobogganing

a bird barn

boneless prime-graded, dry-aged strip
    steak in a black mantle of char

checking your fortune-cookie message to
    see how it matches up with your
    mate's

a bunch of broccoli, red onions,
    cauliflower, white onions, English ivy

baby chicks scurrying underfoot

baby's breath and velvet ribbon

cabin fever

the gift of every day

pocket books

the kitchen

the occasional screech of a gull overhead

packing a flask of coffee, hot chocolate, or
    your favorite chili recipe

archaeology

backroading

India tea, wafer-thin sandwiches, and
    cakes, served by the fire

an old warehouse restaurant with
    stained-glass windows

ordering French fries

looking down on the world from the top of
    a Ferris wheel

red, orange, and purple flowers

rediscovering croquet
the deceiving dark ring around the
     bottom of soda-pop bottles
Old English lettering
sidewalk cheese fries in large paper cups
cedar-stump furniture
stocking fillers
ice crystals so small, so light, that they
     float like mist and shimmer in a
     January sunrise
keeping the scorebook
one rose in a tiny bouquet of wildflowers
the color and contour of sheets
the corn being up but not quite in tassel
overtipping
pre-Christmas hustle and bustle
pressed-tin ceilings, arched doorways,
     and a winding stairway
seeing objects formed by clouds
steel bands
Nerf balls and hoops and Nerfmobiles
picking up your favorite cheeses
the salt of the earth
the shaded quiet of a Victorian gazebo
     and the tranquillity of the woods
when your ship comes in
where to get ideas and stimulate
     thinking
Viewmasters
hot potato salad

the fogging of bathroom mirrors
cleaning windows with squeegees
creamy mushroom gravy
the supermarket meat department
the whole day on skis with a picnic lunch
flea-market furniture
officiating
soft drinks
softening brown sugar
buffalo wings in barbecue sauce
coffee urns
inglenook = a corner by a fireplace;
    chimney corner
edification
drifting off to sleep
leg warmers
a school of fish
magical mushroom lamps: conjuring up
    dreams of romantic South Sea
    islands, lush mystical forest,
    woodland elves
pigeonholes in a desk
sugar-free chilled orange juice
big, round metal hospital trays
eggbeaters
lighting up the place
engineer-stripe jeans
fog mists over violet moors
juicy red apple color
prize finds

refinishing furniture

rain rattling the roof and banging at the
window

the skirling of a bagpipe

sliced pound cake with butterscotch
sauce

swimming in a country club pool

things that might come in handy

white spring flowers, green and white
Chinese vegetables, and bottles of
wine in crushed ice

tying your hair back with ribbons

"ring around the collar" Wisk detergent
commercials

white sales

writing a love letter

University of Alabama

being happy

being offered a football ticket

Clint Eastwood, actor

an inaudible slurp while eating spaghetti

drinking champagne punch in the
afternoon

etiquette observation

going back to the drawing board

hair "rats"

a taproom with bare floors

being sent home from work early

taking in a classic tear-jerker rather than
the latest film from Europe

miles of ribboned highway tied with
    cloverleaf bows
"selling like hot cakes"
tall people
wildlife preservation
believing in miracles
someone calling and inviting you to
    lunch
something that is one of a kind
temptations
camera bags
Camden soup
commodities
long, flat berry baskets
a man's Timex on grosgrain ribbon
    watchband
mini-breaks
miniature petit point furniture
nonchalance
lazily drifting on a raft; lying back and
    looking up, up
running out after dinner for an ice cream
sunny retirement in the Sunbelt
tiny satin pouch bags
wandering on brick-paved lanes lined
    with 18th-century houses
binding books by hand
mint juleps
someone fixing something without being
    asked

bun baskets
candy cones
sleepy babies and teddy bears
denim belts
Donald Duck
gently floodlit trees
looking for an answer
Porky Pig
neon lights
people who eat corn on the cob in a left-to-
    right or "typewriter" style
phosphorus
monkey bars at the park
promenading
scones, delicious when served warm,
    split, buttered, and spread with jam
Peoria farm equipment
a plank steak for two
sloping expanses of white sand meeting
    the blue waters of an inland sea
snow-lathered cars being shaved
auspices
choosing a new ensemble for a Barbie
    Doll
clodhoppers
the secret urge to expedite the person
    ahead of you through a revolving door
typographers' drawers
a pond that freezes into a natural ice-
    skating rink

spot checks
a pub lunch
cloth kites
clearing your head
morning coffee and juice brought to the
    guest rooms
parsley-butter patties on steak
sane living
Perseid meteor shower
strawberry sandwiches
tortellini in white cream sauce
striped awning fabric
turning off all the lights except those on
    the Christmas tree
vertical barren rocks
World Tennis magazine
apples, trees, country sky, the snap of fall
    in the air
a red canoe
herbed cottage cheese
a room to retreat to for listening to music,
    puttering, looking through books,
    and clipping magazines
Gray's Anatomy, unabridged 1901 edition
being barefoot on the grass
power tools
barnswallows swooping
getting lost on purpose when you were
    little
luggage carriers

cork-popping evenings

garlic barbecue sauce

Forest Hills, former site of the U.S. Open
tennis tournament

spareribs spiced with herbs and honey

outdoor cafés on Chicago's Rush Street
and New York City's Columbus
Avenue

listening to old rafters, creaky doors, and
loose floorboards

a sand-between-the-toes walk on the
beach

mischievousness

pistachio cake served warm with ice
cream

an off-the-cuff compliment

Nashua, New Hampshire

a small, attractive courtyard built around
a gazebo

corn relish

letterheads

a stormy weekend to get reacquainted
with the most comfortable chair in
the house

basement family rooms

dishes of Dairy Queen ice cream

the ease with which we fall in love or fall
in love all over again

hospital scrub shirts

birthday celebrations

intramural basketball

short letters being better than no letters

motorized spice racks

outdoor pit barbecues

trekking out to the woods for a walk and
    coming home to potato heaven,
    sausages cooked in maple syrup, and
    nut bread

an antique red hand-stenciled wooden
    sled with dark pine runners

astronomers observing

getting the best news of your life

between errands, spending private time
    in the car reading, listening to the
    radio

cut-crystal decanters

eating crow

getting through the last chilly,
    housebound nights of winter

hitting a tennis ball against the wall
    for practice

Denver, Colorado

saucer golf

Borden's milk

snugglier, snuggliest

young, spring-grown, just-picked radishes

a bouquet of straw flowers in a big basin
    aglow with bee lights

countrified furniture

cherry tree = education

living in Connecticut

seven-foot TV screens

sitting on an outdoor patio overlooking a
    duck pond

giving the perfect gift: a private
    reflection about someone, and a deep
    desire to please him or her

pewter serving plates

towel racks

"A wise man makes more opportunities
    than he finds" (F. Bacon)

cowboy bars

luxuriating in velvet, cashmere, or full-
    length fur

buying soft furniture

dry wood for kindling

flying off the handle

jazz dances

pizza dough

"I'd rather play tennis than cook"
    (slogan)

a Rhode Island barrel clambake,
    including scalloped oysters

baby's-breath flowers

steel drums

a Sunday morning car wash with the
    radio blaring and a picnic lunch of
    cold chicken and white wine

leaves in great golden drifts as crisp as
    beaten gold foil

learning the language
orange soda
plain ice-cream cones
plastic or paper cups
rearranging furniture
standing at the window and seeing the
    snow, the flakes of crystal perfection,
    feathering from the sky
old-time, hard-to-find, bona-fide lamb's-
    wool dusters
swallowing your pride
fresh water
Scandinavia
transistors
travel agency windows
knowing what to do when the power fails
Arabian horses
bran muffins with raisins and a giddy
    kick of spice
"Have a nice day" from a checkout
    person
class rings
Charmin toilet paper
cracked tennis courts
diamond stud earrings
dragging out an old washtub, sitting
    under a tree, and tipping the hose in
flaky-crust meat loaf
flashcards
hearth glow

heaters for bathrooms

old American wedding custom: shivaree,
    mock serenade with pots, pans,
    cowbells, outside the newlyweds'
    window

a big bag of Hershey's Kisses

a bird feeder hanging outside the guest
    room window

payola

bobolinks

bubble gum and hard candy pieces in
    bags of a hundred or more

receiving forgiveness

accordion decorations and lamps

bacon and cream-cheese tomatoes

casement windows

old-time corn popper with rotary agitator

Old English sheepdogs

needlepoint dollhouses

teddy bears

wide-mouthed toasters

cider mills

ice buckets

one-room schoolhouses

steak, corn, potatoes, and beer

stereo-radio headsets

peach denim

stew in a pottery pot

quarts

sweethearts

the "armchair public"

staring at the figures on restroom doors
    to determine men's and ladies'

the Nixon transcripts

fieldstones

sleek limos

saucer eyes

the boxed area on a U.S. map where the
    49th and 50th states are located

freestanding full-size mirrors

fresh lemon juice

the cardboard rod on a hanger that
    prevents creasing in pants

the color, scent, and deliciousness of
    strawberries

useful, preventive measures—fruits of
    experience

when you build a fire outside and it pops

average of 1,800 thunderstorms going on
    in the world at all times

the eerie appearance and ascension of the
    bubble in a watercooler

the folding process that allows Kleenexes
    to emerge from the box one at
    a time

Canadian pro football

the world being at your command

tree swings

breathtaking skating over transparent
    ice

the headlight on a vacuum cleaner
clearing the table after a meal
deep-dish apple pie served with a pitcher
    of cream or a wedge of cheese
feeding a hummingbird
sheet music
fresh pleasure at being outside
guesthouses
bright white paint
daffodils looking like a carpet of yellow
hefty, well-fatted ham with ripe melon
the lawn settling into the sleep of frost
ingredients for cooking
magical winter places
the love of the good things we ate in our
    childhood
the song of a man in the shower
signs on old jalopies
sugar ice-cream cones
beginning to feel the faint touch of
    autumn's brush
egg cartons
Johnson & Johnson's baby powder
joining a health club and getting results
nailing everything to the floor
psychology = philosophy
rain rivers
ski jumping
thick, buttery sweet pea soup fortified
    with potato

spice boxes
things becoming clarified once we
　　nurture ourselves
offshore fishing
writing a love poem or letter
"firing up"
being a lexicographer
wagons
being happy as a clam
chicken roast with a light coating of
　　thyme, tarragon, and onion powder
chili butter for corn
the whole kit and caboodle
crisp morning cereals
fairy tales
flight suits
going to three museums in a row
hair becoming blonder in summer
being attracted to someone when you
　　least expect it
Kissimmee, Florida
taking piano lessons and never practicing
baklava and pistachios
hiking into the woods
jello cakes
roller skating around the block
selecting ripe melons
self-sticking stamps and labels
velvet-backed pillows
Wilson sporting goods

believing in yourself
cold, blustery nights to invite friends over
    for popping corn and games
colorful exotic birds
the delicious cool of the uplands
dollar pocket watches
falling asleep while contemplating
    dinner
filling a woven basket with dried baby's
    breath, statice, horsetail ferns,
    pinecones, or fresh fruit
immediate materialization of the cat
    when the food is brought out
being shipwrecked with your overnight
    bag
remembering Father paying $4 for a full
    tank of gas
someone dependable and solid with
    dimples
camping out
homogenization
long skirts
nine-year-old navy blue blazers
pints of steaming tea
renting a slick sedan
sunny sands
vinaigrette
wind whipping the sand at the shore of
    an ocean or lake and piling it into
    dunes

bingo games
bunches of asparagus, tied with ribbons,
    in a basket
candleshine
workaholics
burnt toast
childhood friendships
doughnut shops with perfect coffee
hand-painted planters
scoreboards
frosty nights and blue-sky days
honey-basted duckling
abet = encourage
your own butter cookies
people who offer you their seat
snow on the side of the road
spontaneity
book bag with notebook, Shetland
    sweater, Cliff Notes, *National
    Lampoon*
books on posture, body language
"Lola" (song)
drop waists
the superior taste of food cooked over a
    charcoal fire
frost whitening lawns
grocery store posters
lip glosses
paper dolls
top bananas

zippy limes
apple cider
happy times
being able to drive and fold a road map at
    the same time
knitted slippers
Morton salt
spreading blankets in the yard, chasing
    fireflies and talking
pyracantha with bright, shiny red berries
streetcars
tortellini salad, sliced mozzarella and
    prosciutto roll, escargot puffs, and
    meat en croûte
mint = virtue
warm sun and seaspray
a romantic train trip
agreeing with anybody bigger than
    you are
staying on the fringe of politics
apricot mustard sauce
burgundied meatballs and dilled
    mushrooms
dormitories
earphones for stereos
Early American pine fruit boxes
Love Story (movie)
post-election parties
resort wear
buttered raisin sauce

restaurants
Sesame Street muppets
visiting a law school
a squirrel's forepaws swiftly excavating a
    new hole
dishes of beach glass
lattice-top pie crust
plate racks
shades of velvet blue
letters from France and Belgium
little faces punctuated with the round o's
    of wide eyes and open mouths
combination metal towel rack/chair
not burping at the dinner table
being "on the beat"
an old-fashioned pole with a metal
    grabber used for retrieving items
    from high shelves
satin vests
watching a big moon skim in and out
    of the clouds, smelling the thick,
    fragrant country air
afternoon pick-me-ups
Batman's enemies: Catwoman, the Joker,
    the Penguin, the Riddler
butter upon bacon = extravagance
frozen apricot mousse
It's a Wonderful Life, A Christmas Carol,
    and *Miracle on 34th Street* (movies)
peach jello

gut-spilling softballs
hot prepared chili on a hot dog
laughing till you cry
round steak casserole
Summer of '42 (movie)
Southern fried chicken and cream gravy,
    hot biscuits, small new potatoes, a big
    salad, and a huge helping of peas
an aquarium in a snifter
church pews
crumpets, straight-sided, pale, round and
    hot, honeycombed with holes and
    ideal with absorbing butter
double-cut lamb chops
Nova Scotia
savoring a quick "fix" from a novel or
    leafing through a travel magazine
    at lunch
pewter wine decanters
getting lots of sleep
power-roar of the sea
a watercolor of the Maine landscape:
    rocky terrain and sparse foliage, lit
    by a full moon
a wicker chair discovered outside a
    countryside antique store
May baskets
buying all new pencils and pens
Dayton cash registers
a 35-bottle wine rack

NBC Studios, New York
UPI and AP tape machines
leather held to armchairs by brass
    upholstery nails
peanut butter in jars
playing hooky when it snows: making a
    snowman, going sledding, sticking
    out your tongue and catching
    snowflakes
seasoned butter molds
Scandinavia's climate
travelogues
squirrels building nests low in the trees
black and dark purple
pear relish
brand-new dominoes and checkers
clamming
beachcombing
a beautiful old hotel in London
flamboyant typography
the best cheerleaders
Dial-a-Joke
heavy china camp mugs
tableside steak Diane and beef
    Wellington
the hard-fought decision on what
    toppings to order on a pizza
a bonfire by the lake
a bravely patient tree leaning leafless in
    the wind

buckets of golf balls
pea jackets
bubble-packs of honey
cubbyholes

mocha tarts
packing weeks ahead of schedule
the icy green sky at the horizon, pink/
    blue above (skim-milk blue) and near
    the zenith, a half-moon
the medieval city of Siena, which
    gave "burnt sienna" to the artist's
    palette
wicker trunks containing patchwork
    quilts
decorating a bachelorette house exactly
    as you want
ducks fishing for their dinners
escaping to a country inn with your child
December: turquoise or zircon
    birthstones; holly, narcissus, or
    poinsettia
individually wrapped sandwiches
old records
radio knobs
doing something against all odds
Radio City Music Hall
wide-open floor space
ice carving
keeping fresh flowers by your bed, fresh
    herbs in the kitchen

needing a hug, a cuddle, and love
Oneida silverware ads with beautiful food
sleepy dogs
the sweet and simple indulgence of an
    afternoon nap
steak: sirloin, fillet, or rib eye with choice
    of cut, size, and degree of doneness
the one who loves you
playing horsey
the sticky sweet steam of a sugar house
    boiling off
when your fingertips have shriveled like
    prunes and you're clean enough to
    put on fresh pajamas
cream jugs and delicate porcelain teacups
the whoosh and roar of the wind
creating exotic life stories for people who
    walk by
dreams of singing in a club or restaurant
Cream of Wheat cereal
field glasses and bird book by the window
the refrigerator in the kitchen
freshly cracked black pepper in spaghetti
    carbonara
drivers' education classes
the song of the mower
the sound of feet crunching through new
    snow or frozen leaves
waffle knit
light meals

dressing for pleasure
the promise of untold adventure
being late to classes
log rollers
night music
rug shampoo
egg wedgers
"The Night Before" by the Beatles
moist gingerbread and cranberry nut
    bread
Maine clams
quixotic = foolishly romantic,
    extravagantly chivalrous
corner-fitting tables
swirl parfait glasses
Snidely Whiplash, Dudley Do-Right's
    enemy
Trix cereal
walking downtown
University of Uppsala, Sweden
whipped cream topping a vanilla
    milkshake
white cotton T-shirts
being silly and funny, serious and strict
a bridged bath in the living room
ceiling lamps fashioned from inverted
    maple buckets
children absorbed in quiet play
doing things together
going to watch a prom

taking care
baked Swiss steak in dill sauce
pulling out some old favorite games:
    Monopoly, Clue, Parcheesi
reliability
rolling up your sleeves
salespeople
silky pants
Polaroid Land cameras
split-collar sweaters
Silly Putty
velocipedes
velvet-starred nights
well-worn stone steps
bald lights
deliciously odorous onion rolls and an ice-
    cream scoop of creamy butter
lemon wedges for fish
remembering good times together
same-day dry cleaning
the Boston Children's Museum
lunch boxes
Minute rice
"Ninety-nine may say no, the hundredth
    yes"
pinecones dropping in the fall
pineapple, cream cheese, and crisp bacon
    on a burger
sending an unsigned card or valentine to
    the person you have a crush on

sangria ice
bike covers
Melba toast
sinecure = a position requiring little
work but with profitable returns
coupons for groceries
sunburst-yellow color
tender, loving touches
vine fruits
winning a blue ribbon
candlewick bedspreads
handmade ski sweaters
loose strands of hair
moonshiners
people who pay Visa bills with
MasterCard
shorebirds
wood-grained cabinets
bookworming
broken corn blades drifting in the breeze
knowing your cholesterol level
choosing a watermelon
egotistical people
Chris Evert, tennis player
flowers for nurturing your soul
sunglasses and shades
candies under pillows
grouping pure white candles in the center
of a table wreath of pinecones,
heather, or moss

food debris under a high chair following
an attempted feeding

Hula-Hoops

map reading

opportunity

paper-airplane flying

tiptoeing into a room

apple cinnamon flavor

morning dew

pork-and-onion kabobs

straw-blown paintings

top-opening notebooks

striped cooks' aprons

throwing out the towel at wrestling meets

warm-weather dressing

workers picking corn, harvesting flax and
broomcorn

airport suitcase tags

first college weekend

furry booties that warm your feet like
little ovens

garden pots

horse prints and hunting scenes

artists' pencils

listening to the lowing of cattle in a
nearby field

mists of Spanish moss, statice, pink
strawflowers, baby blue velvet
ribbons, sprigs of lace, and calico
bound in a wreath

drawstring pants
Massachusetts leather
a sunny day
Bobby Riggs, tennis player
intramural swim meets
late Sunday breakfast
metal trays
cobblers' aprons
sitting around the dining room table
after dinner and enjoying long
conversations
sitting on a bench to watch the billowing
sails of the yachts negotiating the
sparkling blue waters of a harbor
watching the sun rise and set aboard ship
having a scratch for every itch
watermelon-pink color
a time for all things
water mains
art classes
bottle opener/knife/corkscrew
combination
Better Homes & Gardens magazine
cut flowers
eating in the kitchen
extra-large sizes
getting out of the got-to-tell-all, lay-it-on-
the-line syndrome and remembering
how nice it is to have a secret
hating shredded wheat

loud radios
clubhouses
nourishment
soup spoons
a tulip-shaped cup of icy metal
southern New England cherries and
    peaches
squooshing ice-cream sandwiches
blueberries 'n cream
bouquets of old-fashioned country flowers
cauldrons of sauces and gravies
country inns, castles, old coaching stops
sun porches
fluffy puff animals that squish, squiggle,
    and flop
"knock, knock" jokes
living in a treehouse
having your car warmed up by a loving
    soul before you go out on a cold
    winter morning
having the time to reread *Little Women*
unwrapping sandwiches
a wind-surfing regatta
six-layer eggnog cake
secondhand books
layering of patterns and colors
buying all new spices
Q & Z: letters not on the telephone dial
in-a-nutshell reports
white 100% cotton sheets

meats garnished with parsley and small
    red tomatoes
Italian marbled paper
planning your future with the help of a
    Ouija board
plastic colored Easter eggs that split
the magic of play in a relationship
poached white peaches
practicing basketball at a park
real coffee, home-roasted and home-
    ground
searching in cookbooks for something
    new for dinner
that vacation feeling
trampolines
rakes, trowels, and spades
rereading a book you loved 10 years ago
sleepy eyes
poinsettia-red pure silk crepe de Chine
    boat-necked shirt
brandy Alexander pie buried in fluffy
    whipped cream
claret wine
cuddly white rabbits
drag strips
foals and horses
fraises des bois = wild strawberries
glass beads
roast beef sandwiches
"Goals should be written in sand"

heading for the warmth of a blazing
 hearth, pulling a sled of redwood to a
 refurbished home
tablespoons
a baby falling asleep
bar lunches
a bowl of potato-and-onion soup
sociability
acclimating oneself to a cold swimming
 pool, one body region at a time
cocktail hour, when the fiery sun
 drops behind the peaks and singes
 their edges
bacon sauce with peas
decorations
kidskin and snakeskin
Indian berry and potato baskets
Indian-chief haircuts
Modest Town, Virginia
red mittens
underwater limestone formations
Chateaubriand for two
needing a little love
openwork silver caskets and unusual jars
quesadillas
seedlings opening paired leaflets on the
 windowsill
brass horns
classroom instruction
drawstrings

seeking knowledge to plan, enterprise to
    execute, honesty to govern all
the cry of a killdeer
ends of the rolls of newsprint free at the
    printer's
Greek foods
"The early bird catches the worm"
the foxtrot
umpires' outfits
a bubble of quiet air
baby leaves
hobby shops
kick or punt = indentation on bottom of
    wine bottle
the missing last piece of a jigsaw puzzle
when you pull the shade and get caught
    in it, or it falls down, or zips up with a
    bang
the night-day switch on a rearview
    mirror
the regular harbor contingent of mallards
a tan people notice
the thirst-quenching deliciousness of real
    lemonade
watching it snow
the writings and etchings on school desks
Twelfth Night punch: apple cider,
    pineapple and orange juice,
    cinnamon, cloves, nutmeg, honey,
    ginger

aged cheese
an electric presence lingering in the air
cheese and crackers served from atop an
old potbellied stove
flagpole sitting
electric heating pads
clouds with silver linings
fiery south-of-the-border chili
freebies and cheapies
the great thing about humans being their
ability to change
green grass and the smell of it
offering apples and vegetables to birds
and animals in winter
Tiffany-style glasses
old-fashioned waffle-weave kitchen towels
coffee server on stand with votive candle
jogging with a friend
night prowls with flashlights at
Halloween
taking a blanket and something to ward
off chills out to the dunes
organizing your goals
sighs and whisperings
negotiating
sugar mills
foghorns and sea gulls
inhaling maximum amounts of sea air to
stimulate the appetite
knitting worsted yarn

Irish fishermen's pullovers of heavy,
    cream-colored wool
rainbow-colored fires
snipping sun-bleached peppergrass next
    to the river
swirl-pattern crystal bedside carafe with
    glass top
"little dinners": combinations of soups,
    salads, and vegetable dishes
Adidas tennis clothes and shoes
being aware of wonder
dried bouquets of hydrangea, statice,
    baby's breath
going barefoot around the house
taking a covered-wagon vacation in
    Kansas
cake stands
lily pad with lush pink blossom
salad with hot bacon dressing and a
    basket of tea-roomy rolls
Dictaphones
silly times
Salerno butter cookies and milk
walls overgrown with a green cloak of ivy
yellows, oranges, and rusty greens of the
    hickories, sumac, and beeches
bolts of calico fabric for sale
columnists who run out of ideas
juicy, golden oranges
immersion cup heaters

jumbo stuffed ravioli
Romney lamb-pelt rugs
compulsions
ham loaf with brown-sugar syrup
lunch-counter cooking
menservants
pandemonium
inviting your mom to lunch
a penny on the pavement
pinafore dresses with back ties
singing in the shower
the tantalizing odor of barbecuing pork
    chops
tennis on clay courts
Sun-In spray for lightening hair
vanilla meringue filled with ice cream
    and fresh strawberries
candlelight bath for two in a Jacuzzi spa
window seats and bready-smelling mazes
    of bookracks
Wonder Bread wrappers
bunches of drying herbs dangling from
    the rafters of a shady side porch
pizzazz
hanging balloons in the windows
riotous coffee breaks
stopping to rest under the drooping shade
    of a river's edge willow tree
woodsy, outdoorsy skating rinks
an old covered bridge

taking care of plants
apple, peach, and fruit country
bell towers
an old sled
blond guys
browned garlic and pine nut sauce on
    pasta or big, flaky baked potatoes
exotic fresh fruits served cosseted in
    bowls of vanilla cream
floor plans
winter woods whitening silently
Scotch eggs
frost-touched streets
grosgrain ribbon for bookmarks
grouping chairs around a fireplace or
    near windows
maple, butternut, apple, and locust trees
paper kites
a place of golden canyons, apricot sands,
    terra-cotta mountains, and mauve
    shadows
harem pants
a pot of apples, cinnamon sticks, cloves,
    and brown sugar on the way to
    becoming applesauce
irresistible softness
serving warm, soft pretzels to guests who
    come expecting ordinary snacks
street food
tar shampoo

stockings hung from the chimney with care
tire swings
growing luffa sponges
turtlenecks
Virginia country ham served over
    cornbread and covered with maple
    syrup
"Trouble" after-shave
a rooster weathervane
aeronautics
bar cookies
carrying a piece of apple pie along with a
    glass of cold milk out to a freshly
    painted deck
cork-wrapped tumblers
slide rules
dart boards
earthquakes that are exciting but don't
    do damage
ferry boats
fireside log lighters
the first drops of rain on the roof
patio carts
hiring a charter boat
horses breathing ostrich plumes of air
no sound except the branches clicking
    together and a vast, far skein of wind
    flung down from the sky
researching and planning getaway
    weekends

a wood fire
As the World Turns (soap opera)
dolls in a doll
the apple of your eye
a split of champagne with lunch
intramurals
patching and sealing a driveway
a state of continual "becoming"
a survival kit for someone who is sick:
    favorite magazines, books, remote
    control for the TV, soup, juices, and a
    handmade "feel better" card
desk lights
a romp in the hayloft
corn shucks
dishwashers
in the autumn, ravines aglow with the
    fiery brilliance of sugar maple and
    witch hazel
potato patties filled with meat and onion
a tatami used as a bulletin board
a turkey sauce of cooked cranberries and
    ground whole oranges
19th-century opulence
attending a production of *The Messiah*
butterscotch brownies
doing things by the book
deteriorated cookie particles in the milk
entering your name in a local
    sweepstakes

hot cider, scalded English slaw, and
    homemade soups
hot prime ribs of beef and sliced turkey
    sandwiches
moving to a new house
stuffed mushroom caps
country-style oatmeal
crunchy knit mufflers
double knits
drumming of hooves and neighing of
    horses
hauling out photo albums dating back to
    high school
revising Yellow Pages headings
savoring cool summer mornings to relax
    and energize
advertising
covered butter dishes
having tea or cocktails in a super deluxe
    hotel or restaurant
new sandals
being rowdy
a walk down a pine-needled path
reminiscing
a warm, crackling fire
mixed greens topped with chunks of
    chicken, tomatoes, and sprouts,
    served with honey-mustard dressing
Mexican jumping beans
box offices

on your lunch hour: listening to music,
    visiting a planetarium, ice or roller
    skating, touring a ship, dancing,
    shooting darts, going to the Y,
    learning a foreign language, taking a
    bus ride, visiting a health spa, taking
    a tour
daydreamers
McDonald's chef salads and ranch
    dressing
a Morbier farmer's clock
Santa's Helper (book)
peacock throne chairs
real cream—thick, tenderly yellow,
    perfectly sweet
realizing you were wrong
rearranging the house
crab houses
roasted French fries broiled with a
    delicious crunch of Parmesan cheese
checking the faces of departing
    moviegoers in an attempt to
    determine the quality of the film
sea or woods patterns
peas and carrots with sour cream, lemon
    juice, chives, dill, and pepper
reading the newspaper
seafood Newburg on patty shells
soapbox derby racing
toasty warmth

train stops
Spanish-style coffee tables
transoceanic airlines
old-fashioned summers
"painting" with water
beating your own drum
blackboards
classic Seville and coarse-cut orange
    marmalades
elaborately patterned wallpaper
goat cheese
gravy boats
tabernacles
a beer can opening on a hot day
small-boned people
a breakfast tray complete with bud vase
    and crossword puzzles
baby-sitting
bobby socks
cubed steak
in cold weather, simmering apple cider,
    cinnamon, cloves, and tangerines to
    make the house smell cozy
kick pleats
Lucite cutting boards
mock pearls
sub shops and fried-clam stands
orchards heavy with blushing red apples
    and flocks of turkeys being fattened
    for the approaching holiday feasts

brand-new Teflon pans
clam shacks
tickling and silly songs and cookies and
hot chocolate in bed
bacon slabs
bucktoothed kids
Hedda-Get-Bedda dolls
Judy Garland, singer/actress
old-time piano stools
puddles perking in the downpour
riding in the basket of your bike
today's special at a restaurant
a Dedhamware bunny lamp
the nights beginning to draw in
seeds and herbs for kitchen use
the three-day weekend
sleeping on the porch in summer
the delicate content of recipes
spending an afternoon skating or
sledding
weeding and grooming the garden
graduations
steak-bite appetizers
the sting of salt air
sweetshops
the cacophony of typewriters in an office
tennis hats
the only sounds at night being the
conversations of tree frogs, locusts,
and owls

buggy rides

the silence and big logo before a movie

when salespeople admire the picture of
your mate in your wallet

the early dry dark of an October
Saturday evening

when the cake is caved in, vegetables
scorched, gravy flavorless and lumpy,
you've used too much salt, you've
ruined the icing for the cake, and the
dessert is a disaster!

wren houses

"Geronimo!"

shared experiences and private jokes

bread, cheese, and wine on a hillside

"Heaven Sent" cologne

breakfast-in-a-basket

cheese and fruit lighted by a candle in a
wine bottle

the dew, the air, the sounds of the birds

chestnuts roasted over the fire

finger paintings

cleanliness

when you squirt the toothpaste and it
comes out the other end

cream cheese frosting

free throws

fresh orange juice squeezed into slender,
sparkling cut-crystal glasses

gleaming light on swift ripples of a lake

sapphire = wisdom

sweet dreams at the end of a journey home

green grass reaching for sunlight through cracked pavement and vacant-lot rubbish

French blue

infatuation

soft French-style cream cheese flavored with herbs and garlic

life without Frisbees

Oxford blue

soft-lighting effects

pagoda umbrella lamps

having your cat come when you call her

big county fair signs

vanity license plate and a college decal on the back window

joining hands at midnight on New Year's Eve and saying a special prayer for the coming year

quiet places: a garden, a reading room in a library, a corner nook in a café, a botanical garden, a chapel, a rotunda at a museum, a terrace, a hammock

ship models

thinking of ways to deepen your knowledge

soft lettuce, sun-dried tomatoes, and fresh mushrooms in a hot dressing

using dried summer flowers in cards and
   letters during the winter
the whisper of an excited gathering
French lace
white pines, firs, and native spruces that
   remain green; intermixed crimsons,
   oranges, and rusty greens of the
   hickory, sumac, and beech trees
chili dip with fresh vegetables
making a list of things that have been
   bugging you all winter
coin pinball machines
singing old hymns in church
handwriting
pineapple-ham skewers
Chinese chop haircuts
crisscrosses
doing whatever you like best to relax you
driving through a giant sequoia
snapping turtles hibernating side by side
   on the pond bottom
hair-setters
adjustable chamber candlesticks
making a tape of favorite songs
quarts of milk
milquetoasts
oil and vinegar jugs with corks
pulling pantyhose out of the drawer and
   finding them run-, snag-, and hole-
   free

killer Scrabble games
roll-top pencil boxes
selling subscriptions
silk organza blossoms
telling someone your dreams and
fantasies
Wall Street
molded glass compotes
balancing on one foot
towel-dried hair
collecting newspapers
filling out a "How was the service?" card
gold-threaded jewelry
tame animals: burro, camel, cat, cow, dog,
donkey, dromedary, goat, horse, ox,
pig, reindeer, yak
camp shorts
bright sidewalk cafés
ham sandwich sauce: sweet-and-sour red
tomato gravy, redolent of cloves
menu design
ornithology
pantalettes
pink-and-blue sunsets
punctuality
the ring of the telephone
sand castles
sunshine and weekends
wind-combed fields of goldenrod
wine stomps

Converse tennis shoes
finding a seat in a crowded movie theater
hanging basket chairs
honey graham crackers
Frosted Flakes cereal
shopping for new and used books
spoon bread
making plans just to go outside
John "Records" Landecker, radio
    personality
Snoopy standing on a beach ball
obtaining that which is elusive
tools and workbenches
violent, paralyzing snowstorms—
    midweek
broiled cheeseburgers
cool, cooler, coolest
foot powder
groves of lemon trees
paper lamps
repotting your plants
sipping coffee in an antique cup and
    saucer and stirring with a silver
    spoon
lazily wiping your hands on your shirt
a pocket survival kit
carrying a spare tire
In and Out trays
asparagus vinaigrette
dipping your toes in a fountain

jar cozies
Harvard and Radcliffe
strawberry = perfection
serif = cross strokes on letters
fireflies blinking by
strings of miniature lights, strands of
    cranberries or popcorn, red ribbons
    tied in bows around leaves, icicles,
    paper snowflakes that you've
    designed yourself
turkey legs
a porcupine, half asleep up in a big pine
turning on the porch light to watch an
    evening snow sift down
bare trees revealing each small
    movement of birds and animals
curious and expectant travelers
early summer: deeper yellows, stronger
    blues, some orange, and a variety
    of reds
fireside pine benches
sorting clean laundry
forerunners
list-lovers
pick-me-ups
listening to an adult
master keys
missing someone but knowing you'll be
    together soon
pasta salad

a silent, peaceful room with a rocker in
    the corner
at a turn-of-the-century apothecary, a
    soda dispensed at an ornate marble
    fountain
chili in green peppers
fall leaves
a sustaining hot breakfast on a cold
    winter morning
being bushwhacked
Boston baked beans in huge pots
designing a stage set
being in the pink
intensity and abandon
Mattel toys
potato and cheese blintzes as large as toss
    pillows
Mother's Day presents
The National Observer and *National
    Enquirer* newspapers
sitting on a moonlit deck for a few hours
    with a bottle of wine and no sound
    but the lapping of water
listening to the news
turning your pillow over and over, looking
    for a cool spot
with camera and binoculars in hand,
    putting your feet up on the rail and
    settling back to watch the harbor
    drama unfold

a special coffee shop
butter bowl with ladle attached
a tea table on wheels
bath sheets
gleaming gold buttercups and wild
geraniums turning pink faces toward
the sunrise
catching every breeze
cats exploring in bushes and walking
along the tops of low garden walls
bowers of honeysuckle
cowl-neck sweatshirts
eating dinner, watching videos and late-
night talk shows from your pillowed
haven
getting B's in a math course like
geometry
blue-and-white chintz
countertops
fluffy sweet potatoes
lavish buffet spreads
rowdy times
a waterfall with submerged colored lights
fixing up a scrapbook
Pez candies
a wood-paneled saloon
knowing it's almost spring when people
are starting to panic about income
taxes
buying shoes for kids

St. Joseph's aspirin for children
reading a magazine with someone
a New England baked bean supper on
    Saturday night and a roast chicken
    dinner at Sunday noon
learning to swan-dive
trains
playing sailor
plant signs on sticks
a Vermonter
real estate
planning a visit home
roadhouses
sea gulls sailing over the dunes
the driver's seat heater in a SAAB
slabs of boned chicken with melted
    cheese and mashed potatoes
small at-home dinners
playing badminton without a net
Quaker Oats
Car 54, Where are You? (TV show)
beaches that are red in the east, honey in
    the middle, and tawny in the west,
    sloping gently to the water, backed by
    bluffs and dunes and cut by bays and
    harbors
saying "Sure"
grated peels of fruit
a black-and-white speckled spaghetti
    cooker

the blatant lies and illogic that mothers
    use to discourage "dangerous"
    activity among children
chandeliers
glazed fruit pastries
charcoal-broiled fish
a book nook
graph paper
clam shells
graham streusel cakes
Frank Sinatra records
a breath of fresh air
umbrella shade tables
a buckboard
bobèches around candles to catch
    drippings or on chandeliers to hold
    suspended glass prisms
pecan rolls, butterscotch twists, Danish
    pull-aparts, fruit bars, cocoa cake iced
    with fudge
old clothes
picnic buns
recipe-card libraries
succeeding in not raising your voice
    during a fight
riding a chairlift up a ski slope to enjoy
    the exhilaration and fresh air
deck chairs
escargots, fondue bourguignonne, and a
    luscious grape dessert

duck decoys
midweek cocktail time
the name "Holly Beth"
the onset of a peaceful feeling
old wood to burn, old wine to drink,
    old friends to trust, and old authors
    to read
the academy chair in all colors
TV dinners out of the microwave
Daddy smoking his pipe in the family
    room
Ice Capades
open-toed strapped wedgies
pleated dinner trousers and lounge shirts
spending a night at a farmhouse
steam rising from a cluster of casseroles
lottos
a snowman on the football field
the difference between New England and
    Manhattan clam chowder
fishermen's boats cutting patterns in the
    sun-gilded water
the hazy Chicago skyline growing out of
    the horizon
bacon curls
the lacy pattern of twigs against the sky
reed organs
the perfect outdoor café where you can
    hang out with a newspaper, sip,
    nibble, people-watch

indentations that appear in carpets after
    a piece of furniture has been moved
the rising or setting of a star at sunset
side dishes
drop-leaf tables
the momentary confusion in a dog whose
    owner has faked throwing a ball
the point on a potato chip where it breaks
    off and stays behind in the dip
the whisk-broom sound of footsteps on
    fallen leaves
Palmer House, Chicago
wheat cradles, candle molds, corn beds,
    flax shuttles, wool cards, dough and
    oatmeal chests
Weeble toys
bleached sand dollars
when Walter Cronkite was host of
    Twentieth Century
breakfasting outdoors in a thatch-roofed
    restaurant
cheese soup
cream puffs
feeling wonderful after washing your hair
soft snow gathered into clotted masses
    like cotton batting entangled in the
    grass
the screams of people riding roller
    coasters and splashing in the flume
the slow lap of water at the moored boats

making wine
definitions
chicken, golden and crisp, and a pile of
    tender, bright green snap beans
lighthouses
ragamuffins
tugs-of-war
going to Tiffany and trying on rings
cigar boxes
far corners of the earth
The Waltons (TV show)
Bohemian prep schools
Irish linen place mats
skinny ties
spinning quite a yarn
trigonometry
going for 'za (pizza)
using the library's periodicals
being devoted to something outside
    yourself
brick-paved residential streets with
    restored Victorian homes
wrought-iron ice-cream parlor chairs
dainty French daisies
going to church on Christmas Eve in the
    New England tradition
making love
oak rockers
taking down badminton and volleyball
    nets

tepee playhouses

baked coffee custards

pillows, thick comforters, antique linens,
    mohair throws, lace curtains

political conventions

making believe you're somewhere else, in
    a different era or role

salt-cured ham steaks

silos, like giant thermoses on the
    dairyland table

wild blueberries blanketing coastal
    Maine

mingling over wine and hors d'oeuvres
    beside a crackling fire

Volkswagens

coleslaw dressing (a lifesaver)

hardware stores with an inexhaustible
    supply of eminently useful items

collecting pinecones

a half-moon-shaped desk like Noah
    Webster's

lumberjacks

camellias like starched organdy

camp stoves

homemade jam on toast

linebackers

longing for certain happinesses

manhandling the "Open here" spout of a
    milk carton so badly that you have to
    resort to using the "illegal" side

comfortable armchairs
ham-and-chicken salad
miniature hors d'oeuvre cutters
January in California
the panes of a greenhouse
cuddling up to your lover for warmth
sun brightening the brick wall of a house
pine deacons' benches
Montana: bitterroot, wind-sculpted
    buttes, snow, copper, sapphires,
    pasturelands
sandstorms
running a corporation
sun-drenched climates
Senator Howard Baker, Tennessee
mulled wine
country auctions
Sunday supper waffles
tintypes of grandparents in silver frames
wind circles in the sand from beach grass
banana bark
Aunt Jemima
being recognized for doing your own
    thing and respected for it
cinnamon-scented yams
cone shells
strangers you see so regularly that you
    feel they're almost friends
containers of homemade lemonade
fending off a pushy salesperson

ginger beer
honeysuckle
looking at the western sky in midevening
moonbeam blue, sunset pink, star-white,
    and Astroturf-green colors
mushy talk
people who have it all together
showing sensitivity and concern
the Procrastination Club of America
stopwatches
"Morning mouth, when it tastes like the
    inside of a sneaker" (commercial)
blood banks
choosing a chandelier
frozen ice on a stick
ground beef
snow swirls
leprechauns
an old Union Crawford six-burner
    kitchen wood stove
larch trees
maple syrup
typecasting
apple-silk cheese pie
Gerald Ford, former president, "throwing
    a baby and kissing a snowball"
large etched-glass bowls for serving
    salads, fruits, ice cream
marriage certificates
parachutes in the air

serving breakfast or brunch to someone
     you love
modeling schools
strawberry ice treats
terry towels big enough for two
throwing a roof party
a roadhouse
pins made from cookies
barbed wire
B. Dalton Booksellers
arranging a work area
strip sandals in white or brown
carrying books to class in an airline bag
dark green upholstery
Christmas trees lining the street, their
     lights reflecting in the frost that
     covered the cobblestones
earth shoes
fireside tray suppers
formal walking-sticks
harmonizing
horses with snow on their back
insulated bottles full of cider spiced with
     hot cinnamon
Gustave Stickley, Duncan Phyfe, and
     Brewster chairs
natural-wood soap dishes that drain
     themselves
listening to chamber music on the
     veranda

carrot tops

rising earlier than the others, puttering
softly and quieting the beasts

T-shirts on backwards

a stream laughing as it tickles its own
snowy banks

not worrying about what's going to
happen

note-taking in college

petunias and green leaves in a gravy boat

the yellowing pages of old books

putting on heavy ski socks and a good
warm bathrobe

rattan doll furniture

sitting in chairs on the porch and
watching the sun

tattersall shirts with bow ties

water pumps

old medical or legal texts

Betty Grable, actress

butterflies

putting things back where they were
found

cut the deck deeper = provide further
explanation

times when you have to eat-and-run

getting more freckles

mountain-edge flowers

stubby little glasses

young colts

lover's-knot doormats
navy heroes
never anticipating wealth from any
    source but labor
getting really good meat from the
    butcher
savory food
keeping each thing to its season
low-calorie ice cream
rows of glass-fronted boutiques
always losing tic-tac-toe games
bowls and baskets made out of bread
    dough
fawn-colored trousers
mixed vegetables in onion sauce
box springs
plain yellow and plain green gelatin
    cubes
kayak races
special introductory courses
Pizza Hut restaurants
the fizz of a soda syphon
a sharp paring knife
"Hi, there"
no-bake pies
learning to make the perfect cup of coffee
peach butter
planning a weekend of doing something
    you usually tell yourself you're too
    unadventurous for

reading the paper outside on the porch,
     curled up in a big old rocking chair
Niagara wine
circular couches
scarf hats with visors
orange juice in champagne flutes
seaside teas
a slatted wood staircase
spaciousness
basketball socks
staying in the tub longer than it takes to
     get clean
toast and apple butter
yeast-raised doughnuts
an after-dark ramble to search for
     fireflies; listening for night sounds
blazers and white pleated skirts
challenging your lover to a game of
     checkers or Scrabble, baking some
     cookies and adding Spanish sherry
     and mellow jazz
really thick eyelashes
champagne butter sauce
classically cut trousers with pocket on
     seam, straight leg, 1 1/4-inch cuffs
"Layla" (song)
gratefulness
pleated gauze curtains
gray New England winter mornings
Frankenstein

heavy glass humidors with solid-brass lids
ribald humor
tubs of Pepsis and ice
unbuttered green beans
a beaver dam
baby dresses
bib overalls
Fibber McGee and Molly
lace-edged napkins and old hammered
    silver
a mockingbird singing on the chimney
the racket of garbage cans
filbert = reconciliation
secret lands
social security number: first 3 numbers
    tell in what part of the country you
    were born; next 2, a code for the year
    you applied; last 4, your citizen's
    number
red leotards
wading pools
wedding cake
knee patches
pie throwing
precariously tall lemon meringue
locking little fingers
preparing for tomorrow
pretending to take down an "important"
    phone message
sleeping sprawled out on the bed

the hot-stove league in baseball
sleepy times
the first nip of clear, cold air
steeplechase
big joys and small pleasures
the rainbow and sand colors of pretty hair
Certs breath mints
the unmistakable message of love
when the pink of the sunrise reflects on
    the snow of a glacier
treating yourself to a new purse
wheat fields
"When things get tough, the tough get
    going"
Weekly Reader magazine
crème de menthe parfaits
dreaming of dancing at the royal ball and
    midnight never comes
the stirring beat of a fife-and-drum corps
dressing to the max and flirting
hunches
feeding bread to birds in winter
Johnny Carson
raised potato biscuits
free hot dogs
life's great pleasures
refreshments
children in knee-highs
soft luggage
coffee cloud sponge cake with coffee icing

effort activities: debating society, hop
    committee, literary magazine,
    newspaper features or cartoons,
    drama club, cheerleading or pep
    squad
high ceilings, beautiful fireplaces, and
    old-fashioned molding
johnny-jump-ups
Kahlúa chocolate torte
John Dean, Watergate conspirator
The Banana Splits (TV cartoon show)
"The Rail" to congregate at in high
    school
Irish oatmeal muffins spread with a little
    whipped maple syrup
Susan B. Anthony
orienteering
quilts wrought during long winter
    evenings
raising kids
spice-colored kitchens
swing-away can openers
things you don't have to work at to enjoy
this thing called love
children's stainless sets
a stationery embosser
coincidences
crisp blue-and-white plaid and rich
    yellow upholstery adding to natural
    wood and brick tones

prisms
hair ribbons
ink etchings
Dairy Queen Dilly Bars
taking a complete rest
fried green tomatoes with bacon and
    cheese
the individual squares of a waffle
the purple of heather and yellow of gorse
    that inspire the patterns of Irish tweed
going to the movies in the afternoon
    when you're supposed to be at work
asking him to breakfast: croissants or
    warm rolls, good jam, sweet butter,
    hand-squeezed orange juice, an egg
    dish, ham, sausage or country bacon,
    and good coffee
mopping up the last trace of gravy with
    the last piece of corn bread
fake glitter
mullein, wild yarrow, broom sedge, dock,
    and black-eyed Susans
July: National Ice Cream Month
silver beads
the area between the highway and the
    exit lane where cars go when drivers
    can't decide what to do next
velvet brown, chrome yellow, suntan
    colors
silver rings

all of the bobby pins falling on the floor
all-night white-hot wiener shops
cold cucumber soup, made hot, then
    chilled
collecting postcards, beachcombings,
    wine labels, magazine covers, teddy
    bears, favorite cartoons, matchbooks,
    old *Life* magazines, baby chairs,
    necklaces
delicately blooming orchids, colorful
    azaleas, and pineapple plants coming
    to fruit
filling tartlet shells
gold-panning
hula, lei, muumuu, ukulele, luau
lemon butter
pomanders grouped with pinecones,
    mandarin oranges, and gourds
rambunctiousness
going up on the roof and examining your
    neighborhood
remembering a birthday
Funny Face comic books
lining up beautiful books on a
    mantelpiece
mini baskets as containers for small gifts
non-aerosols
pink satin apples with green felt leaves
    and grosgrain loops for hanging
men's shorts

sandwiches and canapés
Pennsylvania and Swiss chocolate
tuna chowder
wine coolers
winter's ice-cream sea
conch shells
Central Park in winter
fennel-specked sausage
fine cuisine
smoke curling out of 200-year-old
    chimneys
Snowballs: chocolate-filled cakes
violets and dandelions
wood-burning cookstoves
wooden fences bordered by colorful
    peonies
brown-sugar or maple-sugar toast
chocolate ambrosia pie
flower seeds
good thick steaks and stone crab claws,
    with pickles and chopped liver and
    onions on the side
ground chuck
a puppy at the gnaw-it-all stage
the richest of seasons
copper color
Jerry West, basketball player
perfectly textured hot chocolate
scrambled eggs with five cheeses
shredded cabbage salad

warmed bread
workbenches
a relish tray with a cheddar spread and
sweet-and-sour cucumbers
open house in a new home
surf fishing
boroughs of the City of New York
burnished, russety, cool, quiet wood tones
carrot-and-raisin slaw
corn patties
errant clouds chasing each other across
the blue sky
fire escapes
instant atmosphere: small scented
candles for bedside; tall, slim tapers
for table
care labels on clothes
listening to the radio
mashed potatoes with butter and sour
cream
passion and compassion
rising early
a three-chair barbershop with shelves of
colorful shaving mugs
tissue paper
tossed salad
sour ball: apricot brandy splashed over
ice, topped with juices of half a lemon
and half an orange
castles and fortresses

dusk-time twittering of swallows
get-acquainted parties
your tummy wanting something yummy
not expecting too much
knowing that nothing can be too warm,
    too generous, too brilliant
nutmeg and Worcestershire sauce
    sprinkled on London broil or flank
    steak
Little League baseball
setting sail
water sports
a trio of Thai bamboo birdcages
wet T-shirts
a trouser trolley rack
antique Chinese porcelain covered tea
    bowls for sugar or candy
Betty Jean Perske: Lauren Bacall's real
    name
automatic transmission
a butter brique for cooling butter
cotton candy
cut-the-cake sand game
enticing back roads for motoring
extra kisses
getting a library card
plucking tomatoes sun-warm, giving
    them a hint of salt and a breath of
    pepper
sautéed Canadian bacon

"Hush Puppies aren't such a fancy shoe
or a pretty shoe, they're just dumb"
(commercial)
city squares
chunky cranberry sauce
buying hardcover books
houseboating
living alone
navy pants and light blue shirts
a very sharp moonlight
devil's food
a morning tea party: lighted fire, small
clove-studded apples floating in hot
cider, homemade toast with honey
butter, and breakfast sausage cooked
in maple syrup
low, rolling thunder in late fall
new stanzas to the poems written on the
hillside, meadow, and riverbank
powder mitts
cow tails taking batting practice
down pillows
Max Factor and Fabergé cosmetics
Tex-Mex food
the Olympics
buying soap bubbles and
blowing them at an
unsuspecting person
Dr Pepper baked beans
L'Air du Temps cologne

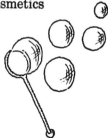

a Bad Day Survival Kit

Granny Smith, Golden Delicious, Cortland, McIntosh, and Jonathan apples

leaves twinkling in the sunlight, spangling in the moonlight, dancing to the special music of raindrops on their thickness

meat that is buttery textured, tender like pot roast

peach cream-cheese pie

dress shirts

play being a rest from the world

quail in wine sauce with grapes

reading all night and sleeping all morning

learning to pot plants

roads becoming black velvet ribbons with winking frost sequins

scarf skirts

small venison steaks studded with red peppercorns, sautéed and then wrapped in herbed crêpes and served in brown sauce with red currant brandy

thatched roof cottages

Spanish rice

wrapped-bodice, cowl-neck, or raglan-sleeve leotards

amateur psychoanalysis

on an autumn weekend, wrapping
   yourself in a blanket in front of a
   fireplace
beach scenes
changing self-defeating behavior
cracking a secret code
draft horses
foamy clouds
"Made in Japan" labels
medical research
robins' eggs
table linens
music in the air
tubs of daffodils and other spring flowers
a broad porch, ideal for rocking
Bibb lettuce
debating half in jest
an old-fashioned herb bed
accepting a compliment
the Sunbelt
backgammon sets for four players
bacon, eggs, sausage, coffee, cereal,
   pitchers of milk, apple butter, two
   kinds of fresh rolls, and gallons of
   apple juice
the last shy bloomings of wild rose in
   already fading brambles
the moon etching whimsical
   hieroglyphics on the snow beneath
   naked trees

medicine men
mod paper flowers in pop bottles
an old-time rocking horse
red Ferraris
the roar and crackle of a log fire's
    beginnings and the whispering
    snicker of its slow dying
Andy Capp comic strips
keeping a smile on your face till the
    shutter clicks
one of those lucky days when there is a
    ton of stuff in the refrigerator
the Parker House Hotel in Boston
freewheeling characters
bring-a-friend banquets
thin pretzels
the pastiche of a colorful fishing village
white grapes
the nickname "Boo Boo"
pheasant in port sauce
scented oils
Frank Lloyd Wright designs
challenging your own assumptions
the splintery crack of new books
status quo institutions: piano lessons,
    ballet lessons, dancing school, French
    lessons, tennis lessons, sailing
    lessons, riding lessons, summer camp
the structure of texts
the texture of cream

unmowed patches of grass, discovered
    after one has put away the mower
treasure-hunting with a favorite
    youngster
beef bologna
brewing a pot of cinnamon coffee
creamed onions baked with a cheese
    topping
creamy cottage cheese with a toasted
    bagel
dreaming of going home
fresh supplies of wood
parrots
sugar and creamer sets
sugar wafers
old-fashioned soda-pop cans with rings
    that come off
Keith Magnuson, hockey player
quilted cotton jackets
quince honey
rain forests
the custom of puddings and pies for
    breakfast treats
the fragrance of wild strawberries in the
    summer sun
Switzerland cheese-and-onion pie
thinly sliced cucumber sandwiches, fresh-
    baked scones with a dab of
    strawberry jam and whipped cream
white organdy curtains

going to a sporting event with some
    chubby Dagwood sandwiches and a
    jug of sangria
whitefish baked in wine and served in a
    champagne butter sauce
little ducky tummies
being scared of someone pushing
    your swing
epistemology
glimmer yarn
using a big word
pencil boxes
locking glove compartments
waking up New Year's Day and knowing
    you didn't make a fool of yourself
baked potato for lunch
malted milk waffles and pancakes
nylon tricot
palindrome = a sentence or group of
    words that reads the same backwards
    as forwards
pulling up your collar
silk anklets in different colors
solecisms, catachreses
allspice, aniseed, bay leaves, bouillon,
    cardamon, caraway, celery salt,
    chives, cinnamon, citron, cloves,
    coriander, curry, dill, garlic, ginger,
    honey, horseradish, hyssop, leek,
    lemon, lime

PENCILS

well-buttered crumpets
calorie-intake control
colors and textures borrowed from
  outdoors
hula-hooping
dart boards
arms control
long walks across the frozen lake to the
  post office
munching cookies and sipping colas
reading between the lines
pantry carts
shower gifts
abracadabra
sons mowing the lawn to earn a down
  payment on an MG
wine country
banana breakfast bread
Bonanza, Ponderosa steak houses
"Indian Summer" by Emily Dickinson
dinghy boats
cooking demonstrations
finding a four-poster at a country auction
short shorts
fines herbes
gingerbread-flavored memories of
  childhood
shopping at Macy's for two hours
shortbread: buttery, crumbling Scottish
  biscuit-cake

dinner bells

the snort of a nose-blower

store-bought potpourri tucked in a pretty
hankie and cinched with ribbon

wooden bowls

boo-shoo-bop

chocolate-dipped cones

dropping out of something important

food candles

crocheted cord choker necklaces

food prepared at hibachi tables

frosted-glass coasters

topstitching

zipper teeth

apple kuchen

something as pretty as a picture

a quilt on a brass bed

party plates

pork sausage

stripteases

terra-cotta Mexican candlesticks in gray-
blue, sand, and white

surprising your partner and picking him
up from work

turning points in life

Vermont goat meat crêpes, lobster
quiches, maple-apple-sweet potato
casserole, golden curried potato soup,
and a whole roasted turkey with
bourbon-pecan stuffing

Turkish silver goblets

work corners

a room overlooking the lakeshore

barbecued pork chops with tangy pear sauce

April chills

perfect baked potatoes

borrowing a friend's child for a few hours to allow her an afternoon off

a bell to ring when you enter an office or store

as a youngster, enjoying the romping, tumbling sport of careening down steep, sandy slopes of a dune

carving sets

Burberrys outer jackets

corsage pins

Coricidin cold medicine

Farmer Brown

hard cheeses

insulated windbreakers

listening to the tinkle of Taiwan bamboo wind chimes

making mushy valentines for your lover

raspberry, orange, pumpkin, lime, coffee, chocolate, and cherry chiffon pies

Mrs. Butterworth's syrup bottles

a self-indulgent lunch all by yourself in a grand restaurant with a marvelous book

a sliced steak sandwich on toasted bread
cast parties
a pastry board with patterns for rolling a
    tart to a 10-inch pie
custard cups
kitchenettes
nature walks
oatmeal days
wire baskets
outdoor glow
Little Red Riding Hood
patio tables
rattan trays with rims
watching out for traffic, holding hands,
    and sticking together
a trout pond
butter-grilled mushrooms seasoned with
    salt, pepper, and lemon
button shoes
cotton velveteen jeans
date and cream cheese sandwiches
eating alone
getting a back scratch
hot biscuits
Mount Vernon
blue-glazed stoneware canisters, corked
    and numbered *une* to *cinq* in a
    French country kitchen
hot chocolate at an outdoor café
double-hung staircases

blueberry pancakes made with stone-
ground whole-wheat flour, granulated
sugar, homogenized milk, and
blueberries
country-crusted breads
a county fair wheeling by in a Technicolor
blur of sawdust and cotton candy
gluing a puzzle onto a cookie tin
having the ducks at the zoo eat the bread
you've thrown to them
buying a hat, gloves, and boots for a
three-year-old
pizza bricks
J & B Scotch
"101 Dalmatians" (story)
Amish quilts in a double wedding ring
pattern
T.B.A. = to be avoided
a Barbie Doll lunch box
a Crayola beginner's set
"I love you"
khaki and wheat colors
eating peas with a fork
planetariums
Texas toast: thick slices of white bread
brushed with butter and grilled
ivy-leaved toadflax stretching to a bank
of wild strawberries
playpen toys
roast pork, fried potatoes, baked tomatoes

a clam shell for a pen tray
standing up for yourself
country pies
toast and honey butter
track shorts
an asterisk with no corresponding
    footnote
at a 6 A.M. breakfast, watching the sky
    perform
black lights
places to go antiquing
bramble: raisins, cranberries in pastry,
    topped with ice cream
"Happy Birthday!" yelled as you enter a
    crowded room
L.L. Bean blucher moccasins
drawing the curtains on a leaden
    afternoon sky, turning with relief to
    an open fire
glazed pears
a brick walk
recipes from old books
secret mazes
succulent baked chicken or country ham
    accompanied by fresh-baked rolls
accomplished musicians
bacon grease
bucking a trend
out-of-order escalators
facial masks

made-on-the-farm taste
mud-thick Greek coffee
order of Presidential succession
red licorice
saddle-soaping leather
soda fountain memories you'll never
lose
the deposit that beats your rubber check
to the bank
sleepthings
the dignified face of a woman well into
her 80s
wide ruffles
beds with original mosquito nets
knee warmers
meeting someone special at the Customs
gate
needlecrafts
shells in a shadow box
speedwriting
the field hockey team in college
goldsmithing
the flavor and ambience of the Maine
woods
thirsty children kissing water from a
fountain
the pasture gate, fashioned of frozen mist
Swedish baked potatoes
the very best tea, the very blackest coffee,
and the very thickest cream

sterling-silver initial pendants
the wind whistling and moaning at the
    window and the stove with its
    steaming teapot sputtering a
    contented reply
"The Farmer in the Dell" (song)
toe clippers
tweed slacks
wheelbarrows
keeping score at a wrestling match
braised beef
beer = beevos, brewski, greenie, road
    brew, roadies, road sauce
the cinch belt
credit cards
feet sticking out of a sandpile
the nickname "Bucky Beaver" because of
    buck teeth
free kittens
fresh flowering plants
green thumbs
thermal blankets
taffy-pulling contests
café au lait
magic tricks
signet rings
being fresh from the shower in a big robe
    with wet hair combed back
argyle socks
keeping a secret

the small bar that turns an "O" into
    a "Q"
the sound a yawning dog emits when he
    opens his mouth too wide
an hour or two fly-fishing in a quiet pool
raisin-and-apple rolls
shivaree serenades for newlyweds
Oriental bowls with a fish motif
colored snow
skinned knees being easier to fix than
    broken dreams
spirit lamps
twisting someone's arm
uninhibited statements
using a telephoto lens
coffeehouses
whispering in the dark
fences
Highlights children's magazine
knowing the absolutely right way to do
    something
chimney pots
a 25¢-off coupon
hoisting the sails in Florida in brisk blue
    early mornings at the marina
making chocolate curls
chilled cucumber-and-tomato soup
picking up tiny seashells, filling them
    with wet sand, and poking in the
    stems of little flowers

writing in a wonderful hand
being frugal
baking in a brick oven
Eskimo cider
Galileo slow thermometers: crystal orbs
    rearranging themselves
inlaid mahogany tables
a kaleidoscope of colors
milkweed pods beginning to float
    and burst
rolling magazine racks
Oklahoma: cattle, hardwoods, oil
tall candles
a grill in a brick niche
bright yellow yolks
Saltine crackers
colorful stationery in the pigeonholes of
    your desk
yellow cheeses, fresh brown eggs, glowing
    pumpkins, tangy russet apples, farm
    butter proudly stamped with the
    maker's own mark, fat purple turnip
    globes, superb smoked hams, chicken
    with the flavor of Sunday afternoon
    family dinner—all snapped up in
    local markets
volunteering to help out in a soup kitchen
below a meringue, a lode of banana
    cream, butterscotch, lemon,
    chocolate, or coconut cream

well-coordinated charm
colonial wick lanterns
billionaires
colors intense against pale sand
golden champagne punch
lime marshmallow salad
oompah music
something new and bright to wear
army surplus
walking shady paths in the woods
    surrounding the inn
Dom Pérignon champagne
"A man thinketh, so he is"
long Edwardian jackets
miniature orange trees
pincushions
Continental beef steak
finger bowls
pine needles tipped with teardrops of rain
running down the dunes
senior proms
Pennsylvania scrapples
sundresses and pinafores you can layer
    over T-shirts
San Francisco strawberry parfait
vintage cabs
the periodic table
winter, a time to emulate nature
conversation whipping gaily around a
    table like rags in a wind

finding a good butcher
Fonzie from *Happy Days*
hand-cranking a freezer of peach ice
    cream
knowing where all your books are
rookie shows
shoe-shining
smokestacks autographing the sky
a small picket fence in the snow
woolen mills
snow peaches
acorn squash
"tossing your cookies"
booby hatch = mental institution
chocolate-dipped graham crackers
choosing a luxury ship
a silly stretchy snake
croque monsieur sandwiches of ham and
    cheese, bananas with rum
flowers and champagne waiting in your
    room
frost before November 23 auguring bad
    weather
puppet shows
supper clubs
a pretty table for Easter dinner
apple butter
small-town cafés
expensive unlisted phone numbers
explosion of fireworks

corn-poppers
mirrors inside closets
parsley and watercress
Mercedes taxicabs and limousines
portable refrigerators
strawberry-pink shirt and tights
turkey tacos
warming milk for cocoa
a rambunctious rooster
a runner made out of small-print fabric
    and lace for the table
surrendering
cool limestone cellars
airy netting
carrying groceries in a backpack
corn-on-the-cob dishes
early-morning eateries
fern gardens
garden ferns
herbs to use with beef
hog-calling contests
kisses: love's punctuation marks
masked balls
pastry carts
tastefulness
a shingled water tower
solid-brass wind-bells
a stalled car catching
storm sashes
Baskin-Robbins ice-cream cartons

getting a tan on the fire escape
horn-rim glasses
litmus paper
Hutchinson bottles with stoppers
notary seals
patchworking
the rattle of an old truck
setting the dining room table up for arts
    and crafts
watching the rain fall
afternoon air that dares you to breathe it
anticipating vacations
"Better safe than sorry"
eating halls
antique glass inkwells
art training
seeing eye to eye
fried, roasted, and smoked drumsticks
    and wings of turkey, hot and cold
    crisp salads, and crusty pies
hot biscuits, oatmeal with cream
laundry soap
plush carpet
Paul Newman and Robert Redford in
    Butch Cassidy and the Sundance Kid
someone being your every dream
brush strokes in artists' pastels
crumb crusts
hot popovers
double-burner griddles

the four basic food groups
new white tennis shoes
buying classic clothes
razzmatazz
"10-4" and other CB talk
hot mushroom turnovers
bebop tunes
Dr Pepper commercials
T.C. (Top Cat)

bowls of sparkling berries and fresh
cream, baskets of popovers and
croissants with little pots of jams and
jellies, steaming coffee and freshly
squeezed orange juice, thick country
bacon, hot maple syrup, pancakes,
and French toast

dew-filled lawns dusted with bairnwort
and baby's-pet-the-daisy before the
heads lay in piles of fresh-mown grass

believing in one great love
the gearshift on a recliner
Italian salad dressing
orange skies
a bowl of matches from watering holes
around the world

seersucker slacks
gas-era lampposts
roasted green peppers stuffed with a
pungent meat-and-cheese filling
dressed in tomato sauce

reaching out to people
seam rippers
shaggy Dartmoor ponies
meatballs in onion gravy or barbecue
    sauce
standing up straighter
starting a wine cellar
Rockefeller Center, New York City
addressing a golf ball
wearing one long braid
an antique-lace hankie
a beach strewn with timbers of uprooted
    wharves and broken boats
bran muffins
drafts scurrying like mice about the
    house
playing Crazy Eights
a flawless sea
heat-resistant, clear-glass mugs
abandoning all your senses to a field of
    wildflowers
heavy Romanian crystal
lobster pots
spending a weekend alone with the cat
Liberty silver dollars
ribbon candy
a balcony resting in the top branches of
    an oak tree
a black suit
baby chickens roasted with herbs

Bob and Ray, comedians

kicking your baggage to the airport counter

picking a sanctuary in your home: a favorite chair with favorite books nearby, a spot to come to and relax all by yourself

picnicking by the pond

Michigan City, Indiana

a brick-paved courtyard with a cluster of gift shops

raccoons raiding a sweet corn patch and filching from the summer garbage

rocks and rye

secret doors

ticker tapes

a canapé and petit-four server

ceiling-hung slatted wood trays

a champagne picnic on a blanket up on the roof under the stars

piglets

access roads

accomplishing what you undertake

backyard screen houses

individual mini crocks

Twiggy, model/actress

old photographs matted with small-print fabrics, a framed doily, and an old mirror

old fancy two-piece pool sticks

red lipstick

the smell of grilled onions in Grand Central Station

cedar boards

hiding behind curtains

overstuffed sandwiches

pleasant autumn drives

seeing *The Nutcracker Suite*

shell prints

opera houses

sleigh bells

spending time in the baby's nursery after everyone is sleeping

the Dow Jones industrial average

fresh vegetable sticks

New York strip sirloin, cut extra thick

the millions of styrofoam wads that accompany mail-order items

Swedish butter cookies

the two-foot-long security plastic device encasing cassette tapes at record stores

unexpected phone calls

when the sky has lost the sunlight but not yet found the stars

beef brisket, barbecued or smothered in liquid smoke

the study of wind resistance conducted by holding a cupped hand out the car window

crème brûlée
fields of June daisies
railroad stations
life choices
white poinsettias
coffeemakers
vegetables served Southern style
wagon trains
the first frost coming without a whisper,
    the glistening leaf, the gleaming vine
big ironed white cloth napkins
English farmhouse cheddar cheese
white clapboard houses
high-gloss white paint
periwinkle shells
playing Yahtzee
achievements
onion dicers
the habit of making distinctions
rain ponchos
cardigan sweater jackets
Oriental grocery shops
pulling a velvety petal from a flower and
    brushing it against your cheek
skinny Christmas trees
thick, golden curried potato soup
things that look juicy
white sneakers and black socks worn
    with khaki pants
an iron tortilla press

being glad you have each other
bringing beauty and meaning into life
the Pittsburgh airport
two-by-fours
chicken cooked in beer
milk glasses
chicken wire
trim on cars
Chinese sandalwood, French
    apricot flavors

flirting for no reason
reading dictionaries
going to the season's first drive-in movie
fresh, luscious fruits
grilled lamb medallions with apricot
    sauce
oaken floors
gardening tools: rake, hoe, hand fork,
    trowel, spade, wheelbarrow, watering
    can, seed box, dibble, secateurs,
    scissors
mulling spices of stick cinnamon, dried
    sweet orange peel, cracked nutmegs,
    and whole cloves
the roller derby
selling lemonade from a big earthenware
    crock set up on a card table on the
    sidewalk
wild Maine blueberries heaped onto a
    crust and topped with whipped cream

the impossible encounters that live in the
    imagination and somehow become
    reality
belt-in-the-back coats
calling bars "lounges"
talking about problems
delicious spiced holiday cookies
Ellery Queen mysteries
holding a jujube up to the cinema screen
    in order to determine its color
pumpkins lit to frighten witches
romantic fashion looks
something springing from mind's eye, to
    sketch pad, to reality
committees of Congress
hams cured the old-fashioned way
snow croquet
many pillows
singing alto in church
cheap formal gowns
sun-dried tomato pesto
tent dresses
soaking down a dog and standing back as
    he shakes dry
wineglasses
conversations on paper
gourmet tools: oven rack push/puller,
    adjustable measuring spoon, bowl-
    fitting scraper, egg piercer, honey
    server, and strawberry huller

winter sports banquets
congenial domestic animals and selected
    wild species
gentlemen rising when a lady enters or
    leaves a room
honey and lemon creams
ironing hair
shoe tassels
a short, squat candle in a tart tin
shower-microphone soap
honeydew and tangerine colors
slow sunsets
a plain, thin bracelet
Garfield Goose
snow picnics
stoneware pouring bowl
toothpaste commercials
wooden kegs for storing beer and keeping
    it cool
a wooden stepladder as plant stand
chocolate raspberry truffle cake
flopping around in a wading pool
goo-goo eyes
maple butternut squash
procrastinations
napkin rings
paper cups of cinnamon-flavored
    applesauce
paper plates
rope weaving

filling stations

when the whole school assembled in the
   auditorium to watch a space shot

poplin "weekend" pants

marina cafés

strawberry-rhubarb jam

string beans

turkey trots

world globes

a romantic holiday with one special
   person

deep purple miniature eggplants, with
   stems and leaves attached, piled high
   on a round wicker platter and placed
   on a violet tablecloth with deep
   lavender napkins

acrylic modeling paste

curling toes

barns sweet with hay and leather

burly country tweed jackets in
   herringbone, houndstooth, or Harris
   tweed

Burberrys for children

Carole King, singer/composer

cords or flannels for men and Laura
   Ashley for women

curly endive

farm trucks chugging into the square
   with loads of fruits and vegetables

garden hoses

listening to Mozart: feeling like tulips,
    warm breezes, boats on the lake, and
    sailor hats
most popular U.S. main dish: fried
    chicken
pastry chefs
testing a bone for fossilization
Baskin-Robbins, Burger King, Carvel,
    Chicken Delight, Kentucky Fried
    Chicken, Dairy Queen, Dunkin'
    Donuts, McDonald's, Wendy's, White
    Castle, and Arby's
casaba melon
notch-collared blazers
getting a check from the insurance
    company
potted palms
a ritual in reminiscence
watching as a raging ocean rises
trustfulness
brushing your son's hair
water-cooling pitchers
a table laden with platters of cider-baked
    ham and roast turkey, crocks of apple
    butter, bowls of green beans with
    smoked side meat, scalloped sweet
    potatoes with apples, sweet-and-sour
    cabbage salad, an iron kettle of thick
    bean soup from the stockpot, a basket
    of hearth bread, and tins of fruit pies

sitting down and really thinking out
an attitude of yours that you're not
sure of
a torchlight ski down the slopes
butter-steamed carrots
reminding yourself that everything you
do, think, and dream matters
cottage cheese with chives, with apples,
with onions and herbs
getting a whiff of that first ocean breeze
sour-cream pumpkin pie
Sturbridge apple bread
touching-the-sky, dreamy, ice-creamy
times
chubby coats
garter hooks
chunky spaghetti sauce
double dares
savoir-faire
Vivaldi in the morning
deviled eggs
rosemary = remembrance
getting up and watching the sun rise
even if you don't have to because of
your job
saying yes yes yes
toy soldiers
cozy jackets
rechecking the mailbox to make sure
your letter has gone down

bowls of vegetables being passed
"Closed" signs
a Sunday feast of pot roast or plump
    roasted chicken
a tin lizzie
learning the harmonica
Italian hot dog topped with tomato sauce
    and mozzarella cheese
playing freeze-tag in the sprinkler
old housekeeping books
quarterbacks
reaching toward greater self-awareness,
    appreciation of beauty, and love of
    others
roast goose served with lemon apples or
    glazed pears
Noah's soup: two of everything
slanting rays of the western sun
small salads
traveling toothbrushes
wearing perfume when you're alone
    reading
clairvoyance
soaking in a bath, reading, and sipping
    orange juice
classic = person or object that is different
    or strange
spiral staircases
framing the best Christmas cards
old political cartoons

grandmothers
Flash Gordon
talking to yourself
baby bunting
haberdashers
sparkling French blue and soft peach
    Spanish poppies
pictures after parties
taco dinners
bucketful of natural-wood kitchen
    utensils
decorating with sheets
tuition
old stock certificates
antique butter churns
red ribbons tied in bows around tree
    limbs
riding well-schooled ponies through
    woods and on the hillsides
Gene Shalit's mustache
the Greek alphabet: alpha, beta, gamma,
    delta, epsilon, zeta, eta, theta, iota,
    kappa, lambda, mu, nu, xi, omicron,
    pi, rho, sigma, tau, upsilon, phi, chi,
    psi, omega
ocean scallops sautéed in a very delicate
    curried drawn butter
seeing a grown man cry
seeing the world through each other's
    eyes

chain stores
drive-in root beer mugs
the Raisin Bran song
English library ladder chairs
stemmed bubble goblets
old-fashioned iceboxes
the Prophet, brother of Tecumseh
the start of softball season
tripods
canapé trays
Cheshire cats
the sound of boats rocking in their berths
sugar houses
vegetable combinations
big checkerboard plaid
egg-shelling
the special symbols used by cartoonists to
    replace swear words
steep-sided fluted brioche, the richest,
    butteriest, and airiest of all breads
Swedish cucumber salad
the things we don't talk about for fear
    that people won't understand
learning to lay a fire
the upward flight of skyscrapers
a toe-wiggling, breeze-blowing day
when he sets the table
when all the company you've got is a
    whistling teakettle
an empty parking space

beer parlors
breakers hammering a rocky coast
cheek-to-cheek dancing
goggles
cherry-chocolate color
the cardboard core in a toilet tissue roll
discovering that there is no real
    difference in the various cycles of
    your washing machine
the history of a four-poster bed
all the tiny bumps that make up a
    basketball
deep country
thinking good thoughts
deer slipping quietly across the lawn to
    eat the fallen apples
life jackets
"go for it" = get carried away and act
    stupid
pegboards inside desks
"The First Noel" (carol)
knit-purl combinations
nail sizes: 2-penny to 20-penny
dimmers for lights
onion domes and stained-glass windows
    against a forest setting
pails of first-run sap
quilted kitchen appliance covers
raisin sauce
slick chintz

a Swiss chalet dollhouse
Thing-Nik toys of yarn
Triumph cars
wienie roasts
white paneling and bamboo shades
the welcome light over the porch
brick cheese
bringing chores and a fiddle into the
    kitchen
chicken cooked in ginger and garlic
    powder
Chinese barbecued ribs
going to a football game with a warm
    blanket and thermos of hot chocolate
    to share
tree sitting
an area that is happily underdeveloped
    and underpopulated
making toast the old-fashioned way: on
    the end of a toasting fork over flames
    roaring in the fireplace
Lake Ontario
making a "balloon dog"
taking back road tours
baking-powder biscuits
milking cows
Milton Berle, comedian
selecting a wood stove
splurging on a great bottle of wine to
    drink on a third-class train ride

wallpapering
valentine candy hearts
Williamsburg, Virginia
fall foliage
gold-dipped rose color
lemon-and-oil dressing
all-purpose flour
pumpkin pie rich with eggs and cream,
    smooth to the tongue, tenderly
    enclosed in a crust that melts in the
    mouth
someone with boots on the wrong feet
summer houses
tomatoes on an orange tablecloth
Bambi's rabbit friends
camel's-hair polo coats
luncheon steak with garlic bread and
    salad
mental files
walking tall
municipal golf courses
your ring size being the same as your hat
    size
renting a car at the airport and driving
    on to the freeway playing the radio
    very, very loud
the ticking of an old clock
sending an April Fools' telegram
Sunday night family-room suppers
feeding and watching the winter birds

wintergreen Life Savers
candied sweet potatoes
congeniality
dance skirts
sunlight making polka dots on noses as it
    spills down through oak leaves
dinner menus
finger cakes
saying what's on your mind
snow crunching under your body, snug in
    its snowsuit and boots
chimney tops
storing notes and memorabilia in a
    family "time capsule" to be opened in
    A.D. 2001
stowing away memories of wonderful
    moments
wooden steps
broiling to perfection
garnet = constancy, fidelity
cookies: the perfume of the Yankee
    kitchen
cross-country skiing through quiet forests
esoterica = singular things, done by a
    small group
two chimneys holding a house like
    bookends
exotic Chinese birds hand-painted on
    cotton
flour scoops

catching a robber
footed bowls
sipping a kir in a Parisian café
zippers of sunbeams seaming up their
    light
a portrait in the snow
food thrills
marble sinks
a pot of tea produced when anything
    momentous occurs
experiencing much love
German marks
large biceps
meringues that melt in the mouth
perfume oils
a personalized leather-bound diary
scrumptious maple bars
working out at the gym
spring nights to look forward to
strawberry coffee cake
pepperoni on rye bread
popover pans
throwing your hair back away from your
    face to feel the sun
a rustic dollhouse made of logs and stones
press secretaries
barbershop harmonizing
caramelizing
Circle Line tours
earthen pots

fireplaces with mammoth andirons
windowboxes
gored skirts
hush puppies
just one day of looking terrific
burgundy mushroom soup
post offices
push-button telephones
strawberries in a pineapple boat
testing a few phrases of a remembered
    song
vast areas of cattails and river bulrushes
vested suits
sailing half-dazed through the air on a
    swing suspended from a tree
baskets of shells on a low table
kitties under blankets
little bits of kitchen knowledge
oatmeal raisin cookies
Highway 1 along the Big Sur coast of
    California
Botswana woven baskets
a butter slicer with wire dividers
paper cups with pull-out handles
catching the breeze in a hammock
a space suit
"It is the greatest of all mistakes to do
    nothing because you can only do
    little. Do what you can." (Sydney
    Smith)

cottage fried potatoes
eating popcorn and cracking nuts
the Cotton and Rose Bowl parades
getting something done by giving it to a
    busy person
hot Cajun pork sausage
hottles = glass beverage servers with
    black-rimmed neck and cap
"Rudolph the Red-Nosed Reindeer"
plump channel quilting
your-weight-and-fortune machines
"Auld Lang Syne" by Guy Lombardo
hot chocolate spiked with Kahlúa and
    topped with whipped cream
church lofts
equal rights
square nails
privacy
housemothers
Vivaldi's *Four Seasons*
Hawaiian Punch and gin
a wall-hung dispenser for plastic wrap,
    foil, and paper towels
feeling shy and wild
waylaying your latest crush on the
    footbridge
Mozart piano concertos
a hoedown
getting out cashmeres and tweeds
pagodas

R.E.M. sleep
leaning on a buck-and-rail fence
platters of fresh eggs
toast points
playing gourmet
snapping the lock on the swimming pool
    fence for the last time
blue daisies
pince-nez glasses
Aruba coffee
stapling papers for the study hall teacher
Bartlett's *Familiar Quotations*
team jackets
weaving cat's cradles and other string
    figures
an auctioneer's hammer
amaretto tea
beautiful things, seldom easy
brandied winter fruits: prunes, apricots,
    figs, nuts, raisins, and dates
clairvoyants
frankfurters
airline stewardess uniforms
a blue ribbon won at a playground pet
    show
a bonfire by an ice-skating rink
cabin lights
toasted sesame mustard
fabric, crayons, and imagination
kickshaws = delicacies

lacy Peter Pan collars
getting up early one warm morning and
    watching the sun rise
microwave mania and not being caught
    in it
cheerleading
greenhouse-fresh roses
softening your skin with cocoa butter
the Katzenjammer Kids
nickel loaves of bread
the desperation of a love letter
the first crossword puzzle, 1913
picking strawberries or tomatoes
recreation and leisure
keeping up muscle tone
ocean wading
suspendered overalls
weird biology teachers
rock crystal Christmas ornaments
sack lunches
a Victorian soap and sponge holder
fact-seekers
models' bags
old maps from a museum gift shop
old-fashioned kitchens
ice-cold oranges and crisp red onion salad
knees quivering when your lover
    comes in
one minute equaling 15 double-spaced
    typewritten lines in a speech

red-dogging the passer
pretty or amusing sleeping masks for
    when the sun's pouring in
scenes from old movies
sweaty football towels
"The best things in life are free"
Shetland crew-neck sweaters
the great elemental sounds of nature:
    driving rain, wind in a primeval
    wood, and the ocean striking beach
the inn dock
rereading a chapter or two from a favorite
    book
the secrets of closets
bridge brunches
the steps of the old post office
an early hunting owl winging close
mocha floats
an enameled breakfront gas range
Ace hardware stores
fresh clean sheets and blankets on the
    bed
dreams and imagination
fleur-de-lis
"The child born on the Sabbath day is
    blithe and bonny, good and gay"
the spiced aroma from the pickling kettle
    in the rural kitchen
soft flour tortillas with chili, cheese, and
    lettuce

great luxury
coffee at a dime a cup from a Bunn-O-
     Matic
lighted makeup mirrors
night lights
the sidewalk sizzling your soles
the smell of vinegar and pickling spices
     drifting out the door
organizing snapshots in an album
Sugar Bear
cooking big chunks of juicy apples slowly
     with cinnamon and sugar, letting
     the white mist carry the smell into
     the day
Swiss cheese
fog: technically nothing but a cloud in
     contact with the earth
school songs
the ride being worth the trouble
Tahitian tans
brick floors
Hygiene, Colorado
miniature fruit crates
What's Up, Doc? (movie)
peignoir sets
quiet green courtyards
being quietly sexy
sliced rosy tomatoes on thin, lightly
     buttered brown bread with ground
     black pepper

smiling at someone who never smiles at
    you
almanac forecasts
trimming logs for cabin building
waiting for the light to turn green when
    you've spotted an empty parking
    space across the intersection
trouser pockets chortling with change
white tablecloths covered with platters of
    scrambled eggs, steaming pancakes,
    warm syrup, compotes of honey, and
    tubs of fresh country butter
brick floors
the first time we helped to bake the bread
chicken and lobster served in a special
    sherry sauce
bridge lamps
chicken coop turned coffee table
crinkled aluminum foil
Edison's "Genius is 1 percent inspiration
    and 99 percent perspiration"
hairpin lace
making a TV commercial
taking baths
bike baskets
pulse points
salt marshes
silk daisies
talking heart to heart
lilacs "mauving" in the breeze

tolerable temperatures
wallpapering the floor
wild flowers
men's cashmere V-necks
willow trees
yellow Goldenrod writing tablets
being all alone with a black-and-white
    movie on television and a favorite
    pair of pajamas, cutting and pasting
    a scrapbook
all-white saddle shoes
cold hands, warm heart
Erma Bombeck, columnist/author
cultivating the habit of success
diligence and industry
felt puppets
gulls spiraling like paper airplanes
    against the sky
helping someone do laundry
electric blankets
Humphrey Bogart movies
romantic nooks for tea or drinks
Roman snails
common sense
compact overnight bags
the Mississippi River
bisque-head dolls
many surprises coming in one day
nonstop cool
Kansas wheat

sending "Snidely Whiplash" cards
London theater tickets
old-fashioned square dances
the ping-pong of batted tennis balls
running a retail store
sentiment and a sense of history
wine and cheese guides
being wonderfully alone on a frozen
    country pond
banana toast
minute hands
candlelight and Gregorian chants
sending small whimsical gifts to brighten
    a long day
conviviality
finding the perfectly ripe mango
ginger trees
Lionel electric trains
pooping out completely
James Bond movies
stone gargoyles
"Sportlight," Grantland Rice's sports
    column
wholesale boxes of Hershey bars, Milky
    Ways, and Tootsie Rolls
wooden baths
candles at the windows
Concord wine
woodspice and maple-frost colors
zoot suits

"Home Sweet Apartment"
broiling tomato halves with cinnamon,
    bread crumbs, and butter
clop of horses' hooves
cross-country trekkers
footed Pilsner glasses
good luck old witch on broom in kitchen:
    a Norwegian tradition
growing food
Japanese fried chicken
popping corn
shrimp color
strands of wood, mother-of-pearl, Iluana
    shell, yellow jade, and coffee bean
    beads
apple wood burning in the hearth
emphasis on handcrafts
a quaint maple mortar and pestle
acquiescence
parsleyheads
purchasing a yard of lavender ribbon to
    tie up poems
strawberry season and summer tea
striped chintz pillows
warmth and cordiality = peppermint
laughing out loud
wire mesh and glass soda syphons
a rainbow of soap bubbles dancing across
    the dishpan
a rasher of bacon done to a turn

a room with an old cannonball bed, a
    steamer trunk, and a view of Mount
    Washington
Bert Parks, former emcee of Miss
    America pageants
christenings
baby grand pianos
corn custard
Christmas tree farmers
Dorothy Hamill, skater
garlic bread
instant soup
mustard and dill sauce
oyster white
pastel skies
Missouri: Huck and Tom, rocky glens,
    Pony Express, watermelons
a sauce chef
rosti: partially-cooked potatoes formed
    into broad pancakes and fried until
    golden
unstringing black currants and seeding
    strawberries
a small fragrant disk of sausage
a straight black skirt
best-sellers
not having to pick up wet towels
centrifugal force
potato tarts
putting suntan lotion on someone

ultra-romantic dresses
a trunk full of patchwork pieces
acting class
cantilevered staircases
cottonseeds
preheating Dutch oven in fireplace, then
      adding bread dough or other item to
      be baked
the refrigerator egg holder
hot cross buns on Easter morning
blue pencils
ancient alphabets
living in a lighthouse
mouth-watering flavors
sautéed onion rings on a hot dog
getting out of class to set up for dances in
      the gym
soup du jour
sour-cream butter cake
truck stops and little country towns off
      the freeway
"tubby time"
buttons that say LOVE
the metal clicker at the top of a ballpoint
      pen
newfangled stacking potato chips
sewing name tags on clothes
Lucite clipboards
Palladian windows
discovering a different route to work

"A word to the wise is sufficient"
cowboy boots
saying "hello" to cows
buying dinner and tickets to a hockey
    game
flying south
"S" pothooks
a Model T bakery truck
planning a rites-of-spring party
a "backwards" party—clothes, invitation,
    and meal
jean jackets
leaves or seashells in your hair
space people
oranges, grapes, and peaches topped with
    freshly whipped cream
playing dumb
poached salmon served with dilled sour-
    cream sauce topped with feathery
    fresh dill
meadowlarks
reading the fine print
sponges
hat racks and hats
microwave cooking
the slap of a closing book
spaghetti with chicken
standing in the doorway, embracing
    sheets brought in from the line with
    an end-of-summer smell in them

"California Dreamin'" by the Mamas
     and the Papas
tractor feet
wrapping a taffeta ribbon around the
     waist of a white tunic or tying pastel
     ribbons around a straw hat
an apple-butter kettle
beach babies
Hawaiian Eye (TV show)
charcoal grills beside the shore
diagramming a sentence
glazed-dough ornaments
the back-and-forth dance of tennis players
the blizzard that hulks beyond the
     horizon
grass stains
hearing Santa and his reindeer on the
     roof
webbed army-type belts
a bright red maraschino cherry atop a
     snow-capped whipped cream
     mountain
ambidexterity
baby cougars
Mickey Mouse
seedless raspberry jam
rock gardens
soccer socks
French telephones
bacon-and-egg skillets

deciding when to bluff
modeling-agency models
seafoam green and baby-girl pink
shaking up our routine way of doing
    things
redwood forests and Spanish moss
sudden confrontation with a huge
    expanse of gentle hills and clusters of
    old trees
"Wednesday's child is full of woe"
cuddling your children
Joe Namath's autograph
paean = song of praise or triumph
presents such as little things from the
    dimestore, secondhand clothes,
    magazines, toys, costume jewelry,
    wonderful bath soap or salts, a week's
    worth of crossword puzzles, a library
    book, an article the person wanted to
    read and could not find
ledgers
the Chicago Blackhawks hockey team
sweeping chimneys, taking up carpets,
    painting and whitewashing the
    kitchen, papering rooms: putting a
    new face on the house, in unison with
    nature
sweet-and-sour chicken
the ability to persist
staring off into space

starting a dream diary
the amusing shaking of a person's bottom
    while sharpening a pencil
clean sheets
the contagious act of yawning
taking a maraschino cherry from the bar
    while paying the tab
the cheery glow of a crackling fireplace
Adam's apple
secret rooms
the lead facial tissue that gets all the
    others going
French cooking gadgets
the neighborhood spaghetti joint
the sedatives of woodsmoke and
    candlelight
rhinestone buttons
shin splints
blackboard menus
the smell of Band-Aids
12-packs
when the dog brings the paper and
    there's a hole in the middle
General Hospital (TV soap opera)
cleaning the birdcage
high school rock bands
executive jump ropes with digital
    counters
fresh batter-fried mushrooms in garlic
    country gravy

French fries
daffodils popping up in February and
    roses that bloom all year
lighted swimming pools
mugs of soup
sniffing the air to see if snow is coming
egg coddlers
high-shuttered windows
the "Think Factory" slogan
Friendship Gardens, Michigan City,
    Indiana
knowing it's "easier" to settle than to
    search out the best
a winding staircase
ski knickers
being alone by the sea
spiked fruit punch, Japanese lanterns
    with Christmas lights, and oldies on
    the record player
stirring up the dust in your room while
    the sun shines through a hole in the
    curtain
using powder
wristwatches
small evergreen hedges
writing dedications for books and articles
being crazy about someone
thinking someone is terrific
being tapped as someone walks by
colorful fishing boats

crisp on the outside, tender on the inside
    food
crisped rice
going to the country armed with books
    and a vision of autumnal walks and
    sunlit garden swings
oak moss, balsams, leaves, woods
raking a big pile of leaves and jumping in
ankle-tied espadrilles
the sudden squeal of hidden pigs
The Monkees, pop group
millionaires
pale peach with orange stitching
selling on consignment
the splash of a pool diver
editing a magazine or an article
mint-frosted brownies
splurging on a spectacular party
tulips, then apples, then peonies
    blooming
holding hands on the way home from a
    concert
willows that look like great honey-colored
    fountains
yellow leather jackets
all the trappings of baking: large bowl of
    eggs, blender, box of oats, brush for
    melted butter, recipe books, tempting
    flavorings
colored hose

delicate asparagus and artichokes, crisp
    lettuce, and new peas
tennis on TV
being one number away from bingo
Chianti wine
salt packets
wild turkeys
shoveling the sidewalk
dollhouses and plastic furniture
gilding with gold leaf
jumping to conclusions
Humptulips, Washington
pumice color
remembering when the highway patrol
    didn't hide with radar at the side of
    the road
summer squash on a sunny yellow
    tablecloth
tomatoes, red and sweet
Tom Watson, pro golfer
camel, spice, and whiskey colors
long, long, blue-skied perfect picnic time
hanging a mirror to reflect the greenery
    and sunshine of an outdoor view
coming out of a supermarket in a good
    mood
innocent colors of exotic fruits
long days at the beach
mineral oils
being kissy

mint sherbet
ornament storage boxes
pink grapefruit with sugar cubes
rinsing pantyhose in almond soap
piña colada milkshakes
running after rainbows
sandbox toys
tiny mangers
sunsets/starry nights/full moons
window seats
mini-stripes
"The Song of Hiawatha" (poem)
bandeau tops
candy stores
denim jewelry and toys
dinner rolls
finding good red wines
gentle light falling through panels of
    frosted glass
hand-hammered cowbells
hanging pans
Grover Washington, Jr., musician
noodles mingled with herbs and red
    peppers
a photo collage
snow shakers
Romance, West Virginia
apron strings for tying presents
correspondence courses
snowscape of a whitewashed house

wooden beads
mood rings
an oversize pouch bag
Honey West (TV series)
close-up photographic techniques
spotless chef's whites
cloudberries
frost-edged grass blades shimmering in
    an incredible variety of patterns
maple walnut
Orphan Annie
stenciled kitchen cabinets
copy readers
happily coping with cobblestones
Liquid Smoke seasoning
going to an observatory on a star-filled
    night
marble-topped dressers
frozen chili
marveling at fairy-tale trees iced in snow
no room in the hammock
perfect summer parties
a landscape sprinkled with lakes rimmed
    by thick forest and soaring bluffs
a radio pouring out a little Haydn quartet
travel games
beauty books
cranky times
airtight stoneware jars with attached
    wooden spoons

flo-thru tea bags
carrying a rabbit's foot
a row of wooden booths
ceremonial peace pipes
firecrackers
gardens past
Early American rockers
music stands
starting the coffee machine in the
     morning
pasta makers
raspberries picked in the garden
rusty slides
fireside conversations
visiting an apple farm
corn shocks tepeed in the fields
a splash pool for kids
abstract art
castor sugar
double locks
agricultural surpluses
playing fair
small steaks
a service counter in the kitchen
casual shoes
dusting off the camera
letting the breezes blow through
sweet dreams
little boxes of breakfast cereal
natural wood

not having to talk just to keep a
     conversation going
patterned silk ribbons
Christmas cards from the Metropolitan
     Museum of Art
littleneck clams on a bed of ice
pottery mugs
Mother Goose
your best friend and a good
     bottle of wine
butterscotch
a hot, damp, smothery day
"Out in the Country" by Three Dog
     Night
plump white berries on mistletoe
National Cash Register registers
an unusual combo: steak and duck
country-manor breeding
doughnut-hole machines
"I'm Not Your Stepping Stone" by the
     Monkees
drum majorette dresses
love under an umbrella
beveling the edge of a mirror to add
     prisms of light
new potatoes with mustard butter
a waterfall cascading amid bright floral
     colors and the sloping greenery of
     wide lawns
a wicker food cover for outdoors

shy goldfish

buying a pair of jazzy gym shorts for
   spring jogging

potbellied stoves

a 4,000-volume library

an English pub in the Berkshires

learning all the words to the songs you
   usually hum or whistle

slapping the bottom of a ketchup bottle
   with too much intensity

learning to service your own car

leaves shedding before they turn

meat markets

oval, pear, marquise, and emerald
   diamonds

pear sherbet

seafoam, coral, bean brown, chartreuse,
   granite gray colors

SpaghettiOs and franks

"Dancing Days" by Led Zeppelin

cocoa butter soap

stabbing a block of frozen vegetables to
   make them cook faster

Thanksgiving, when there may be a
   brush of snow on the ground and a
   hint of frost in the air

a toasty pimiento chamois flannel shirt
   dress

wearing your favorite outfit on tough
   days

what your wedding night was like
beachcombing
clam cakes and chowder
crayons that go through the wash
Coast deodorant soap commercials
sketching food
traveling first class on a train
exam week frustrations
giant slices of slightly caramelized apple
    on pastry
baby showers
glazed chintz, country plaids, tiny prints
tubes of paint in wooden crates
a barn to make love in
a bountiful weekend brunch table covered
    with an antique lace or linen cloth
    and topped with country pottery, a
    napkin-lined muffin basket, stout
    pitchers for milk or juice, and an
    earthenware vase of wildflowers
bobbing markers for lobster pots
sweet-and-sour mustard and sweet-and-
    sour curry house dressing
swell smells
the Indian method, the colonial method,
    and the modern evaporating method
    of converting sap to maple syrup
the Sugarplum Fairy
orchard maps
packing with plastic-windowed envelopes

recreational vehicles plastered with state
    and national parks decals and
    American flags
Oscar awards
being tickled pink
unconventional English
vacationing on a farm in Denmark
the first 12 days after Christmas
    indicating what each month in the
    next year will be like
the green of white pines and firs and
    native spruces
medical kits
old-fashioned firkins for storing butter
    and cheeses
keeping a list of favorite names
leeks with sour-cream dill sauce
opening one's eyes a little more
needlepoint footstools
overnight camp picnics
skewered vegetables: red onion and snap
    or snow peas
Presidential nominations and
    inaugurations
six-lane freeways
the dizzy smell of fresh-cut hay
French jeans
the fine red and blue threads running
    through new dollar bills
honeysuckle reaching upwards for light

the joy of discovering a second layer of
    chocolates underneath the first
the lower chalet at the edge of the forest
old-fashioned striped brown bags
bed bolsters
the old custom of exchanging gifts on
    New Year's Day
an ebelskiver pan for making puffy,
    sphere-shaped Scandinavian
    pancakes with jam or fruit inside
electricians
field hockey
the spin of a football
the uncontrollable urge to lean out the
    car window and yell "Moo!" every
    time you pass a cow
Swedish ivy everywhere
when the fourth wheel on a shopping cart
    refuses to cooperate with the other
    three
Americanisms
the new loaf, warm from the oven
breakfast on the porch
"Health, love, wealth, and time to enjoy
    them" (slogan)
Beethoven symphonies and sonatas
deep footed rice bowls
rain-hatched mushrooms springing
    underfoot
raisin color

French fries, crisp and speckled with
     shreds of skin
reflections of the seasons in constantly
     changing and inviting patterns of
     sights and sounds
soft pretzels with grains of hard, coarse
     salt, served with sunny yellow
     mustard
coffee in a silver pot with a
     silver jug of hot milk
bagels and onion rolls
dog and cat food boxes
prizewinning
rain barrels
raising corn
leis placed on visitors to Hawaii
slices of colored rope
spinning around on a diner stool
white Christmas lights
writing letters to representatives in
     Washington, D.C.
being lost in a sea of relatives
bridle paths
chicken salad platters
faithfulness
adjournments
lake sailing
making plans
making sweet-potato French fries
write-in-the-dark pens

rekindling friendships
asking first
baked candied tomatoes
multicolor paper loops
self-threading needles
splashing ivory, creamy beige, rainrose
    beige, tea rose colors
walking around ladders
shin-kicking fun
dill mustard
café society
welcoming the new girl at school
split-levels
Welsh rabbit with beer
gravity
cold new potatoes dressed with
    vinaigrette
collections of lanterns, rolling pins,
    ceramics, copper, and pewter
gumdrops
plate rails
colored logs
delicate fronds
filet mignon
gallon cans of caramel
secondhand stores
fresh lemonade made from squeezed
    lemons, water, and sugar
Simple Simon
running through the sand all day

women who dress for aerobics class in
    dangling earrings, coordinated
    outfits, and full makeup
bamboo boxes
hamburgers with mustard, lettuce,
    tomato, pickle, onion, cheese, and
    hickory sauce
men who explain their behavior by
    saying "I'm just a wild 'n crazy guy"
mini-tubs of margarine
hand-carved and lacquered coromandel
    chest, in the full spectrum of Chinese
    colors
mint sprigs
Norway, Land of the Midnight Sun
brown sweaters
sangria of white wine, a splash of brandy,
    and pinwheels of lemons, limes,
    oranges
sunsparkles
Tonka trucks
"And now for something completely
    different" (Monty Python)
banana pants
condominiums
scoop scales
center-parted hair
porch swings
Continental breakfasts
Danbury hats

the gentle sounds of a summer Sunday
handicraft centers in New England
honey-colored paneling
Georgia: brown thrashers singing in the
    pines, sweet scent of Cherokee rose,
    tropical flowers floating in swamps
people who take risks, who are creative
    and love to experiment, who
    improvise and make the best of what
    they have
pioneer ways
root cellars
smoked corned beef with apple-raisin
    sauce
snow flowers
tromping around with a candidate
wooden beams
browsing through guest registers
grown-ups with kids' imaginations
impromptu wine-and-cheese parties on
    Friday evenings
popping salted peanuts
apple conveyor belts at orchards
someone calling to check on you when
    you're sick
large, pull-apart rolls
marionette and mime performances
particolored things
porch swings
shrimp salad

country colors in blanket checks: purple,
loden, yellow, red

surviving a summer job

throngs of businessmen in Ivy League
suits

hand-knit wool sweaters

worn plush movie seats

a riverboat restaurant decorated with lots
of sparkling white lights

a rowboat with a motor

"America the Beautiful" (song)

certificates

garlic juice

raspberry and lemon buttercreams

free mints and toothpicks after dinner

bird safaris

corduroy weekend pants

Christmas trees draped with strung
popcorn, cranberries, and candy
canes

eerie lights

garage sales

computer terminals

visiting art galleries

a serving of spaghetti

listening to music so beautiful that it
makes you cry

a stickler for details

cast-aluminum skillets with wooden
handles

cash on hand
a tall London oil lamp
discussing philosophical matters of
    import
gas stations
intelligent life on the planet Earth
not just seizing the day but making the
    day
wet-look rain slickers
a bright red Ralph Lauren oxford shirt
a toast rack
plaid shirts
having your hair frosted
squeaky cars
a traditional cross-country sled
after-dinner coffee and melt-in-your-
    mouth chocolate morsels of truffles
playing badminton well
buttered sandwich buns
catching a falling leaf to make a wish
    come true or for a day of good luck
getting to know people
antique maps
cutting tags off new clothes
mountain climbing over molehills
reusing an old bridesmaid's dress
getting a quick answer
plush parlor and dining cars
aluminum canisters with parqueted
    Thailand teak lids

thimbles
"Because it's there"
the preposterous rituals that people
resort to to get rid of hiccups
living in snow country
Seven-and-Seven drinks in summertime
having a heart-to-heart with Dad
sewing rooms
packets of tissues
always having something to look forward
to—love, life, work, happiness
mixing yellow and red light bulbs
saying grace
pizza places
rereading a good book
an FBI agent
Grade A eggs
learning to love and appreciate easy-
listening music
Italian waffle-weave bath towels
peach leaves
playing favorite records and dancing
wildly in the living room
reading a favorite magazine
road daisies
searching out a piece of solitude and
refreshing yourself with the sound of
absolutely nothing
making files
small, flower-design lollipops

Dark Shadows (TV show)

tea bag tags

an array of dogwood and mauve redbud
    trees

brandy ice for dessert

champignons = mushrooms

soda parlors

cracks in the sidewalk

heavy teak deck chairs

nubby cotton

pub food: sausages, cold cuts, meat pies,
    and salads

people who hold the elevator doors so
    they don't close in your face

rubber rafts

baby bootees

microwave/toaster/broiler in one

nickelodeons

Bic pens

being the greatest putt-putter of all time

secret caves

old catalogs

unconventional tablecloths: country
    quilt, painter's dropcloth, unfolded
    road map, sheet of butcher's paper,
    tartan wool blanket, festive rag rug

cactus pears

decorating a small bushel basket

kids making their own valentines

old satin pillowcases

old tintypes

red-barn red

sad, romantic, nostalgic, wistful, peeved,
   kittenish feelings

Rodgers and Hammerstein's "Carousel
   Waltz"

undulating cane fields

widening horizons, crisp nights, mild
   days

"100 yellow ribbons tied around the old
   oak tree"

daddies cooking dinner

meeting eyes

scenic-patterned paper

one-third pound hamburger topped with
   a choice of avocados, onions, sautéed
   spinach, mushrooms, tomatoes, green
   peppers, bacon, and four kinds of
   cheese

shed-style bay windows

stenographers' notebooks

the cat acting foolish

sweeps of white beach that surround the
   ocean's edge

swell sounds

bringing nature inside

the new math

the Abominable Snowman

the dancing of fireflies as the moon rises

Mother's Day

colors of the 64-crayon box: carnation
    pink, salmon, lavender, thistle,
    orchid, periwinkle, blue-violet, violet,
    plum, magenta, red, maroon, violet-
    red, red-violet, mulberry, brick red,
    orange-red, red-orange, melon,
    orange, burnt orange, yellow-orange,
    apricot, peach, maize, goldenrod,
    orange-yellow, lemon yellow, yellow,
    yellow-green, green-yellow, spring
    green, sea green, green, olive green,
    pine green, forest green, blue-green,
    green-blue, turquoise blue,
    aquamarine, sky blue, navy blue,
    cornflower blue, cadet blue, midnight
    blue, blue, blue-gray, violet-blue, raw
    sienna, sepia, bittersweet, raw umber,
    brown, tan, burnt sienna, mahogany,
    Indian red, copper, silver, gold, gray,
    white, black
the excitement of a storm and the sudden
    transformation of the landscape
the friend who introduced you to
    Mr. Right
getting mail
the memory of a spring afternoon
cheese shops
dreamy music
the gap in the dressing room curtain that
    can never be completely closed

skinny rings
feeling blue
the phone ringing on a rainy day
"as quick as a wink"
the smell of peat moss
the soothing sound of sprinklers
maiden names
Kriss Kringle
onion quiche
the tideline
the turbulent surface of the sun
seeking others' advice
The Old Man in the Mountain, New
 Hampshire
tree-trimmed streets graced with
 antebellum mansions
the loon's distinctive white necklace in
 contrast to its black plumage
American Express cards
cheerfulness
letting go of inhibitions without need of
 excuse
presteaming fresh young vegetables—
 zucchini, yellow squash, corn on the
 cob, mushrooms—and then grilling
 them for a woodsy smoke flavor
Buffalo Bill
coffee-set travel kits
effervescence
species of marine life

jigsaw puzzles: dumping out all the pieces
    on a card table, turning them all over,
    and propping up the picture
light and tender baked doughnuts,
    brushed with butter and rolled in
    cinnamon sugar
lightning-white teeth
night sports
digging clams in Oregon, Washington,
    and New England
dogs nose-deep in wrapping paper
keeping the night light on
an herb-stuffed pillow
"I hear happiness and I know you've
    come into the room" (saying)
leisurely bubble baths
paint shirts
the logbook at an inn
primitive reproduction paintings
quilt blocks
being delayed in an interesting airport
    like Dulles in Washington, D.C.
slices of fresh pineapple and little bowls
    of fresh berries with brownies or
    cookies
jargon
waiters in red jackets
boiled potatoes set in buttered, red-
    peppered cheese
bright-colored mittens

seasonable weather
chicken, avocado, orange, and tomato,
    bathed in oil flavored with
    crystallized ginger
Chinese lacquered bamboo baskets
crisp French fried onion rings on a burger
daisies exercising in the breeze
doing some research on the place you
    want to visit on your next vacation
friendliness
pajama pants
slate blackboards
taking Sunday papers to the park
baking bread in an iron pot at the edge of
    a glowing peat fire
goldfinches
nylon shirts
chiliburgers
dripping wax
Ben Gay muscle rub
silent deserted shores
velveteen pincushions
walking into your dreams and coming out
    a new person
wild orchids
being all dressed up with nowhere to go
dolphins, reveling in the buoyant
    pleasures of water
helicopter sightseeing
baking potatoes in aluminum foil

Humpty Dumpty magazine
memories sitting like lonely men on the
    park bench of the mind
sand sifting
bike jackets
holiday soaps
mumblety-peg
name-calling
rumble seats
simnel cake = fruitcake
summer: falling in love with a lifeguard
Campbell's tomato soup
gumball machine prizes
homemade gingerbread for dessert
linden trees
flannel trousers
miner's hash
Singapore Sling drinks
pine-shingled cottages
Monopoly's 10 most-landed-on spaces:
    Illinois Avenue, B&O RR, Free
    Parking, Tennessee Avenue, New
    York Avenue, Reading RR, St. James
    Place, Water Works, Penn RR
spittoons
renting a winter house
singing "and many more" at the end of
    the "Happy Birthday" song
sun-checked avenue and groves
accidental meetings

Windsor ties
scouting computer stores for a new
    printer
a snail's pace
banana peels
sunken ships
tiny percussive sounds
Saks Fifth Avenue
warm afghans
bending over backwards
Senator Edward Kennedy, Massachusetts
bins for pepper, raisins, currants, coffee,
    kegs of molasses, and canisters for
    milk in a grocer's shop
park benches
candlelight ceremonies
candles glimmering behind cut-glass
    holders that reflect the light 100
    times over
dandelions growing wild: a salad of leaves
    and wine of flowers
snow berries
Tootsie Roll lollipops
finding a café, having a cup of coffee and
    a snack, then organizing your purse
    and agenda book
queries
Georgian silver and Canton china
short aprons
stockings hung on the shower rod

two lamps by the bed so you don't disturb
    the other person
wooden shoes
an old-fashioned tin candle mold
crossword-puzzle books
frosted-cocktail color
hoop rolling
paper angels
wondering what it would be like to be
    rich and taken care of
sponge baths
a pumpkin pie, light and pungent
appreciation
serving wine
expecting to hear some good news every
    day
happy aromas
parrot green
panda bears with white paws
stretching to reach a parking lot's ticket
    dispenser
taking someone out for coffee or ice cream
surviving cafeteria and junk food
    machines
the tart-sweet, sharp-clean scent of
    lemons and oranges in the air
shrimp-shaped earrings
throwing a rolling pin
sunglasses with tortoise-shell frames
Vermont cheddar cheese

warm-weather thirst quenchers
a raft swing
terry washcloths
a real expedition with candles, music,
    blankets, pillows, champagne, cold
    oysters, chocolate truffles, St. André
    cheese, and cold lobster meat
a restored nickelodeon
the ringmaster
barbecuing some meat on a charcoal
    brazier
ceramic marmalade jars
stair treads
trainee hats
weather maps
Virginia jumbo peanuts
corn-husking and pumpkin-rolling
good news for a change
strawberry whipped cream waffles
fire embers seeming endowed with a
    memory of the sun
milkmen
your signature
passing over licorice jellybeans
butter-making
reservation books at restaurants
Russian hats
Yosemite National Park
assuring success by counting on one in
    four things going wrong

bamboo birdcages
cushioned vinyl floors
displaying collections
natural-wood sculpture
outdoor craft exhibits
patio dining in summer
cash refunds
bottled beer
knowing it's never too late to learn
potpourri in a small antique box
a turtleneck, Lacoste, button-down shirt
and Shetland sweater under a
herringbone tweed jacket for a
football game
19th-century pewter inkwell with quill
pen
hot dog buns
hot-chocolate lipstick
laughter being the best medicine
sauerkraut, sweet mustard, wurst,
fresh loaves of pumpernickel or rye,
generous mugs of beer mixed with
lemon soda, apple strudel, and
German chocolate cake
studying seed catalogs
church bells
butterscotch cream pie
a country mile
enveloping yourself with calm;
nourishing your senses and soul

having a story, poem, or article published
buttery suede slippers
having one credit card
always looking people in the eye
jeans stores
fish tank bubbles
saying grace softly at the table
anything simple that you can do well and
    easily
an Italian leather box
a June bride
static cling
buying a dimestore jar of liquid for
    blowing bubbles
believing that crying is good for you
size 11 feet
a 6 A.M. newspaper run
playing pool
peaked roofs
stubborn spider plants
cruise ships
swamp maples in bright red, yellow,
    orange, and crimson flames
the playground of life
pearl onions
plaid skirts
searchlights
starting to make good contacts in
    business
the unique smell of new Play-Doh

team posters
toast with maple cream
wearing something brilliant and
    watching other people's reactions
an art book on a stand
an authentic, artistic, and aesthetic life
beautiful buys in a straw market
Hamburger Helper
chanting singsong lessons in a one-room
    schoolhouse
Charleston chandeliers
public-address systems
Nabisco Shredded Wheat cereal
tabletop croquet games
a baked potato anytime
a black hole
playing kick-the-can
wicker baskets as pencil holders
a chauffeur in uniform
ham basted with Coca-Cola, and spoon
    bread, sliced tomatoes, fresh peach
    shortcake
ladies who don't swear
old English barristers
pilots in uniform
old food cans from 10 or 20 years ago
an old-fashioned brass telephone with
    separate earpiece
wedding buffet suppers
a baby plant

tobacco laths
dude ranches
shells collected from the beach with
    single orchids growing out of them
sweet peas in soft bunches of muted
    colors
the aroma of cinnamon rolls that lures
    you to countless bakeries
sweet-and-sour carrots
restaurants that allow you to bring your
    own wine
canned soups
the cold coming and knitting a film of ice
old-time raccoon coats
riding your bike to work
"Once upon a time..."
the grinding undertone of stones
the hen coop
wide beaches
the lonely sound of a train horn
the new sandscape that takes the
    appearance of weathered wood,
    flames of fire, checkerboards, mazes,
    parqueting
crab soccer and getting your hands filthy
    playing it
hearty chocolate cocoa
doodads
mobile homes
the pick of the litter

treadle-operated sewing machines
20 shades of green in a tree
yawning
an evenly lighted room to reduce
     eyestrain
chef salad
French bread
cleaning off your desk and buying new
     file folders
milk bottles
smile makers
grinding your own beef
talking shop
sock sorter rings
dress gloves
freshly made Italian cheesecakes
French cuffs
cuffed Jamaican shorts
organizational thrills
Mighty Mouse
toga parties
Schlitz beer
"The most beautiful thing we can
     experience is the mysterious"
     (Einstein)
camomile = initiative, ingenuity, energy,
     and tenacity
a leisurely stroll bringing sensory
     delights
painting the apartment

calla lillies
primping and powdering
sliced bread
enjoying a summer moon
spin-dry salad baskets
swing choirs
an intricate Fabergé egg, a world in a
    gilded walnut shell
brightening up one's spirits
chicken barbecue with salads, homemade
    breads, and blueberry baked goods
the Chicago Cubs
Chiclets
driving against the arrow in a parking lot
one size fits all
going to a pinball arcade: loser buys hot
    dogs and soft drinks
enjoying your vacation
acknowledging the corn = admitting
    failure or having been outwitted
multicolored plastic paper clips
Julian and John Lennon, singers
pulling the curtains, putting on some
    music, serving your favorite
    cocktails, and dreaming about what
    it must have been like to sail to
    Europe a long time ago
taking someone to work
self-defense
telling spooky stories

Tilt-a-Whirls at fairs
walking to the baseball field after school
all-cotton terry cloth
California date shakes
colloquialisms and catchphrases
winter fruit
Sunday rides in the country
roll-on deodorant
color wheels
biochemistry
wood and wicker tables
lemon halves
mime artists
Mom food: chipped beef on toast,
    macaroni and cheese, scalloped
    potatoes and sausages, stuffed bell
    peppers, lemon noodles
muumuus
balance of nature
china cups and saucers
good sports facilities
tumbling down a meadow
combinations
home-garden varieties of squash, beans,
    and potatoes
hunting for natural-wood sculpture in
    early morning after a storm or a first
    frost
long, loose-waisted tea gowns festooned
    with lace furbelows

pink peonies
the smell of chalk and pencil shavings
an entourage
concerts on TV
sun-reflector blankets
sunshine coming through a window
tiny tomato juice cans
a wine brique, filled with water and then
    emptied, for maintaining
    temperature of the wine
bananas and sour cream
confiture = preserved or candied fruit;
    jam
dangling between a past that held a
    different future, and a future that
    would require a different past
silence
a generous Continental breakfast of fruit,
    muffins, and warm caramel rolls
gentle, rocking motion
hanging baskets of plants, gay flowers,
    and a waterfall splashing into a
    sunken garden surrounding a dance
    floor
gingham pinafores
looking up words you don't know how to
    spell
shoe buttons
pH
Danskin tennis clothes

photographing children
programming a computer
smoked hams hanging on warped barn
    rafters
thoughts while ironing
violet: eggplants, beets, blackberries,
    mulberries, plums, purple grapes
a wool gabardine Baltic cap with
    commander's "scrambled egg" visor
Wyoming wool
an old farm table in the kitchen
brownie cake
door decorations for each season
foot traffic
"Love is patient, love is kind"
    (Ecclesiastics)
groves of orange and olive trees
wooden curtain rods and brackets
growing one's nails for special occasions
    (like receiving a ring)
impala bucks
sipping crisp wine from a hand-blown
    glass
Pepsi-Cola commercials
supermarkets
pyramids of fruits and vegetables
    arranged in stalls
straight-from-the-dyepot blue Bahamian
    sky
liquid diets

German-style meat loaf
large, round eyeglasses
periodicals reserved for bathroom
    readings
personal investigation and
    experimentation
strolling through a cool, dark pine forest
Strawberry Fields wine
a retreat from the outside world
barrels of duffel bags
April Fools' Day cards
a ceramic ovenproof lasagna server
corn blades rustling, rabbits lying close,
    the owl coursing the crisp meadow on
    silent wings
ear stoppers
farmhouses with silos waiting to be filled
stretch lace
mustard seed
patio lights
corn, spinach, and bacon chowder
corrigenda = corrections of errors
button boxes
curled trees
garlic sauce
installing seat belts on the rocking chair
almond flower = hope
portable talismans
entertaining
fire engines

street lamps festooned with garlands and
      bright bows
master lists
your own spaghetti
postage stamps: first introduced in
      Belgium
reserve-team basketball practice
Russian salad dressing
a small masher to crush herbs or mash
      baby food or pack butter into tubs
the rat race
a swaying sea of grass
basically happy people
letting your hair dry in the sun
belts with whale, geese, lobster, and
      yacht motifs
not being able to fight sleep on the train
pita bread with very thin roast beef and
      Greek salad
cotton balls
boys in caps
a salad with an interesting house
      dressing
satchel bags
sitting on the front stoop after dinner,
      telling ghost stories and trading
      dreams
watching Mother as she cuts apples,
      sews, or prepares the house against a
      hot New England day

a toast to twilight in champagne
butter mints
cat hammocks
eating meals
getting fresh fish from someone who just
    caught them
putting on overalls and getting dirty
hot peach conserve, a bottomless
    coffeepot, and eggs served in
    individual skillets
a hot-water bottle on the back of the door
knuckleballs
Maurice Lenell cookies
soufflé pans
your first love letter
Young America, Indiana
the useless pockets on pajama tops
country mist
double Indian shutters
reveling in a lack of structure
saving money regularly
advertising colors: black on yellow, black
    on white, yellow on black, white on
    black, dark blue on white, white on
    dark blue, dark blue on yellow, yellow
    on dark blue, dark green on white,
    white on dark green, brown on white,
    white on brown, brown on yellow,
    yellow on brown, red on white, white
    on red, red on yellow, yellow on red

having a baby's sneakers bronzed
sword swallowers
sewing all your loose buttons on
Maypo cereal
a crystal jigger pitcher
movable TV stands
bay swimming
buying your first home
a C average
a Saturday morning round of clean-
the-house
leap-frogging
peaked white umbrellas, linened tables,
and a gurgling fountain
answers
an 18th-century wooden splint box
plant-sitting for a friend
roaring fires
skating rinks
beaver lodges
Dutch tulip bulbs
peach muffins
slabs of butcher blocks
Catra (movie)
team studying
"hanging 10"
an appreciation for fine leathers and
imported tweeds
beautiful flower-decorated greeting cards
displayed in a basket

black figure sculptures
playing blackjack or "21"
diamond mines
flag-striped bobby pins
glass-bottomed boat rides
heavy, dark pine captain's chairs
cock-a-doodle-do
a before-breakfast walk
picnic quilts
albino watermelon seeds
elbow pillows
keeping a promise
Jack and Jill
Macy's stores
picking flowers here and there, then
    putting them between the pages of a
    big heavy book to dry
pocket concerts of jingling keys and
    change
recipe chests
succotash: corn, beans, tomatoes, and
    cream
Victorian furniture and lamps with red
    bows
a cake baking
backgammon on the beach
scented clothes hangers
buckwheat mix
etched-glass partitions
a ladies' lunch

old lavalieres

red pillboxes

bodies of water that collect on upturned
mugs in the dishwasher

sweater vests

the gleaming symmetry of a frosted
spider web at dawn

sweet smells that change with passing
hours

freedom

the basic Vermont meal: a piece of
cheddar, a glass of cold milk, and a
stack of common crackers

Shetland yarn

the cakewalk

curtains whispering

the first day of winter

red

the magic curl of waves

icebox pinwheel cookies

shell blouses

last summer's shells from the beach

spending a night on the water in a
sailboat

the metal barrier on a rotary phone that
keeps you from dialing past zero

old newspaper clippings

pedal pushers

the rugby tradition of repairing after a
match to the local watering hole

Help! (movie)
Cheesequake, New Jersey
the tinkling chorus of hand bells
iridescent shapes
the wooden steps of vacant houses
tree-watching
ergasiophobia = fear of work
weeping willows talking of spring
the sun-tanned, crew-cut, all-American
    male
the Berkshire Mountains
bread and butter with pots of jam and
    honey
diet cheaters
the feeling that you're in a totally
    different world
freedom to flunk French
fresh orchids
the wooden steps of vacant houses
waffles made with chunks of apple
coffee yogurt
sugar packets
white and onion-topped dark rolls
togaed Romans
the slow light of a late dawning
angel sleeves
three-gallon ice-cream tubs
eggs hatching
English-style breakfasts and dinners in a
    riverside dining room

white on the evergreens
going birding
onion soup mix and sour-cream dip
baked bananas
Maine muffins
first impressions
waiters smiling when they see you
writing in your diary in a secret code
being an archaeologist in your own
    backyard
cliffs like cathedrals and trees growing
    out of rocks
Chicago Loop windows at Christmas
a rousing rendition of the "Hallelujah
    Chorus"
driving alone
going to foreign movies
adjustable pop-it beads
liking others, accepting others, laughing
    with others
making things into doll furniture
rainbow cakes
ship's clocks
taking a walk in the woods with a field
    guide; learning different trees,
    animals, and birds
baked fruit compote in the winter
melon baskets
pull-up pants
rolling hills

solar heating
telling your friends you paid 8% less for
    whatever it is they've bought at a
    bargain price
wilderness jeep safaris
folding combs
lemon sherbet
pumpkin bread
slumps, grunts, buckles, Bettys, and
    pandowdies
rummage sales
acme = the highest point
relative humidity
the domino theory
butter-fried ham and farm cheese
    sandwiches
"That's the ticket"
jingle-bell donkey rides
menus from country inns
drinking a little white wine out of a
    thermos at the laundromat
insulated bottles
communicating in a foreign country with
    "yes, no, please, thank you, that" and
    numbers
running a country store
songs of the meadowlark
small, sun-drenched houses overlooking
    a bay
tan poplin trench coats

tiny gold heart lockets
vanilla-colored beaches
winning games
candlelight processions
tennis shirts
a pretty face
candy apples on a plate
conspicuous consumption
fancy hankies
finding an Easter egg in your raincoat
    pocket
baking powder
crew haircuts
gingerbread ring with maple cream
hand-me-downs
watching the moon at night and finding
    out why it looks the way it does
prodigal sons
short ribs served in individual casseroles
    with sauce
stomping in mud puddles
Bozo's Circus (TV show)
pushing your luck
wooden spaghetti spoons
blood oranges for breakfast juice
growing Christmas trees
impaling white bread on a toasting fork
    and holding its face near the flames
    of a good coal or log fire
a sympathetic ear

popcorn popping all over the room
barbershop quartet contests
sharing everying
a parenthesis in time
apple-picking
requesting information on courses
pure fruit jelly squares of apricot, quince,
     pineapple, black currant, passion
     fruit, orange, and fig purées rolled
     in sugar
stretch pants
terpsichorean = related to dancing
a private walk on a snowy landscape
throwing a surprise party for two
turkey salad sandwiches
very romantic things or people
Babar the elephant
working women
a room filled with candlelight at
     Christmas
a rotating toaster or gridiron that lets
     toast and meat cook evenly on all
     sides without being handled
summer languor giving way to a sense of
     purpose
a rolled lawn
birdies singing the same song over
     and over
gleaming copper double boiler with
     ceramic lining

dirndl skirts

foreign coins

fireflies creating an incredible ballet of
soft light

garden vegetables and pasta salad

listening to chickadees

mastering the perfect vinaigrette

mist over the rolling meadows drifting
away

possibilities

restored colonial homes

a sensual afternoon nap

flirting

pet portraits

clutch purses

billing and cooing

hash browns served as a large crisp
pancake

an intimate dinner for two on the coffee
table

kits: cosmetic, first aid, medical,
mending, sewing, shoeshine, tackle,
toilet, tool, travel

oatmeal, ocean pearl, olive, onyx, Oxford
blue, peach, pearl gray, pecan,
peppermint red, pewter, pine green,
pistachio, platinum, plum, powder
blue, primrose pink, pumpkin,
puritan gray, putty colors

an outfitted picnic hamper

patio parties

October: the month to exhale the hot, stuffy laziness of summer and inhale the cool, brisk life of fall

water bottles

a timid tiger

getting a swing twisted and then untwirling

a toddler napping with his blankie

a tray of tiny cactus against a wooden table

doormats

butterflies gathering in bunches in the air

catching fish

eating off glass plates

having your hair braided

getting to work on time

a wave at sea

laughing at soap operas

sometimes just having to say "What the hell!"

young fingers gooey with paste-made baskets

brunch in a dreamy garden setting

purple cow = grape soda and vanilla ice cream

a scene that is highly paintable and photographable

country music

a wind on the way when there's a red sky
    at sunset
double agents
movie star lighting
never being discouraged
reveling in time alone
Riverboat playing cards
leek = vivacity
having a wonderful nurturing side
"Row, Row, Row Your Boat"
a happy snowman
newspaper delivery
idyllic forest settings
S.O.T. = same old thing
Bayer aspirin
"dry as a duck"
frying a steak in bacon drippings
lazing about
pizza samples
stratocumulus, cumulus, and
    cumulonimbus clouds
no-bean chili
X-Acto knives
Be Kind to Animals week
e pluribus unum = out of many, one
picnic scenes
gray T-shirts
a Victorian drawing room with a rose-
    sprinkled carpet
leafy suburban campuses

cowbells

leaving work early the day before a
holiday

on a rainy evening, writing long letters to
old friends

the little store on the corner

prandial (cooking) skills

sweet honesty

reading statistics about the U.S.

parents

slabs of homemade fudge

Plato and Aristotle, philosophers

stacks of old childhood snapshots

dominoes

starchy white material

baa

veal sautéed with butter, fresh
mushrooms, wine, and artichokes

Hansel and Gretel

draping a night table with fabric

flat griddles

smelling roasted sweet corn as you drive

mahogany

glazed grapes

public relations directors for sports teams

the few seconds of pleasure before the
aftertaste of a diet drink sets in

rubber-soled deck shoes

submitting a sealed bid

baby pictures, slides, and movies

cab services that show up on time
synonyms
packets of cotton balls
picture books stacked next to a swivel
    chair in the living room
social skills
a cake laced with apple slivers and served
    with sticky butterscotch sauce
accompaniment
coconut and Christmas palms, gardenias,
    ixora, crotons, and dieffenbachia
duck-egg blue
exchanging enlightening interests
face creams that soothe
kidnapping your lover
midday repast
riding a roller coaster
cathedral ceilings
andirons and fireplaces
beds of nails
hide-and-seek
open-air flower markets
shell mobiles
steaming mugs of coffee
the flashy, robust season of fall
whitefish baked in wine
the glint and glitter of frost crystals in
    the air, dancing like diamond dust in
    the sunlight
running backs

the intoxicating smell of bacon frying in
    the morning
John Lennon and Paul McCartney,
    songwriters
soda-pop cans and rings
a rainy-days-were-meant-to-be-spooky
    plan
waiting rooms
being a pilot
the happiness of heading home
licorice
watching someone take a nap
a snowshoer in the winter woods
bobbing for apples
tie stickpins
the country, viewed through a curtain of
    warm summer rain, taking on
    exquisite watercolor tints from smoky
    blue to tarnished silver
when no day is Friday the 13th
being too busy to notice
three-ring binders
when traveling, taking twice the money
    and half the clothes you think you'll
    need
when you think you're a kid again
West Side Story (movie)
cleaning out your wallet, makeup case,
    and pocketbook
brand new Ticonderoga pencils

cleaning up your own mess
dyed carpenters' aprons
evenings in the recesses of Paris taxicabs
feeding ducks
cheese stores
thistledown tufts riding every gust of
     wind
thick crayons
exercising immediately after work
fresh formats
green lawns shaded by willows carpeted
     with daffodils
the soul-stirring sound of rain on the roof
the verdant countryside
coffee tables
twirling batons
The Little Rascals (TV show)
registered Morgan colts
Fig Newton cookies
painting a watercolor on the bedroom
     window
the swish of a silken dress
thinking caps
using a table of contents or a short, out-
     of-context chapter to spark a new
     kind of logic
being motivated by self-knowledge
chicken broth
driving up and down the main street of
     town

birth certificates
haiku poems: three lines unrhymed
making cut flowers last
wild cherries
belly dancers
taking an hour a day for yourself
baking garlic bread and eating it
Gil Thorpe
oil paintings
delicatessens
falling in love with a brass bed on a trip
    to Vermont
thickets of blackberry bushes and
    morning glory vines
homespun-look crinkle shirts with
    quilted and embroidered yokes
thin-handled silverware
hillsides covered by chestnut, lemon, and
    olive trees, with a wandering
    shoreline dotted with mellow hamlets
    and splendorous villas
hole-in-the-middle cake doughnuts
jumping into bed with a good book
lemon "boats"
remembering all the sweet things in
    your life
The Real Ghostbusters (TV show)
someone who makes you happy by loving
    you, being alive with you, filling up
    your life

Samuelson's *Economics*

bamboo plates

gumdrop bread

aardvarks

long-buried feelings and memories

penny arcades

renting and borrowing for parties

sanding and shellacking

tennis courts

tiny graph-paper checks

venison, rabbit, and duck braised with
vegetables and served in a brioche

wine-dark sea

banister-back armchairs

candlelight, champagne, and pizza

dancing school: learning the fox-trot,
waltz, cha-cha, rumba, merengue,
eggbeater, and frug

dinners including choice of appetizer,
salad, potato, and drink

hand-loomed India madras

zithers

hanging socks on your body because they
have static electricity

George Carlin, comedian

shopping friends, gym class friends,
go-out-for-a-drink friends

resting under a favorite tree

home projects

sport fishing

violets and pansies in all colors
wood carvings
justice
summer melons
band concerts
wool topcoats
"Golden Autumn" cologne
an old-fashioned flavor and honest
    function in a room
browsing in a favorite book or record
    store
chocolate and cambric tea in the
    afternoon
florists' boxes
flower-decked balconies
maple syrup cake with maple icing
sportswriting
rope railings
Speedy Gonzalez
taper candles
finding a pretty spot to sit and read the
    newspaper
appurtenances
being adamant
emptying out the medicine cabinet
tennis whites
cabooses
stone benches
morning weather reports
stretch socks

throwing a 30-yard pass
burying potatoes to preserve them
curling irons
forsythia buttering the roadsides
European square pillows
harp = the metal hoop that supports a
    lampshade
lessening the impact of a horror
    movie by filtering it through one's
    fingers
losing weight
possibilities for refreshment and
    discovery
taste buds coming alive as you savor the
    smells of fresh-baked bread, fresh
    fish, and sizzling steaks
a sunken garden providing sunlight and
    shadow, trees and greenery, stone
    walkways and a rippling stream
letting fireworks send chills up your
    spine
marbelized paper as drawer liners
finding loose change in your purse or
    pocket—especially quarters
pots de crème
T-strap shoes
watching with curious fascination
the clucking of a hen
bouncing back
orange = generosity

sitting on the porch in cold autumn
    weather
watermelon-rind pickles
antique farm implements
a tin of mixed biscuits
butter crocks
cotton clouds
entrance fees
pounding surf
soundproofing
brushing your teeth in the shower
counting tinsel strands
watching old movies with old friends
"Just My Imagination" by the
    Temptations
double-bolting the door
familiar surroundings
The Red Badge of Courage (book)
gourmet clubs
never being overwhelmed
Beverly Shores, Indiana
Dave DeBusschere, New York Knicks
    basketball player
new wallpaper
a wagon wheel
a bowl of fruit and flower blossoms
six
cozy brunches
"It's the pits"
ERA

BLTs on English muffins
learning words to songs
peace buttons
plaster of paris
training bras
causing an avalanche of snow when you
    put the key in the door
beautiful old oil lamps
the rusty greens of the hickories
coin purses
the NFL
the perfume of pines and azalea blossoms
    and fresh-turned earth
class-year numbers on sweaters or jackets
tiddledywinks disks
diamond rings
flailing corn
"Made in Taiwan" labels
gladiolus in acres of waving fields, in
    colorful floats in a parade, and fresh-
    cut in pretty bunches to take home
grape-stomping contests
head lettuce with French dressing
clay-potted English ivy
heat lamps in bathrooms
library books
rubber-tipped doorstops
toboggan runs
a bed of clams, oysters
tic-tac-toe in the dirt

a cast-iron coffee mill
coconut bowls
cucumber-and-bread hors d'oeuvres
decorating paper plates
a duck-paneled magazine rack with *Town
    & Country, Antiques, Smithsonian,
    Gourmet, Time, The New Yorker,
    Architectural Digest, National
    Geographic, Yachting, Fortune, Blair*
    and *Ketchum's Country Journal*
    magazines, and alumni bulletins
huckleberries
middy blouses
old Fleetwood Cadillacs
body language
"Keep thinking"
one
preparing your Christmas card list before
    Thanksgiving
seeing Manhattan outside the train
    compartment window
steam shovels
the Parthenon
cloisonné = the art of blending fired
    enamel and brass
the cheery noise of bubbling pancake
    batter
potato nachos
the crisp, secret rustle of a whispering
    breeze in a cornfield

babas au rhum
the feel of a whirlpool
Bible schools
the one cube left by the person too lazy to
    refill the ice tray
picnic groves
the first scratchy, camphor-smelling wool
    sweater of the season
slalom racing
the thin person inside every fat person
Staten Island
abandoning all civility
the tiny fragments of toast left behind in
    the butter
clear nail polish
toasted chocolate color
the structure of things
a thermos lunch
when the lake is "flat"
breaking even
cherry crisp and butterscotch pie
crème fraîche to serve dolloped on top of
    iced coffee
wooden booths
deep and calm feelings
free-form trees of glistening ice
great escapes
life beginning at 40
wafer cookies
print drawers

seining weirs
two-for-one sales
many candles on a table
pink cottages
log cabin designs on quilts
garlic = courage and strength
no expiration date
rich, sugary cheesecake
toggle clasps
museum shops and bookstores for a quiet
    browse
eight-foot-long scarves
David Letterman
The Roaring Twenties with Dorothy
    Provine
joie de vivre
Irish setters
painted nails
English rabbit: bread with wine and
    butter, toasted, topped with a mix of
    butter, cheese, and mustard, and
    grilled
alarm clocks
railroad ties
spinach salad
Shirley Temple, actress
thin-lined (narrow) writing paper
using lots of brightly colored quilts for
    tablecloths
whiter-than-white angel food cake

writing about whatever you think of
   (things you wish, say, dream);
   observing people and writing down
   what you think they think
an in-flight phone call
philtrum = the indentation between nose
   and upper lip
being stranded on a desert island
an ornate building with gingerbread
   decoration
enjoying fall yardwork
crisp curls of toffee-colored laciness,
   slightly hot-flavored from ginger
doing three or four crossword puzzles
   until 3 A.M.
unicorns
going to the same restaurant often
   enough to be given the same table
making yogurt
"Pronto!"
taking a weekend trip by yourself
melting-pot experiences
July's sailboats skimming the waters of a
   nearby lake
rolled-up shirtsleeves
dingy = dummy
fine-quality shelled pecan halves
prom programs
shopping in factory outlet stores
smoke from the cookfire

self-reliance

TV sets at an appliance store

delectable creations made hot and fresh
every morning

fillets and lamb chops merrily sizzling
away

remembering what you have learned

regional, semi-state, and state baseball
championships

simple-hearted dreams of children

comfy clothes

manicotti, the pillows of pasta stuffed
with pully cheese and covered with
bubbling red sauce

penuche icing

running mates

sunlight creating a dappled pattern
through the trees

confectionery

watching an old Woody Allen movie

sporting gear

Venice, Italy

winter scents

Canadian bacon and egg sandwiches

conchologists

waking up an hour early and
experimenting with makeup

salt and pepper jars with wire bail tops
and matching vinegar and oil jars
with cork stoppers

stone bridges
stopping by the edge of a woodland and
finding dainty-flowered anemones
nodding brightly in the breeze
too-hot-to-cook weather
thwarting troublemakers
crickets at dusk
"No one else will ever love you the way
I do"
an old-fashioned milk strainer for a
farmer
an orangutan bargaining for treats from
the zookeeper
browsing in a toy store
cooking without an oven
frozen amaretto soufflé
sweet basil = good wishes
peppermint whipped cream frosting
zipper-front and button-fly jeans
a portable whirlpool for the bath
cupcake icing
perky teapots
scrubbed and tubbed baked potatoes, not
cooked in foil
air terminals
pastel colors
two or three cabbages opened like flowers
in a basket
watering cans
church choirs

Tinker Bell in *Peter Pan*
spray perfume
straightforward service
Turkish taffy
a wire caddy for paper cups, ketchup,
    mustard, pickles for picnics
Xerox copiers
a romantic garden, an English perennial
    garden, a traditional herb garden
apricot jellyroll cake
Air Force One
carving up a brand-new jar of peanut
    butter or tub of margarine
buying Christmas decorations early
Farrah Fawcett, actress
insulated window shades
just a moment
museum stores
apricot shortbread pie with a glass of
    milk
mushroom identification
balsam = impatience and ardent love
nasturtiums climbing and tumbling with
    bright flowers
a salmon-colored sunset
noshing on hamburgers and watching
        Dallas
post office bins for a collector's showcase
a setting of serenity and comfort
assertiveness

the distinctive aroma of garlic or bell
   peppers
fishing for compliments
hasty pudding
little things
lots of old table lamps
wrapping tape
potatoes swirled with a cake decorator
   into a little tin "skin"
pots of yogurt on floes of crushed ice in
   silver tureens
watching your blood pressure as it is
   taken
a 20-hour workweek
astronaut pens that write on any surface,
   upside down, forwards, and
   backwards
bittersweet's bright orange and the
   lacquered red of barberries
cutting open a grapefruit and finding a
   sprouted seed
old Ford cars
eating an exotic fruit or untried
   vegetable
getting involved with people out of the
   usual circle of friends
mustache-grooming kits
sautéed eggplant slices
putting trouble into a boat of leaves and
   sailing it out to sea

sturdy plastic plates, knockabout cutlery,
    simple gingham napkins, and an old
    blanket to spread on the ground
squirrels with the bushiest tails
trunk lunches
young people's concerts
your first love
the nickname "Puddin' Face"
blueberry cake after lobsters
blunt-tipped scissors, paper, and crayons
    for a child
counting your blessings
South Carolina: stately gardens, white-
    pillared homes, cotton, wood, wild
    rice, sweet jasmine
country-fresh food
fluorescent-lighted luncheonettes
love of books
never postponing till tomorrow what can
    be done today
woven baskets
David Brenner, comedian
new computers
power players
a washtub-size basket with pots of flowers
a waving tide of color
Mexican wedding cookies and cakes
buying yourself a toy you wanted as
    a child
a Ching Dynasty artist's brush jar

shallow bowls holding closely clipped
 blossoms
a May basket hung on the doorknob
lean textures
pretending to be an Olympic swimmer
reading to someone who is cooking
roast goose on wild rice with glazed
 grapes
a shampoo session outside
staging a children's vehicle parade with
 scooters, bicycles, and skateboards
 festooned with crepe paper
toasted marshmallows, black outside,
 squishy inside
wearing three bracelets at a time
chariot races
classic steamer lounge chairs with teak,
 brass, and marine varnish finish
local peaches
macaroni jars
picnic hampers loaded with pâté, caviar,
 cold salmon, French cheeses and
 wines, and champagne
Charlie cosmetics
crazy socks peeking out
wicker knitting baskets
coconut palm, mango, banana trees
muddy baseball diamonds
old-style preserve jars
red wine and one-inch-thick pizza

wooden ice-cream sticks
keeping a child's heart happy
peeking out from under sunglasses
the Library of Congress
ice weighing down trees
the colony of little indentations on a golf
    ball
fishing licenses
writing paper
chaise longues
the corded trunk of a sugar maple
chamber music
the critical period in matrimony being
    breakfast time
an at-home electric buffet server
chain letters
the discovery of a secret view that is
    invisible when the foliage is full
the empty stretches of bun on either end
    of a hot dog
diamond solitaire rings
a bag of doughnut holes
a beautiful display of marigolds, zinnias,
    roses, and larkspurs
fabric-protector sprays
the kind of man summer nights were
    made for
red-checked tablecloths
saddlebag shoulder bags
address books

French tarragon chicken
the nutty flavor of Irish oatmeal
medieval market squares
the roast carved, the corks drawn
at a ball game, the smell of hot dogs and
        ice cream and peanuts, the view of
        the bleachers and the flags flying
        overhead
the sounds of geese high overhead
when the lakes are high
when you had seat belts installed in
        the car
being knee-deep in foam and icy
        saltwater
mail that is not all bills
chemise-type sundresses
the shower, where the acoustics are
        concert-perfect
when your cat had kittens
the small metal ring on a ballpoint pen
        that separates the top from the
        bottom half
clear blue creek waters
cream in coffee, or half-and-half
onion-skin paper
ad absurdum and ad nauseum
Coed magazine
being free-spirited
puffins, kittiwakes, gannets, murres, and
        sea parrots

tying hand-me-down sweaters around
    your waist or neck
refrigerators
buffalo plaid
coffee, light
light-tone wood baskets
nighty-nights
suggesting he come to your place for
    chocolate fondue
a tight-weave sisal bag for knitting
    supplies
angle parking
doggies tumbling into morning,
    spreading early birds and careless
    cats before them
Friday night, usually left open for drinks
    after work
nail polish in a pencil
philosophies on posters
rainbow jello
swinging beds
chestnut reds
being wistful
s'mores: chocolate and marshmellows
    melted between graham crackers
Spike, Snoopy's brother
waiting by candlelight for a special
    person
writing your spouse a love letter
brick-and-board shelves

chicken in a "bird's nest" of shredded
   potatoes with a spot of cinnamon-
   berry jelly for spice
chilled pears
dairy cellars
going jogging at sunset
twilight hour
China-red satin pajamas
Easter egg hunts
crickets in the chimney
doing something spontaneous on a
   "snow day"
idioms
drifting down France's beautiful Canal
   du Midi on a hotel barge
childhood report cards and art projects,
   high school yearbooks, photo albums,
   diaries, and love letters
drinking beer, eating pretzels and
   peanuts, tuning the radio to a top-40
   station
feeding a cat
cabbage = gain and profit
going to a duty event, such as a political
   rally or volunteer meeting, and
   having it turn out to be fun
making an ice-cream pie
the twang of a guitar
taking action
asking simple questions

cakes of soap
hundreds of handmade quilts to be
     auctioned
long after-dinner talks
kaleidoscopes
no loose ends
police car loudspeakers
tulips bursting into bloom in a
     kaleidoscope of color
campfire wood
epauletted Air Force shirts
pineapple pie
frost flowers
choosing a neighborhood
hilltop towns
velvet quilts
walking tours
Adirondack yellow birch
bills of sale
Colorado mountain roads
fall fashions
half nelsons in wrestling
knowing you're absolutely unique
clothesline rope
remembering when bubble gum cost a
     penny, comic books 10¢, hot dogs a
     quarter, and water was free
tomatoes for puffy eyes
commuter drinking cups
men with egos

long-handled hearth roasters for
deliciously cooked meats or toasted
bread or rolls

Kentucky horse-breeding

pencil-striped clothing

banana flambé

the body's first surge of energy in the
morning

handbags with room for everything

handing out invitations

knowing all the answers to a game show
while confined to your living room

looking at all the colors you can see on a
cloudy day

root beer and spaghetti

sporty, casual, exciting, fresh, up, jaunty
feelings

an odd couple

two

an old pickup truck with the tailgate
down, a willow basket chock-full of
sandwiches, salads, and cheese, a jar
of pickles, a crock of honey, a loaf of
bread just baked that morning, a red-
and-white checkered tablecloth, and
sunshine pouring down through the
overhanging branches of a grand old
oak tree

blowing air out the window and seeing
steam

party spreads

straw fedoras

broiling meat or toasting bread on the top
    rack of a wood stove

chopped raisins and cranberries gently
    sweetened and wrapped in a tender
    pastry and topped with vanilla ice
    cream

flowers thriving on love and friendly
    words

frozen yogurt

peppermint-crunch candy

sapphire mountains set into emerald
    valleys

upper-crust restaurants

a portable writing desk with secret
    drawers

hockey teams that use finesse rather
    than brawn

personalized golf balls

Maryland: National Anthem, Annapolis,
    crabs

brown, green, and yellow plastic trash
    bags

Blood, Sweat & Tears, pop group

the clangor of a fire truck

planning a camping trip

battery fluid

screened-in porches with delightful views
    and breezes

curtain calls
striped baseball shirts
interjections
attaché cases
Scrabble
arriving at work with covered dishes,
    huge baskets, towel-draped platters,
    even pails of food
cork tiles for pictures
farmers and countrymen in the pub
records for learning foreign languages
his favorite pipe
just happening upon a parking spot in
    the right place
nasturtiums, all colors
a small fishing village
baskets filled with letter-writing supplies
fashion shows
plate collecting, a booming hobby
small dinners
fishing for panfish from the bank of
    a lake
an intoxicating atmosphere
putting extra raisins in Raisin Bran
    cereal
Notre Dame cheerleaders
satin sachets with hints of lavender,
    roses, and lace
watching the same TV shows as someone
    even when you're not together

watching your clothes dryer's spin cycle
    for excitement
afternoons at garden fetes: flowered hats,
    tables laden with home produce,
    jams, cakes, tempting offerings, milk
    for teas, and cream for scones
authentic Welsh miners' oil lamps
filled croissants, better than store-bought
butter crunch ice cream
entangled rambler roses
sewing groups
extra sweaters, boots, parkas for winter
laundry-sorting baskets
mustache wax
lingonberry and sour-cream crêpes
square dances
blush chablis
country ribs with red chili sauce
courteousness
butcher coats
sautéed fresh mushrooms
hot, crusty, yeasty French bread and
    butter
doughnut conveyor belts
reverse hair permanents
five people reading one newspaper
jewelry and glass booths at fairs
new cookbooks
sawing boards
the riverboat era

a waiter who is not concentrating
a down-to-earth attitude
taxi whistles
beautiful sand patterns
stained glass
waxing floors
Royal Copenhagen Christmas plates
buying T-shirts and short-sleeve shirts on
    the first day of spring, then having a
    blizzard that night
clocks that tick
pizza cutters
P.F. Flyer tennis shoes
D.H. Lawrence
shawl collars
O.O.C. = out of control
playing a game of hopscotch with a
    neighbor
skateboarding
wearing a sand dollar on a ribbon
"hanging out" and remembering why you
    like each other
space heaters
starting an herb garden
brandied eggnog, candied yams, candy
    canes, cranberry sauce, fruitcake,
    gingerbread, mince pie, mulled wine,
    plum pudding, popcorn balls,
    pumpkin pie, roast turkey, and bread
    stuffing

brass buttons
Chanel No. 5 body cream
crackle in the fall air
meeting deadlines
diamond stars
heartbreakers
subtle color gradations
planning things: a picnic, concert, hike in
    the woods
Rube Goldberg, inventor
a baby's ring
propagating bulbs
a booth made out of a beer barrel
country fairs
making clarinets squeak
racing a bike
a brood of chicks, hens
abbreviations
baby formulas
cable spools for tables
itching after playing in the snow
spotting bobolinks and short-billed marsh
    wrens
a calendarium
muggy dugouts
toilet waters
a celebration breakfast
modular storage systems
old maps and large farm tools hung on
    walls

old-fashioned door keys
understanding
endless days of raspberry picking
the inertia that overcomes drivers when
   they see police on the road
art supply stores
a one-pot meal including boiled potatoes,
   fresh corn, oranges, lemons, onions,
   garlic, and spices in a savory broth
peeling fruit
Sesame Street (TV show)
pleasing colors, shapes, textures
prepping your bath with scented sachet
   cubes, bubble bath, soaps shaped
   like shells
filigree pens
"The Lord giveth, the Government taketh
   away"
using five free minutes to start an
   important project
whitewashed wainscoting
brimming glasses of ice-cold milk
kennels
crisp, leaf-scented air
flitting around for pleasure in the
   evening
the ability to cut a piece of cake with a
   little plastic fork on a flimsy paper
   plate while holding a drink, napkin,
   and cup of mints

the area on a windshield that the wipers
    cannot reach
Irish soda bread on St. Patrick's Day; hot
    cross buns on Easter
painting drawers different colors
the smell of hot coffee
the solid sound of a good car door
    shutting
fountain spray
the tractor on the farm
George Balanchine, choreographer
the energy to squeeze some juice, grind
    some coffee, and stir up a batch of
    muffins
treasuring private time
coat styles: trench, princess, toggle,
    duffel, blanket
when Mr. Right trips over your beach
    blanket
when the last sherbety blob falls
an egg wedger
looking your best
cheesecake and espresso
foliage tours
clear crystal
crème brûlée with tropical fruits
feeding a cow
fields of tall yellow flax stalks
the language of flowers
old silent movies

treating yourself to a new toothbrush
fresh, romantic, tender moments
guest rooms furnished with a decanter of
    wine and French country antiques
puffy sleeves
soft pale-pumpkin color
hub caps
magazine correspondents
wagon-wheel chandeliers
the sea's monumental indifference
scheduling appointments
Tahitian Treat soda pop
achieving parents having achieving
    children
Mai Tais on the terrace at sunset
prints of dogs, ducks, horses, boats, birds
quiet free hours to sit by a fire
Oriental rugs
ski-bobbing: riding downhill on a bicycle
    frame mounted on skis
Phillips Exeter Academy
when the rain stops and the sun comes
    out
an echo
grilled meat served with salty French
    fries
making your own junk food at home
waking up early and having breakfast
    together outside
bikini season

salty stories
jellybeans in an Easter basket
Holland bulbs
pullover tops
rolling the package of bacon before
    opening
cool moisture
silver-plated baby mugs
people on a sidewalk watching TV in a
    store window
velvet voices
cold asparagus tarragon
a colorful windjammer sailing fleet
colored scents that fill the air
falling asleep to music
helping each other grow
chewable vitamins
curling up in bed on a Sunday afternoon,
    then reading a book until dawn
truck headlights that invade your motel
    room at three in the morning
Roman candles
tomato paste in tubes from France
come-as-you-are parties
dumpling soup
gaming tables
homey touches
long-stemmed carnations
men
Linus the Lionhearted

supper salads
pencils, pens, a sketchbook, books to help
    identify wildflowers or birds, and
    maps
"A penny for your thoughts"
pincushion-topped jars
run-sheep-run game
sun infusing the atmosphere with
    rich light
a window jungle of plants
Scotch pine trees
singing along to the movie *Carousel*
Benton Harbor, Michigan
confetti-pattern dishes
consuming M & M's by color groups
finnan haddie
a fun-to-be-fit attitude
window-shopping in the fall
honeymoon bridge long years later
people who make you listen to an entire
    song or comedy routine before you get
    the beep on their answering machine
shoe = top drawer, very acceptable
sports arenas
"Topo Gigio," mouse puppet on *Ed
    Sullivan Show*
wooden or fake fruits and vegetables to
    pretty up coffee tables
a chopping block with attached dish
cooling off at the pool

floor buffers

Good King Henry, wormwood, woodruff, parsley, garlic, savory, camomile, fennel, comfrey, mustard, tansy, vervain, mandrake, thyme, tarragon, cowslip, southernwood, sapphire, sunflower, geraniums, jasmine, and lime

sitting and watching a plant grow

imported Holland cheese

papaya with lemon cream

September = aster or morning glory

cypress trees

exploring a parking lot

Northland hockey sticks

strawberry-frosted doughnuts from Dunkin' Donuts

Warren Dunes State Park, Michigan

a romantic scavenger hunt, steering your lover to a restaurant or back home for a private celebration

agreeableness

barbecuing steaks, chops, burgers summer-style on a cold winter night in a fireplace

dark blue Indian cotton

apricot butterfly rolls

dark wood floors warmed by Oriental, kilim, or needlepoint rugs

firefighting apparatus

fortune cookie pendants
the gurgle of running water
harvest brown, heather, heaven blue,
     honey, hot pink, ice blue, ivory, ivy
     green, jade, and kelly colors
listening to Tchaikovsky's lilting
     "Nutcracker Suite"
Ball mason canning jars
poster colors
T's and jeans
a solid-oak Chinese checkers game
spider saucepans, whose legs keep the
     pot above hot embers
Easter breads
jottings and musings preserved in
     one place
not having any cavities
potato slices
Mutt and Jeff
returning library books
sets of artist's colors
who, what, where, when, why, and how
getting up at the cusp of morning
sitting in the kitchen with your hands
     wrapped around a hot cup of coffee
     and musing on your life
a tiny restaurant that specializes in
     lunches and afternoon tea
"stolen" time
autumn bonfires of gathered twigs

cuticle cream
getting your picture in the paper
laurel leaves
sourdough French toast, dipped in cream-
     thickened eggs
studying a student pilots' manual
getting the gist of required reading by
     reading the first and last chapters
     and Cliff or Monarch notes
aquamarine = courage, truthfulness
chunky tomato-dill soup
fruit or vegetable pictures for the kitchen
inviting someone special to tell you a
     secret wish
love between two people
slanty floors
bicycle hikes
pear pancakes
tongue-and-groove walls and ceilings
serpentine linked necklaces
Davy Crockett, pioneer
having a private picnic
sewing-machine stitches
a train huffing and puffing out of the
     station
window seats
bowling balls
layered salad
saying you're sorry when you hurt
     somebody

heavy blackberry blooms

styrofoam picnic chests

buying a wonderful piece of furniture and enjoying it for years

pizza with leftover French or Italian bread

cozy robes, morning newspapers, chocolates on the pillows, milk and cookies at bedtime, and coffee 24 hours a day

a down-easter

leaf patterns

food for thought

planning a cheese plate

plants and shells as centerpieces

scarlet flowers in hair

small, moist, bite-size muffins served slightly warm

tea tarts: delicate, sweet pastry with jam or mincemeat filling

at a hotel, unpacking a romantic picnic, sprawling out on the bed, and listening to the quiet

patchwork calico

black- and blueberry jam

drawing a self-portrait

an enameled pierced-steel pie keeper

glass apothecary jars with multicolor or different-shaped shells

grass flowers

sybarite = anyone who loves luxury and
    self-indulgence
tobogganing: sitting down, getting close,
    hanging on, and go!
a barn filled with hay, swings, and
    tunnels; playing hide-and-seek on
    rainy days
barley
playing drums
Thumbelina dolls
packing a frosted cake for a trip
society girls
Rocky the Flying Squirrel
a calico shop
tickets to the symphony
wicker trunks
a cat named Marmalade because it's
    orange
back soothers
bacon presses
picking your own Academy Award
    winners beforehand and opening the
    envelopes when they do while sipping
    champagne
dicing onions
scot = a tab for drinks
taking the extra minute to notice
white leather
foulard bow ties
old-fashioned stick candy in jars

riding the wind

vodka gimlets

traveling in the off-season

Oneida silver

the authentic Victorian color scheme of
cream with coffee brown and dark
brown trim

Riesling wine

the Avon lady

the Campbell Soup twins

love returned

the chipmunk lining his winter bedroom
and stocking his granary

packing twine

veils of rain

the final gasp of a coffee percolator,
alerting you that it's ready

raffia baskets

the condition of waking up with your
pajamas turned 180 degrees

reflecting at the beach

Tiffany lamps

the first hours of sunlight: time to
twinkle and strike sparks from frosty
twigs and icy ponds, time to pencil
long shadows on every tree-lined
meadow

the first star quietly coming out

big parties with beautiful people

"Nice socks!"

the freshest dairy butter, farm eggs, and
ripe lemons
laissez-faire
painting a dream
the language spoken by fast-food
restaurant employees
colorful calorie charts
people-watching from a park bench
a baby's yawn
searching for pumpkin perfection
the slight trace of criminality one feels
when having a lover's keys duplicated
when hiking through snow, using the
footsteps of one who has boldly gone
before you
the smell of newly mimeographed test
papers
treating everyone with civility and
respect
when the lights come up
where writers, artists, and tourists
gather
the way your lover looked at you the first
time you met
an evening of zero productivity
creamy and sharp cheese
the library's summer book club and
earning gold stars
squirrels in reckless treetop chases
Ecclesiastes 3:1–13

falling asleep on the couch
French francs
wafers with the slender stripe of green
    mint through the center
coffee served in enormous bone china
    cups and saucers
the meaning of a bird's song
suggestions for romantic evenings
primitive and untouched things
reincarnation
spider plants
opening clams
stirring coffee with your finger
the morning newspaper at the door
being motioned to come sit by someone
thick pine snack tables
using pink, yellow, and green satin
    ribbons to tie around napkins,
    champagne glasses, and invitations
going to the beach with cucumber
    sandwiches
University of Stockholm
white collars and cuffs
an incorrigible browser
being swept away by sheer delight
chicken in cherry sauce
dripping BLT sandwiches
gaining energy by exerting energy
grilling over slow coals
majolica ware

farm markets with the best fresh milk
Baby Boom (movie)
making eggnog
Sunday papers
relaxing with a half-hour of yoga
asking a child to sing you a song
the posts of a picket fence
baking a crock of beans on a Saturday
    night
Goosey Gander
multiplying sunlight with mirrors
a polished acrylic tic-tac-toe board
pulling all-nighters before exams
men playing "tough guy"
rolling the rugs back for dancing
splurging on a midweek dinner out
window sashes
making lists at bedtime
taking advantage of Indian summer
dance studios
tulips pushing through rain-soaked soil
fireflies winking their undecipherable
    messages
hangers
college rings
halved melons filled with strawberries
    or raspberries
lamb souvlakia
chicken with hard cider
someone's secret summer

tomato sauce and Parmesan cheese
   on a hot dog
humble abodes
lingonberries
penny loafers
Noodle, Texas
Gallo pink chablis wine
sunsets scooped between the dunes
Groundhog Day
vanilla bread pudding with nutmeg
a winter breakfast: steaming bowls of
   oatmeal topped with raisins or sliced
   bananas
banquettes with onion-shaped backs
Candy Cane Lane, LaPorte, Indiana
denim blazers
finally realizing that your mate will not
   close the closet doors so you stop
   nagging about it
hand-blended larch and lemon potpourri
   in an embroidered pillow
ivory almond bark candy
spot removers
mentally going through rolls of film
perfume vials
smoked bacon rashers with a brown-gold
   rind and deep pink flesh
Treasure Island
storing vitamins in a ceramic jar
wood-burning fireplaces

amphitheaters

running your hand along fences or walls

Depression furniture: blond wood with
rounded corners for dressing tables,
wardrobes, and bureaus

hoping that someday you'll cook a steak
to perfection

wrong numbers

"Woodstock," the bird in *Peanuts*

an old-fashioned roasting kitchen

cooling swims

the scientific method

snow in March

an organ loft

broad-leaved evergreens

cooking your first turkey

flour sifters

hot, gooey chocolate-chip cookies

tapioca/Tap City = broke

a post office and grocery store being the
only services on the island

a private collection of pleasures

large textual databases

Herefords standing knee-deep in lush
grass

porch gliders

home-fried pork tenderloin and breakfast
vegetables

knowing when to work and when to play

spring onions

throwing a coin in a well and making
  a wish
getting a family heirloom fixed
a restaurant where guests cook their own
  steaks, lobsters, and shrimps on a
  table grill
apron dresses
barbershop-tiled floors
turn-of-the-century corked medicine
  bottles
birches that look like paintbrushes whose
  tips have been dipped in rouge
burning a Yule log only halfway, saving
  the rest to light the new log the
  next year
careless ways
dark blue sky
earthenware butter tubs
tiny, woven fortune-cookie baskets
listing names and page numbers of
  favorite recipes inside cookbook
  covers
passing a car
Boris Badenov and Natasha Nogoodnik,
  arch-enemies of Bullwinkle and
  Rocky
washing your hands before you eat
a snowdrift curled in the shape of the
  storm's breath
team pennants

baskets of tomatoes, squash, and
cucumbers clustered on the kitchen
steps

cast-off time when sailing

easy-out ice-cube trays

a smile from a stranger

a tiny shell picked up in Jamaica

fishing lines

Gatorade kegs

the rich, deep purples of late August

enjoying the morning sun on the patio

pattern books

Nat King Cole, musician

setting the table with cloth napkins and
napkin rings

a tray covered with a snowy, cutwork
cloth

peppermint sticks

after supper, lying in the grass and
watching the fire die

antique icebox hardware

batting cages

fast learners

singing voices: alto, baritone, baritenor,
bass, coloratura, contralto, dramatic
soprano, lyric soprano, male soprano,
mezzo-soprano, soprano, tenor, and
basso profundo

antique books

stately homes

eating crullers, pork chops, apple butter,
     persimmon ice cream, whole-hog
     sausage, beans, and cornbread
extra-duty tennis balls
getting something fixed
mounds of blueberry, apple, pumpkin,
     and date muffins
pruning trees
"butter" suns
bouzouki music and blue, blue sea
country gourmet cooking
double boilers
equinoxes and solstices
a four-hankie flick on the Late-Late
gaudy tartans
deviled ham and relish sandwiches
having a really good photograph taken
     of you
new friends to help us stay young
a window shade that allows itself to be
     pulled down, hesitates for a second,
     then snaps up in your face
bowling lawns
chunky wooden bracelets
planting corn
small snowmen with twigs for arms
boxes of live daffodils throughout
     the room
layered seeds and nuts in an apothecary
     jar

pizza, stamp, poker table, and gumball
   jigsaw puzzles
7X: Coca Cola's secret ingredient
a Chippendale secretary
orange crates
playing among big trees and rocks
All the President's Men (book, movie)
real turkey on an overstuffed triple-
   decker
roast beef sandwiches with lettuce,
   mayonnaise, and salt/pepper
sharing things: toys, fun, giggles, secrets
when the lights flicker
a cat purring
striped canvas beach chairs
staying fresh
pleasing yourself
translucent hair color with subtle
   shadings
unarguable fundamentals
an antique pie cupboard
chestnut trees, heavy with blooms
third basemen
writing thank-you notes
an aromatic puff of frying onion wafting
   out the door
old Bible racks hooked on a cabinet to
   hold cookbooks
bracelet-length sleeves
clapping of an audience

elaborate coats of arms
murfles = freckles, dimples
heather-cloaked heights
library steps
Tabasco sauce
a baggy-eyed baker on the night shift
a bushel of oatmeal made into thin cakes
    and bannocks
babies' quilts
hobby shelves
going for it lock, stock, and barrel
a canopied pontoon boat
"accidentally on purpose"
ancient gray stones and white picket
    fences
back-saver snow shovels
decorating your home with mistletoe or
    fresh pine wreaths; hanging
    Christmas lights or lighting a menorah
hickory spice
kids keeping you moving
the quiet spirit of holiday music
the smell of old school buildings
old farmhouses with tall ceilings
red rubber boots for walking through the
    streets and woods after the rain or
    snow and hearing the wonderful
    sound your footsteps make
riding horses
cider presses

theater tickets for two
one-act plays
spending a day when you take cabs
    everywhere or walk everywhere
presidential autographs
stereopticons
sweet potatoes with a glaze of sugar,
    cinnamon, margarine, and cornstarch
the plastic tray used to organize and
    separate silverware
the cardboard snowflake you made when
    you were little
iced mint tea
oceanfront dining rooms
the crunch of snap peas
open-minded uncertainty
seeing your breath exhaled as a frosty
    puff
the fairy-tale factory in your mind
old-fashioned lemon pie
ordering a cord of wood
red geraniums
the night smell, feel, and wonder of
    October
Caesar salads
freewheeling
shirt jackets
Wrigley's gum
fresh-baked raisin and raspberry cream
    pies

guest rooms done up with bright floral
    print wallpapers and draperies,
    antique quilts, thick carpets, and
    period furnishings
the squeak of a hammock
clearing the underbrush
the take-your-picnic-indoors plan
tree-lined streets, fireflies, nighttime
    sounds, and aromas stirring up
    feelings of nostalgia
when, in the middle of a quiet, milder
    than usual night, the accumulated
    snow on the roof slides off with a
    thundering crash
an encampment of tepees, lean-tos, and
    pioneer wagons
breakers so huge that they seem to move
    in slow motion while wind blows
    spray back in gossamer white arcs
    and mists the air with spindrift
breeches, tall boots, and a riding jacket
chenille caterpillars doing push-ups
    through the lawn
clear-glass candle cups
electric football games
the tea table
the third pancake of a batch being the
    first good one
elephants sliding down a slope for their
    morning bath

fresh Key lime pie, strawberry meringue
glacé, peach Melba, and pecan pie
soft pretzels kept toasty on a warming
tray
coffee served with a pitcher
of thick cream
big paychecks
Irish whiskey
a mahogany stationery box
jogging on a carpet of leaves as the sun-
dappled trail winds through a thick,
hardwood forest
pigeons gargling on a fire escape
sugaring off = gathering sap from maple
trees and boiling it down over old-
fashioned wood-fired evaporators
onion holders
when physical fitness was related only to
gym class and President Kennedy
paintbrushes
quilted seaside spreads on wooden
platforms
rainy days, ideal for special projects
you've been procrastinating about
raisin bread pudding with fresh lemon
sauce
endlessly winding backroads
bread rising
skivvy skirts
thick bark on the trees

using candles
white birch logs in the fireplace in
    summer
a set of sharpened colored pencils on your
    desk in a glass for doodling and
    jotting notes in something other than
    gray lead
being happy sharing quiet moments
coffee-colored kitchen appliances
brick porches
holding hands
fresh produce
Chinese brocade diaries
making pizzas
pillow fights
bright rivers winding like silver threads
    through the soft, rich tapestries of
    growing fields
homemade cheese-and-sausage pizza
indirect lighting
bringing home the bacon
chili sprinkled with strong chopped
    onions and triangles of orange cheese
chives, bergamot, sweet cicely, purslane,
    pennyroyal, betony, mallow, dill,
    coriander, saffron, anise, borage,
    caraway, marigold, violet, bog myrtle,
    alecost, clary, soapwort,
    meadowsweet, rose, and lemon
    verbena

crinkly nylon swimsuits

a fait accompli

hairpin curves

making up dreams in bed

poker parties

taking a bus to a small town with an
interesting name; staying a few hours
and exploring

taking in a stray puppy

jelly for morning toast

Louisiana: bayous, New Orleans, creole
cooking

polished ash and walnut

pull-apart bread loaves

believing in yourself when no one
else will

roll-on antiperspirants

Blazing Saddles (movie)

tall French doors opening onto a terrace
that looks out over the river

balance beams

Bill Cosby's Jell-O commercials

celery and cream cheese

fall visitors

holiday mints

summer homes in Vermont

I: the commonest word in conversation

gumball banks

homemade pea soup in a restaurant

king-size Danish rolls

lengths of knotty pine for a paneled effect
men's collarband shirts
Kentucky: blue grass, the Derby,
    limestoned valleys, Cumberland Gap
pancake shops
sending Christmas cards
sand dunes and thickets
mandarin rice
coonskin caps
sending someone an article you know will
    be of special interest
Reno divorces
Santa's Village, Dundee, Illinois
want-ad weeks
bentwood chairs and hanging lamps
paisley
finding the start of a roll of toilet paper
ivory animals
the silver screen
looking for the best and enjoying
cardigan sweaters
proms, gardenias, and moonlit dance
    halls on the lake
"God Bless Our Home" wall mottoes
root beer floats made with homemade ice
    cream every Fourth of July
Noodle-O soup
showing a dog
"a nickel for all the times the ice melted
    waiting for him to come home"

"NaNaNaNa-NaNaNaNa-HeyHey-
      Goodbye" (song)
adopting a parakeet and teaching it to
      talk
an old railroad station
blowing out all the candles
floor pillows
chocolate wafer cookies
feeling cool and serene as a country pond
exotic coral seashell and barnacle
      clusters
cargo pockets
little feet in the sand
frosty shades
"Good morning, sweetums!"
serving the senior dinner at the
      fraternity
popcorn in plastic jugs
sipping a passion punch
Ripley's Believe-It-or-Not
a pulsating shower head
the "upper crust"
happy unplanned moments
an irresistible party mood
large, messy submarine sandwiches
part of you always being a child
March: jonquil or daisy
porch sitting
scraping snow and ice off the car
stretching muscles in the morning

terrarium coffee tables
a romantic walk through the
    neighborhood to look at Christmas
    decorations
barbecue pits
ceramic beads
Carvel ice-cream stores
for red dye: beetroot, bloodroot, dogwood
    root, hollyhock flowers, madder root,
    St.-John's-wort flowers
the luxury of a fresh towel
a sense of humor in bed
just-picked vegetables and fruits
pistol-handled flatware
rosy mornings
vision checks
a surprise burst of joy
cases of beer
a cosmopolitan atmosphere
easy-to-eat finger food
fishing lures
Disneyland, Walt Disney World
hostess gifts
international cookbooks
the cooing doves of morning
noted artists
on the prod = looking for trouble
pets in line for the fire hydrant
wet-hair sets
a tired Santa

getting something fixed that's been
    broken all winter
autumn feasts
city britches
playing house, school, restaurant
peas amandine
stately palms
cotton shirts
eating at the boat dock
getting a free soda or a cheaper one from
    a machine that still has someone
    else's money in it
Dutch scenes on the ends of demitasse
    spoons
getting asked out on a date early
things we can not be without
white place cards
hot dogs, paratrooper pants, bowling
    shirts
the sense of promise inherent in the start
    of a new year
laughing as you remember good times
    together
mouthwatering descriptions
sauerbraten: pot roast marinated several
    days in vinegar with vegetables and
    spices
studying in the library
"You can't go home again"
blueberry jam

church spires
moving into town from the suburbs
savoring an achievement
a vast underground cache of wines
Elvis Presley, rock star
New York City
children sewing on paper plates
a wondrously fleecy towel
"as warm as summer roses"
luxury hotel stationery
toys on sticks at amusement parks
drying gourds
Mr. Magoo's Chinese cook, Charley
I.D. pictures
a SAAB convertible for graduation
the Hi and Lois comic strip
an Italian vetro verde wine decanter
peach and cranberry muffins and sour-
    cream coffeecake
hayrack rides
lazy evenings
breakfast at the bird feeder
seaside amusement parks
team pictures
double-decker sandwiches
FTP = fall to pieces
tearing cartoons out of the paper
"saucering" in the snow
an antique quilt in reds, greens, browns,
    and yellows

the chambered nautilus shell
big red barns
using a razor
whiskey sours
brick streets
talking intelligently, possibly brilliantly
an authentic Irish wool tweed tie
chair circles
flared skirts
flat, smooth, cool sand, just out of reach of
    the incoming tide
glazing a pot
liberation from grown-up routines
rib-eye steaks for lunch
unbelieveably tender filet mignon
tugboats
the funny feeling that you already put
    sugar in your coffee
a beehive oven capable of baking many
    loaves of bread at one time
Mickey Mouse timepieces
Occupant mail
a calm before the storm
ancient ruins
back-scrubbers
award frames
a cabin by the side of a huge northern
    lake
tractor pulls
free stuff from a hotel

stiff collars
bacon and pork sausages
decorating a flowerpot
The Addams Family (TV show)
riding in a wheelbarrow
Rodgers and Hammerstein
today's promise becoming tomorrow's joy
cider sherbet
inexpensive music boxes
one-day hikes
steak joint/rock-Muzak places
sweater coats
fresh air and good food
the Chicago Seven, 1968
a sewing nook
the *Oxford English Dictionary* and its
    Supplements and the *New Oxford*
    English Dictionary
vodka glasses
a trellis of sweet peas
the best climbing rocks
the plastic wand that launches soap
    bubbles
a clean litter box
deep-fried French toast
erect posture
feeding a parking meter
the stars having a frosty twinkle
the sugar-scented green of leaves
pizza parlors

the sun's warmest tones
coffee barefoot (black)
the uses of a yardstick
theatergoing
when there's a thick gray rim of thawing
    ice lining the streets
Friday = "weekend eve"
a checkerboard cake baker
chefs' knives
fresh flowers, crisp vegetables, hot
    popovers, hearty portions, lots of bath
    towels
al fresco = out of doors
color schemes
jugs of fruit
organization of closets
big armfuls of dried wheat, bulrushes, or
    dunegrass arranged in a country
    milk can
eager beavers
high school sweethearts
"Thank you for not smoking" signs
rainy leaves stuck like emblems on the
    walk
sipping homemade apple cider
joining clubs in school
paint rollers
rail-splitting contests
wine spiced with lemon, cloves, sugar,
    cinnamon

wild black cherry trees
stirring up warm, friendly feelings on a
    cold morning
twin theaters
using the cat to remove crumbs on
    the floor
writing down all the different roles
    you play
tin lizzies
animal sounds
telling people you've been afraid of
    exactly what you think of them and
    having the situation get better
bright rubies
bright, sunny cold days
chiffon cake with ice-cream balls
fringed jeans
going to bed early with a new mystery
    novel
making something from magazine
    instructions
using pokers to pick up paper
oak moss, citrus, quiet spice, woody
    smells
raking leaves
being as idle as a languid brook
melt-in-your-mouth food
milkshake with a muffin
a salad-and-relish buffet
selling your first house

splurging on fresh flowers, flowering
plants, scented candles, and a fresh
batch of magazines
"Blue Rhythm" painting by Hans
Hoffman in the Chicago Art Institute
walking through fresh snow and listening
to it crunch
couriers
Valentine's Day aluminum-wrapped
shoeboxes for school
wild violets growing profusely and
making the prettiest of small
bouquets
calling someone at home
collecting milk bottles
full freezers
taking a cat to the vet
watching kids ice-skate
ceramic glaze
getting in the right line at the store
lemon pancakes served with fresh
raspberries or raspberry syrup
sundae dishes
hill climbing
Humpty Dumpty
romantic tables for two
summer storms
aiming for more quality
familiar sounds of the Deep South
long sojourns

manger scenes
minerals that color stone formations deep
    black and red, purple, green, and
    orange
pony trekking
sunken Spanish galleons
Tennessee: Nashville, marble, green,
    horses
leaded glass doors
candelabras entwined with garlands of
    holly
finding things when you need them
a hanging place for wursts, bagged
    cheeses, and strings of peppers
ivory chokers
knowledge of arcane whys and hows
looking toward tomorrow
room settings
snow accumulating on the pavement
an 1805 lap desk
spotted sandpipers with long bills
    and legs
once-in-a-lifetime chances
wooden scoops
"Oooh doggies, the hoggies are out!"
an old French black steel boulangerie
    rack
over-the-sink cutting boards
"Hound Dog" by Elvis
floating flower candles

hoop earrings

super showers

a plate of hot buckwheat cakes with
transparent syrup

your first room at college

booths in park bench style

serving dips in seashells collected on the
beach or found in import shops

struggling with algebra

transcontinental telephoning

mufflers

Bergdorf Goodman stores

burgundy wine

caring for new woodwork

strange paw prints to investigate

fingerbreadths

chrome-and-glass tables

dark clouds settling on the mountain
ridges

when, for the moment, the crowd is
somewhere else

gardens planted with cold-weather
crops: turnips, broccoli, cauliflower,
and peas

listening to the magic workings of a
flower, of a butterfly, and of man's
intellect

massive old breakfronts

misty mornings

redwood trees

leather mules
playing poker
little boys in white boxer shorts
natural-wood milk pails
mosquito kerosene lamps
pushing car lighters in
responding to challenge
a shady, babbling brook
a stable with a dozen island-bred
    palominos
peut être = maybe
assorted-size canvases
basketweaving
bus terminals
easy-to-peel tangerines
Gothic and Cotswold-style quadrangles
    for old-fashioned schools
kitchen sinks
network sports introductory music
not begrudging others what you cannot
    enjoy
not despising what you cannot get
a stroll on the lakeside footpath
potato fields
National Newspaper Week
J.J. Audubon's *Birds of America*
cream cheese and watercress triangles
a terra-cotta flue pipe
afternoon tea in London
Betty Crocker cookbooks

the rambunctiousness of boys
getaway cars with empty gas tanks
industry
blueberries and Asti Spumanti wine
the klunk-klunk of a windshield wiper
your nest egg
an unusual setting for a candlelight
    dinner
the feel of a scarf against the neck
coupons for information on foreign travel
    spots
hours of climbing trees
invisible ink
bouquets of silk flowers all over the house
Blue Onion serving sets
Nevada silver
giving an affectionate nickname to
    someone who doesn't have one
a Cape Codder
IBM
towels that absorb well
a world of action toys: Ghostbusters,
    G.I. Joe, trucks and cars
layering on favorite old sweaters
trying every ride at the carnival
lazy inner-tube floats on the looping river
B & M railroad lanterns
100-watt eyes
a snow softball
plastic cups with built-in straws

meat platters
Gothic novels
ice-cream store posters
Chantilly whipped cream
drawing hopscotch lines
Cracker Jacks

small tidal pools in which you can see
      bright green moss and species of
      marine life
palm-fringed beach
the snappy bustle of pelicans and donkeys
tearoom lunch
Shaker crafts
silvery milkweed pods opening
toast under the broiler
the whack of a bat against a baseball
alacrity = cheerful willingness,
      liveliness
plastic ponchos in rainbow colors
clippity-clop, jingle-jingle sounds
shadow boxes in kitchens
pictures leaving stickies on the walls
giant turner/fork/tongs
heading north
the first day of biking
the haven you escape to for hours: sitting
      curled there, dreaming, reading,
      building yourself a life, a world
a boy who follows in his mother's
      footsteps

a bright, cheerful breakfast room

handwoven fabrics, tinted with rich, earthy colors from the juices of fresh berries

nachos served with guacamole and sour cream

apple pie and the Fourth of July

shutters

red carnations with green candles

pickled beets

playing Old Mill

eating TV dinners while sitting on the floor

hooded and zippered sweaters

iced scallop salad, lemon noodles, roasted green beans, and sautéed cherry tomatoes

open-to-the-sky freedom

pie-iron pies

pretending the hallway has stairs

the "light/dark" knob on a toaster that makes you think you're in control

ice-skating at midnight

the Chipmunks, singing group

picnic brunch

the cidery tang of windfall apples in the country air

the honk of car horns and car alarm systems

recognizing the obvious

the accumulation of junk in the attic

auctioneering

Midwesternese

the part of the envelope that tells where
to place the stamp as if you couldn't
figure it out

charisma

alkaline batteries

the start of a good classical record
collection: Bach's Brandenburg
Concertos, Beethoven's Symphony
No. 3, Brahms' Symphony No. 1,
Chopin's Piano Concerto No. 2,
Debussy's *La Mer*, Handel's *Water
Music Suite*, Mozart's Symphony
No. 40, Stravinsky's *The Rite of
Spring*, Tchaikovsky's Symphony No.
6, and Vivaldi's *Four Seasons*

the uncurling of a fern

treadle sewing machines

bee-drone days and firefly nights

the satisfaction of lifting your own
homemade waffles out of a steaming
waffle iron

show-and-tell

lemon extract

every fair and flea market having a fried
dough wagon

field mushrooms, fried in butter and kept
warm in a chafing dish

the creak of an old door or gate
disco dancing
freshly laundered jeans
cherub cheeks
air-conditioning
taking a dare
French country pitchers
cafés with gaily striped umbrellas
offering to do a Tarot card reading with
    scented candles and Irish coffee
something as fresh as candy mints
coffee-flavored soufflé ice cream
organization of errands
sugarless gum
clean windows
coffee "with socks on" (with cream)
ungodly hours
big baskets for magazines or yarn
the *Tonight Show* song
knife-sharpened pencils
onions keeping best when roped and
    hung in a dry, cold room
"smile" buttons
whizzing down hills with wind on your
    face and sun on your back
White Castle hamburgers
chic sneakers
enough china and silver to serve an army
dried flowers, fresh fruit, poetry books,
    and herbal sachets in each room

Chip and Dale Chipmunks
going roller-skating on a Saturday
    morning with corny organ music in
    the background
lake steamers
taking a walk downtown on Saturday
    night to buy the Sunday *New York
    Times*
taking someone a bunch of violets
ankling T-shirt dresses
baked pears for dessert
getting a passport
milk boiling on a blue-tiled charcoal stove
mulching leaves with a lawn mower
pale radar screens flickering with
    activity
political consciousness
self-awareness and self-discovery
Pallas' cats in a Himalayan pass
"Well begun is half done"
ball earrings
going to a palm reader or having your tea
    leaves read
gallons, bushels, pecks
Felix the Cat
streaked hair
limbering up for sports
remembering people's names long after
    they've forgotten yours
romper and boxer shorts

smiling in phone booths
birds huddling on the ground
balm = sympathy
time for cozy dinners of soup and bread
    and indoor games by a toasty fire
yummy-to-lick envelopes
bamboo chairs
compulsive crossword-puzzle doers
mango chutney
ten
Ionic columns
flower and garden shows
pan pizza from Domino's
serene, sun-splashed scenes
tennis on public courts
Sunday school
gingerbread houses outlined in white
    spun sugar, peppermints, corn candy,
    jellybeans, and mint patties
tunnel vision
winning a war
a candle in a cluster of rock candy
Loving, New Mexico
defusing a bomb
pink lemonade
contributing to a lending library
dinero = money
getting adequate recognition for a job
    well done
ginkgo and willow trees

spotting a city slicker
the moon-baying of hounds
playing Jeopardy!
people who try to have their freckles
     removed
root crops: potatoes, peanuts, onions,
     beets, carrots, turnips, rutabagas
showing off collections
sports shorts
"You turkey!"
chopping fresh vegetables on a wooden
     board
floating in tender clouds of silk
"cool" notebooks at school, i.e.,
     "Go-Ports"
flowers in an empty mustard or cheese
     crock
football pins
grosgrain ribbon for headbands,
     watchbands, and belts
pipe cleaners
the snall rubbery pads on the bottom of a
     cat's or dog's paws
fig = longevity
empty bottles
saffron = marriage and cheerfulness
morning light
parting your hair crooked
Marilyn Monroe, actress
a porkpie hassock with knob on top

portable Scrabble games
spring salads
street hockey
three-layer carrot cake
Tarzan, Texas
sitting on the deck of a sailboat
your adrenaline starting to pump at
    the thought of leaving work and
    going home
chenille
the tweet of a whistle
the bark of a dog
harbor houses
coral and white fabric flowers, tied up
    with a pretty grosgrain ribbon and
    placed in a grapevine basket
satiny shirts
Barnacle Bill
burgundy, rust, and peach comforters and
    dust ruffles
carrot strips and cucumber slices
seasonless corduroy, cotton gabardine,
    velour, denim
corn beginning to ripen
formal terraced gardens
herringbone twill pants
curling up with a book while the hubby
    is out playing golf or watching sports
    on TV
horses in nippy weather

visiting his alma mater
a sense of dignity
learning the ropes
basic recipes
cotton towels
squash courts
baskets of cloudberries
desperados
hash browns in the form of a charred
    pancake of mashed potatoes
not being able to face one more winter
    clearance sale
rational, clean, spacious, joyous settings
settling into a lush green valley to
    dairy-farm
Ritz crackers
a tall octagon aquarium
attending to your own business and never
    trusting it to another
biting into a croissant
a tray of scones and pot of honey
cutting bangs
vaulted rooms
aluminum foil
estimating the temperature by counting
    the number of cricket chirps in
    15 seconds and adding 37
getting a job
poultry cooked in cider
squirrels hoarding nuts

an underground railroad
blueberries and raspberries to freeze for
    winter pies
banana oil = foolish or insincere talk
handkerchief linen
a fruit bowl with cardamom dressing
inviting a friend over or out for breakfast
living in the woods near the edge of
    a lake
never having used training wheels
saving money on almost everything
November: chrysanthemum
divorce sales
arts fanatics
bifocals
setting aside time for relaxation
crates of fruit jellies
New Hampshire primaries
a weekend afternoon taking photos
a well-wishing attitude
Mexican pesos
attempts to communicate with the
    doughnut waitress on the other side
    of the glass case
pizza pot pie
a Swedish country inn set well off the
    main road
picking the right lane for once in a traffic
    jam
the old Chevy

leaving the mistletoe up all year
meat pounders
Italian menus
learning to be free, willing to take
    reasonable risks, open to others and
    new ideas
plants on cinder blocks
children playing "radio station"
reading guest registers
beach lunches
realizing you forgot your rubber duck
    when you get to the beach
standing out in a crowd
teas tailor-made to individual
    requirements
Shaker pantry and sewing boxes and
    piggins (boxes with handles)
braising food
Crate and Barrel stores
featherweight flapjacks
heading south
Labradors that think they're lapdogs,
    Great Danes that eat off tables,
    golden retrievers digging huge holes
    in the rose garden, and basset hounds
    sunbathing on the highway
kids' imaginations
scarred desks
red knit caps
leather sofas

a string of ponies
being blessed
a blueberry farm amid corn and wheat
    fields
intellectual rigor
a bowback Windsor chair
lace curtains, pillows, napkins, clothes
pocket caddies for reading chairs
tacos with tomato juice
vacuum bottle holders with straps
a baccalaureate
hockey boards
medicine kits
ordering books by phone
radish spread
Underdog's girlfriend, Sweet Polly
    Purebred
wading knee-deep in fallen leaves
faded palaces
French phones
French-milled soap, fresh flowers, and
    fruit
seeing cows milked, chicks hatch, and
    lambs drink from a bottle
blue gumdrops
slatted doors
beating around the bush
the Acropolis
sherried sweet potatoes
sleepy people

the Cubs' Bleacher Bums
breakfast quick breads, warm from the
    oven, puffy and delicious
cheddar cheese pancakes
the combination of fall colors and
    waterside atmosphere
greengrocers
the frost-flowered surface of a silent lake
interrobang = a combination of the
    exclamation point and question mark
the red leather chair on which the dog is
    not allowed
safety razors
cafés along the blue water's edge
coffee steaming gently from the spout of a
    tall blue enamel pot with a hinged lid
the retort "Don't make me laugh!"
a sense of continuity
the season's first drive-in movie
red and white
the shine of old things
using a brass corn popper on the hearth
    for roasting chestnuts, baking
    potatoes, or grilling sandwiches
writing menus
being tickled
the smell of a coffee can opening
baseball hats
the vacuum tube used in drive-through
    banks

when the person ahead of you pays
 your toll
bread, still warm, in an unmarked plastic
 bag tied with a snippet of wire
Shirley Temple in *Heidi*
cherub faces sticking out of multicolor ski
 jackets and hats
deep red dogwood and sourwood, yellow
 birch and beech, orange sassafras and
 bright red maples
dwelling in possibility
being free to change and express yourself
the wonder of life
magic carpets
piglets and swine
eggdrop soup
English muffins, split and toasted hot
 with lots of butter and golden jam
high ceilings, ornate moldings, and
 massive windows
school dances
Athens marble
sciences: anthropology, astronomy,
 bacteriology, biochemistry, biology,
 botany, chemistry, ecology, geology,
 mathematics, metallurgy,
 meteorology, oceanography,
 paleontology, psychology, space,
 zoology
ship models, nautical memorabilia

bringing a bowl of berries to bed
skinny breadsticks
flickering candlelight
begonias
hairy traffic
the sound of sneakers squeaking against
the floor during basketball games
the turning earth, the blazing sun, the
restless wind
making a child's settee of a crib
melted butter
silicon chips
"Well, I'm a dirty bird!"
yellow boys' raincoats with hoods
balancing the checkbook
leaves starting to turn
Belgian endive with chicken or Swiss
cheese
collages
filling a glass bowl with fresh apples and
tangerines
Delaware wine
lemon shake-up drinks at the fair
"Time is money"
memories that revolve around food
romantic beds
timing your garage sale
women who say, in reference to their
husbands, "We never fight"
avocado trees

computer cash registers

families that spend leisure hours
together having a chance to grow and
understand one another

people who ask you Trivial Pursuit
questions instead of trying to make
conversation

shop doorways

Woodward and Bernstein, Watergate
reporters

Gnomes (book)

MasterCard and Visa

candlelight dinners at eight instead of
neon-lighted dinners at six

wine tastings

candy stripes

using canning jars as kitchen canisters

finding a drive-in and watching from
behind the fence

hanging popcorn balls on the tree

the Road Runner

pelicans

men who shave every day

running your first mile

spring skiing

tangy fresh-pepper hash

winds, the unseen tides

compliments to the chef

broiled corn on the cob

chocolate cream liqueur

lamps with wicker bases
tan and brown suedes and leathers
block bazaars
park concerts
chopping wood
aspen-covered mountains in golden and
     amber hues against a backdrop of
     dark green fir, spruce, and pine
good evenings
rope hammocks
apple peeling
bop
lemon-lime milk sherbet
a copper-and-brass coal scuttle used for
     kindling or small logs or as a sewing
     caddy or popcorn bowl
Harvard beets
remembering when leaves were raked,
     jumped into, or burned and not put in
     plastic bags or giant vacuums
morning music
parrot tulips
Norman Rockwell's "Stockbridge at
     Christmas" painting
pure folk art
scrub brushes
finding your own private pleasure
sleep learning
turned-up shirt collars
a wire Easter-egg dipper

working wives
a rainy Sunday with your children
city planning
spas
airline meals
an African stone game called Mankala
carte blanche
a farmers' market with sausages and
    cheese ready for slicing, country-
    cured bacon, and baked beans
    simmered in sweet molasses
forecasting the weather
geranium pots
European pro basketball
a room filled with art and sewing
herbs and plants used for yellow dye:
    alder leaves, apple bark, aster
    flowers, bayberry leaves, camomile
    flowers, horse chestnut husks, catnip,
    peach bark
hiring help for a party
playing Password
a set of 30 cotton turtlenecks in a rainbow
    of colors
a sun-toasted colonnade
basketball time buzzers
peaches 'n cream ice cream
discovering a secret country lane or
    peaceful bend in the river
a really good hamburger

hash browns, red-spiced and salted
kitchen bags for onions and potatoes
letter sweaters and pleated skirts
little paper cups of honey butter
not being embarrassed easily
Katharine Ross, actress
blueberries, pine cherries, woodbine,
    raspberries, cranberries,
    honeysuckle, wild roses, and beach
    plums
outdoor decking for inside floors
watching a thunderstorm
achieving more, but possibly doing less,
    with rest
a thermos of frozen fruit "slush"
picnic grounds
antique water meter box
getting artsy-craftsy
attentiveness
cats that sleep all day Sunday
cotton tunics
Spanish olives
cutting boards for serving breads
extra innings
getting stuck in a beanbag chair
hot coals in the hearth for toasting toes
round trays for serving
true beauty being timeless
your own energy as a letter of
    introduction

extra-summery clothes
"super" diets and exercise guides
churns, copper kettles, oak kegs, wash
    pots, buggies, wood stoves, cider
    presses, coffee mills, kerosene
    lamps—all sold at the general store
taking a child to the park to feed the
    ducks
house-sitting
movie posters
having the Sunday funnies on hand
Howard Johnson's motels
powder blue/lemon/peach/fresh mint/
    peppermint/suede/bone colors
Tweety Bird
a wintergreen toothpick
a wood-smoke smell
wax paintings
falling stars after midnight
do-it-yourself projects
1954
Patton (movie)
jeans with clean patches
peanut butter and cranberry sauce
    sandwiches
plates of lettuce, peppergrass and chives,
    interspersed with white and red
    radishes and balls of buttermilk
    cheese
soaps in dresser drawers

crescent rolls
generics
crackered eggs
stars outside the airplane window
analyticalness
an arabesque of vines braiding the door
beach plum jam
the chatter of talking women
coal shoveling
drawing tables
a black jacket
cleaning out your emotional closet
a bowl of 'red' = chili
fabric collage paintings
mice
secret closets
uncrinkled aluminum foil
vacuum bottles
a capiz shell minaudière
1¢ sundae sales at Dairy Queen
"Knowledge is power"
decorating in "early college," "early
    hotel," or "early married"
crafts to sell
Indiana Dunes State Park
old-fashioned tea wagons
fads
French-speaking Belgians
summertime stripes
old-fashioned sock dolls

needlepoint napkin rings

wind chime with 100 brass bells

daybreak

sherry, cheese, biscuits, and a Bette
Davis golden oldie on a rainy Sunday
afternoon

spending money on small things: real
maple syrup, fancy bacon, *Vogue*
magazine, expensive soaps

arqo: the crossbar that turns an 'R' into
the drugstore symbol

laughing to keep from crying

the cool breezes of a New England
summer day

herb vinegars

thunderstorms

crocuses

Gnaw Bone, Indiana

the first blush of falling in love

going sockless

the high voice one uses when summoning
a cat

snowflakes twirling through the treetops

treasure boxes

when you start wanting to eat breakfast
outdoors in the sunshine

breath-catching evenings

cheering, sipping coffee, and taking in
the bright colors, enthusiasm, and
excitement of a football game

an elegant military ball
beef
cheese-stuffed mushrooms
the least attractive side of a Christmas
    tree that ends up facing the wall
crease-resistant clothes
green rivers, strawberry banana boats,
    brown cows, and pink elephant punch
dipping slices of pineapple, banana, and
    apple into chocolate fondue
lying in bed at night, picking out one
    thing you did well for the day, and
    congratulating yourself
coffee and doughnuts, their outsides crisp
    and sugary, their insides light and
    spicy
swallows returning
the long, weary walk up the aisle at the
    end of a movie
magic lanterns
pegged coatracks
the line you draw on a check to prevent
    someone from writing "and a million
    dollars"
sugar snap peas
dogs that guzzle beer from a dish, shed
    profusely, nap on the living room sofa,
    and sleep on a family member's bed
the Bay of Fundy, with the highest tides
    in the world

rugged clothes
sailing on Lake Michigan
the smell of freshly brewed coffee
skippies = white sneakers
the newspaper or magazine at the top of
the stack that everyone passes over,
believing the ones beneath are better
slipping away from shore on a boat
triple-layer jello molds
twig furniture
white chocolate bunnies and Santas
writing a book
being remembered long after the holidays
are forgotten
the red light in the church chapel
being soothed when awakened from a bad
dream at 3 A.M.
boiling water for coffee
devilish grins
the savory simmer of mincemeat in the
making
dried greenery
being told you're beautiful when wearing
a grungy T-shirt and jeans
going to a pizza place for a Singapore
Sling
taking an elevator friend to lunch
rolls served with plenty of butter and
jams, heaps of fresh fruit, juices, and
delicious coffee

"I just had to fall in love with him"
salt
Palm Springs, California
transmission fluid
walking on ice
balancing the checkbook at a sidewalk café
celebrating self-invented holidays
cold roast beef, rib of lamb, one ham, two roast duck, three baskets of salads, nine small lettuces, sparkling white wine, and lemon kept cool in a nearby stream
feathers
lemon ice cream and cake
Limoges ashtray and matchbox cover
someone who looks right at your eyes and smiles a huge, sweet smile
time to browse
women's sports
components of a romantic evening: iced oysters, chilled vodka, champagne with a bubble bath, fresh flowers, candles, and silk
families who summer in the Hamptons, the Vineyard, and Nantucket
homemade maple syrup, real cream, real butter, and heated plates
manhole covers
mint

tangy iced tea

bringing towels and soap

chicken spread

tennis challenge matches

candied apples, pickled beets, buttered
potatoes, string beans, and a half-
dozen hot biscuits served with a
pitcher of honey

dinner at noon

Morris, the finicky cat

iron, calcium, vitamin A

moonbeams on the water, like
fairies spawned from light

people who bob up and down in the ocean
trying to stay dry above the waist

poo = champagne

two layers of chocolate candies

zoos

Ordinary, Kentucky

aloe

"God Rest Ye, Merry Gentlemen" (carol)

an occasional trash breakfast, like a bowl
of Trix and a dip into a juicy novel

people who know exactly where they're
going

an outboard motor gargling at dawn

bronze mums and red carnations, brown
eggs, and bronze daisies

a door on a base, used as a coffee table or
desk

choral singing
floor-to-ceiling windows
frozen lemonade and orange juice
    concentrates
good farm food
Shetland sheepdogs
maple-blueberry corncake
peppermint-stick ice cream with a
    whipped cream topping and fudge in
    a small pitcher on the side
Pop-Tarts breakfast food
tape recordings
types of beds: baby, brass, bunk, canopy,
    crib, cot, davenport, double-deck,
    feather, hammock, Hollywood,
    hospital, iron, king-size, Murphy,
    double queen-size, roll-away, round,
    single, trundle, twin, vibrating, wall,
    wooden
apprenticeship
"Let's see what we find in the fridge"
large, framed pieces of seascapes,
    landscapes
Harvey Wallbanger drinks
marrying money
portable desks
North Carolina: sands, Smoky
    Mountains, rhododendron, dogwood,
    tobacco, Kitty Hawk
nursery school

penny loafers with the pennies stuck in
strapless bras
tartlet tins
percale sheets
cork
stream fishing for trout
streusel-topped pear pie
throwaways to play with or collect
turning over to even out your tan
barefoot beach barbecues
carol singing, children squealing, New
    Year's toasting
a string of really bad luck finally being
    broken
forever-green dieffenbachia plants
garbanzo beans
breeze-swept rooms
girl reporters
herb-lined pathways where one pauses to
    squeeze the lemon balm
horticultural techniques
inserting tabs
less strenuous pleasures
listening for the sound of a key in the
    lock
corrugated green velvet landscapes
musk
postcard views
reserved seats
a special weekend brunch

a struggling bag carrier
busy-day meals
Boston blueberry muffins
disguising your voice on the phone
natural pine paneling and shutters
a flower-laden outdoor bar
a pitcher of sangria to go
rattan hangers
a tan in April
button jewelry
cat toy makers in Vermont
cubed potatoes fried in bacon fat, salt and
    pepper
cottage cheese and sugar
Chevy Chase, actor
the kangaroo, koala, and wombat
Louisiana sweet potatoes
squash players
touch football
fruit trees in glorious clouds of red, white,
    and pink
unusual decorating finds
"cut the mustard"
aluminum-foil reflectors
blueberry cake
borage = courage
reviving tired furniture
Shakespeare's seven ages of man: infant,
    schoolboy, lover, soldier, justice,
    pantaloon, second childhood

caviar servers
five
having two magical days with no
    conversation, only contemplation
high IQs
new patent-leather shoes
paws
sawdust floors
things Mother never told you
mixing a drink
keys
bays and marinas jammed with boats
buying a good dictionary
pizza bicolore
a June-in-February party
59¢ grills
an alpine horn
G.I. Joe dolls
a New England meadow, green with the
    freshness of April
gumball dispensers
a Swedish whip
playing possum
playing your cards right
real fur coats
a bowl of cornflakes and cold milk
really thick, really special books
seascapes of southern Rhode Island
snatched sidewalk kisses
traditional Easter bread

aviation windsocks
a classic picnic of cheese and fruit
Charlie Brown and Snoopy
tobacco stores
a bed left guiltlessly, spontaneously
    unmade
"as brittle as spun glass"
feeling lucky to be born a woman
picking a passion flower
after-effects
raccoons and squirrels scampering in
    the bush
uncharted seas
a clandestine meeting at a hotel
uncrowded places to shop
bacon frying in cast-iron skillets
bicycling in the evening
old-fashioned washboards
sewing buckets
red convertible Alfa-Romeo Spiders
riding stables
wading through paperwork
body elements: aluminum, arsenic,
    calcium, carbon, chlorine, cobalt,
    copper, fluorine, hydrogen, iodine,
    iron, magnesium, manganese,
    nitrogen, oxygen, potassium,
    phosphorus, silicon, sodium,
    sulphur, zinc
French vanilla

the first few snowy mornings of any
   winter, wonderful and crisply
   beautiful
gifts at graduation time
pies
pretzels, hunks of supermarket cheddar,
   and potato chips with onion dip, jug
   wine, a fridge full of beer
skeet shooting
the doughnut shop where everyone
   hangs out
steak platters
a stamp for printing your name on brown
   bags, etc.
the dark line of a storm on the horizon
   growing wider and closer
magnolia trees
organizing a sleigh ride
big, hooded trench coats
the original Equal Rights Amendment's
   ideals
digging out a piece of lawn and putting in
   a garden
the head-for-the-beach-anyway plan
being someone's pillow
the warming of the heart
lemony islands
the symphony of the wind
spring suiting
painted barges

the wind picking up, blowing the trees
     around wildly, then rain starting to
     pour, pounding the surface of a lake
     and creating rivers in the dirt
"Lefties are better lovers"
soft cowl-neck pullovers
"Before the rising sun, we fly; so many
     roads to choose"
soft maples in the swamp
dogs wearing college mufflers
an English brass bed warmer
school lockers
Where the Action Is (TV daytime show,
     June 1965 to March 1967)
Maine potatoes
walnut = intellect
sailboat sails
Ohio: glass, pottery, steel, tires, mound
     builders, fertile fields
skipping among the waves and diving
     beneath the swells
collards
thick sweaters
potato mashers
effortlessness
making an animated movie
sliding shorts
tying a dozen helium-filled balloons to a
     friend's car
white and pink

slipping out for a walk in the snow
and cold

white wicker furniture contrasting with a
patterned brick floor, jungle plants,
and a fountain

writing with chalk on the driveway

being charming

ignorance being bliss

a child's wagon

climbing a fire watchtower for a
panoramic view of the rolling
countryside

doily cornucopias filled with baby's
breath

drinking a whole bottle of wine and
playing all your old records

liking rain showers

"All that mankind has done, thought,
gained, or been: it is lying as in
magic preservation in the pages of
books"

drive-in trays hooked onto windows

melon or grapefruit served with honey
instead of sugar

Milano, Lido, and Brussels cookies

rules of thumb

making champagne at home

silk stockings

silver trays of fresh fruit grouped in fans
and slices

yellow cheeses, fresh brown eggs, glowing
     pumpkins, tangy russet apples, farm
     butter proudly stamped with the
     maker's own mark, fat purple turnip
     globes, superb smoked hams, chicken
     with the flavor of Sunday afternoon
     family dinner—all snapped up in
     local groceries
"blinky milk" = sour milk
at least one night having Lean Cuisine,
     Chinese food delivered, or delicacies
     picked up at a specialty store
the Atlantic Ocean
calling a friend to go for a bike ride
     together at midnight
college basketball teams
gels
the doldrum months
self-portraits
Hamilton, Joe, Frank, and Reynolds, pop
     group
full-skirt bathing suits
gold rice-paper ceilings
halftime bands
osmosis: rubbing minds with informed
     persons
ramekins for baked eggs, tiny shrimp, or
     chocolate pots au crème
something more powerful, universal,
     peaceful

tomato chutney
lunch served at poolside
lynxes
monogrammed wine carafes
pincord slacks
sending home a menu, canceled
    Metroticket, brochure from a hotel
sunbeam yellow
tiny Mateus wine bottles
dolman sleeves
vanilla-frosted, maple-frosted, and
    strawberry-frosted doughnuts
fontina cheese
henna for hair
remembering being picked up and rocked
    to sleep in someone's arms, then
    carried up to bed
banana royales
Centurion inkwell, English antique
finding the doll of the child you used to be
"Rocky" movies
sponge fishing
looking at old family photos
snow patterns on windows
chocolate pops
closing your eyes while riding on a
    motorcycle
burger presses
fishing booths
choreographers

football terms
frosty brown-sugar color
good food for a cold afternoon: piping-hot
     chocolate and crispy, home-fried
     doughnuts
paste-on rhinestone pins
choosing an alcoholic beverage and
     sticking with it: beer for men, white
     wine for women
maple-braised pork chops with pineapple-
     mustard relish
popcorn-and-tears movies
wolves' and dogs' pups
September in the country
alpine breezes
growing onions
portable drafting tables
spring buffets
apple blossoms
happy holidays
requesting the pleasure of a dance
"More isn't always better"
parasol-sheltered tables
pork and apples coddled in a nostalgic
     ginger-raisin sauce and creamy corn
     pudding on the side
straightening the pantry
throwing the windows open during a
     blizzard and enjoying the air
warm firesides

deep green viridian glass pitchers

zories = Oriental sandals

a ripe apricot

a round oak table with a single candle
on it

fire escapes slashing down sides of
buildings like wrought-iron lightning

air so crisp and clear, it draws you
outdoors

Nordic patternings

strolling in Sunday best after the
noontime meal

corn butterers

fireworks effects: Chrysanthemum,
Weeping Willow, and Battle in the
Clouds

mashed-potato sandwiches

for a happy marriage: never speak loudly
to one another, unless the house is
on fire

proverbs

garden benches

instant cocoa with cinnamon sticks

just a beach, your cat, and the wind

kissable glows

messy piles of shoes in the closet

gooseberry jam

reserving a window table

a spa vacation

red-and-white saddle shoes

assembly lines

dish brochures

fish fry and beer on tap

historical buildings, quaint squares, and
flower-trimmed alleys, all lined with
restaurants and shops full of English
woolens and china

jitney service

your body being eight times the length of
your head

season tickets

hose

kitchen chores

lots of little balls of different flavored
sherbet, icy cold and rousing

motionlessness

not minding the silences

stamp machines

nutmeg graters

sitting cross-legged in the window

the blare of a band

classic French blue cheese dressing

seeing an apple fall from a tree

a tearful tune

better results from order, form, and
harmony

Saturday night

peanut brittle

computer nerds with a large collection of
pens in their shirt pockets

a porch swing cradling a puddle of cat

four

extravagant lawn parties

getting skates sharpened

stage managers

hot dog stands

studying trees, buildings, scenery

young marrieds

blue blazer, gray flannels, Weejuns, white
     shirt, and red-and-blue rep tie

five different kinds of cakes and breads,
     plenty of whipped cream, jam
     and butter and a pot of tea under
     a tea cozy

low wood beams

the "Twister" game

love

a weekend gathering spot

waxer machines

Jayne Mansfield, actress

small pieces of toilet paper applied to
     shaving wounds

AMC Pacers

sharing in the planning, shopping, and
     cooking of a dinner party

VCRs

the U.S. Air Force

sparking nonalcoholic grape juice

a T-bone, served for two

luxe

orange and lime sherbets
scatter baskets of bread
playing dodgeball with a Nerf ball
space-saving ideas
reading all the books you never had
    time for
staying until the candle burns out
reams of paper
spatter prints
swapping fried-chicken recipes over the
    backyard fence
tea for drop-in visitors
small painted wicker baskets filled with
    daisies
classic shirts
teakwood plates for big, crisp summer
    salads
an apple and a candy bar in your
    Christmas stocking
blackberry ice
action photography
cracking open a new book
crayon-striped sheets
drafting tools
the smell of a baby's skin
flat notebooks
what a goodnight kiss can do for your
    dreams
grabbing a pen
cranberry bogs

gray flannel skirt and navy blazer
the rub-a-dub of a washboard
a basket on folding legs
Utah: Salt Lake, Bryce Canyon, clean,
 wide streets, choir, honeybees
lobster boats coming in under the
 drawbridge
mobiles moving
robust parades
picture phones
the LOVE stamp
secret diaries
social workers

a cake shot through with crackling bits of
 brown sugar
the Sunday crossword puzzle and the
 ultimate country pleasure: a tractor
 inner tube
a cheese board
bachelor's fare: bread, cheese, and kisses
cycling derbies
exchanging news over tea
kids: a very sweet lesson in enjoying life
icebergs
lady ferns, maidenhair, wood ferns, and
 cinnamon ferns
old spool beds
the New York City ballet
old-fashioned spice cake
the taste of cake batter

singing "We Gather Together" on
    Thanksgiving
red plush establishments
idea exchanges
Tightwad, Missouri
oven-baked potato sticks
pledge "names"
shell planters
the setting sun creating great red and
    orange streaks over the snowy hills
skeins of yarn
a steaming pot over a crackling fire
the Audubon Society's gift catalog
white shutters
the irresistible fragrance of toasting
    bread
being forgiven
making a movie
the practice of eating the cream center of
    an Oreo before eating the cookie
    outsides
treasure hunts
the weeds going berserk and lawns
    growing way too fast
when the salt-shaker cap comes off
a baby grand piano in the front parlor
the sunny side of living
"Let me bring lollipops and confetti
    and silly things and place them at
    your feet"

creamed skillet potatoes
deep-sheared terry cloth
white ash tennis rackets
dreaming of sinking into a comfortable
    chair
elegant white bed linens
hybrid day lilies, Resurrection lilies
election night
variety being the spice of life
digital clocks
fog lathering up the stubbed field
juicy barbecued delights
original gas chandeliers
painting bedrooms yellow
Maine snowshoe furniture
raisins in rum
scientific understanding
tying colorful ribbons around things for
    the fun of it
writing a final sentence
being moved by a book or by nature
bridal showers
Labor Day weekends
hailing a taxi
chicken wings, celery stalks, and blue
    cheese dressing
glisteny stuff
going to sleep
hair-flying, shirt-tossing, sun-dripping
    days

adjusting the sugar/cream level of your
        coffee, only to have a waitress come
        along and ruin it
making love after tennis
pomp
taking off to a place you've never seen
        before
airy, Frenchified cakes and pastries,
        extremely pretty, creamy, and rich
no line for the restroom
luge
the swirly, splotched-paint pictures you
        can make at a fair
wildness
tomato gardens
balloon racing
culotte flares
fully rigged ship models
hillsides painted gold and crimson
rams
tomatoes as big as soup plates; tomatoes
        by the bushel
Arm & Hammer baking soda
gumdrop breaks
the do-something-you-haven't-done-in-
        years plan
lending a hand
linking oneself with a great cause
men whose license plates read "Big Guy"
        or "Ace Lover"

the inability to stop spelling the word
   "banana" once you've started
Lincoln wheat-cent coins
synthetic airplane pillows and sober navy
   blue scratchy blankets
Tinkertoys, Play-Doh, Etch a Sketch,
   Fisher-Price corn popper, Lego
   blocks, Monopoly, Scrabble, and an
   Erector set
anniversary remembrances
band marathons
dinners that include a green salad and
   French bread with butter
finding the most luscious piece of fruit
   you can and savoring it
hand-wrapped silk flowers in a willow
   basket
a great cat named Hooper
loons yodeling
Romeo and Juliet (movie)
shopping at garage sales
slow snowfalls
hanging windows with lush curtains of
   velvet
bright buttons
hens
whole carrots baked in maple syrup
finishing wood
stovepipe hats
violin lessons

"Together, Let's Find Love" by the Fifth
  Dimension
woodland paths
the heightened awareness of the sheer joy
  of nature, the stillness, the changing
  patterns of light and shade, the small
  sounds of honeybees, the gentle
  cooing of doves
broccoli-stuffed chicken
wooden bridges
a school dance
kerosene lamps
sipping a Coke
doodling
hypochondriacs
impulse buying
literacy
napkin folding
popcorn stitching
a pot of steaming chili served with a
  dollop of sour cream and grated
  cheddar in pottery bowls
alpine trails above the timberline
closing your eyes and breathing in
brooding about the meaning of life
the suitcase that keeps going around and
  around the luggage carousel
being more open, less helpless
party sounds behind a door you're about
  to open

the rare pileated woodpecker
Perrier-shaped glassware
straw brimmers
Stroh's or Miller's beer
varying your study spots
a reputation for the best fresh fish
    in town
bar towels for polishing glassware
April evenings
cereal cookies
floats in a parade
dark and cushy carpeting
first-aid kits
forthrightness
outlawing gerrymandering
jasmine flower
muskrat houses
being chosen formal-dance chairman
unscarred snow
visiting someone you haven't seen in a
    very long time
West Virginia: twin panhandles, Harpers
    Ferry, the Potomac
a seasonal collage of pictures of your
    house
a sink cabinet with a cistern pump
riding a steam train around the park
    periphery
a sweets trolley with lots of tarts
cast-iron pans

dessert picked off trees
a space heater
when you drop a glass and it doesn't
    break
platform shoes
touring glee clubs
dish towels on cup hooks
dust
sitting on a stoop, watching dusk change
    to darkness and counting the stars
watermelon-seed spitting
Watermelon Day at camp or the park
a tomato press
a treasure hunt for red raspberries or
    running vine blackberries
eating cookies and milk in the car
rough brick walls and oak surfaces
revolving lights
stuffed shoulder of lamb
touch-and-guess exhibits
wildlife in its natural habitat
educated grace
marizipan
living with the knowledge that you've
    done your best
movie theaters
reverie and conversation
rhubarb = advice
pewter casting
sewing circles

Lexington, Massachusetts
the six sides of a snowflake
"My Girl" (song)
cayenne pepper
flying kites in the bold March sky
pizza crackers
a sizzle-red skimmer dress
24-hour stores
praying for a sick child
reading menus
1964
a Chinese basket of spring clover and tiny
    peach roses
a Sunday breakfast of eggs, Canadian
    bacon, and pastry
BMWs
a Thomas Edison Ediphone
italic writing
Health-Tex children's clothing ads
opal or tourmaline = hope
a plastic inner tube with a duck's head
reading *The New York Times* and *USA
    Today* every morning
real mashed potatoes, peeled on the
    premises and veined with melted
    butter
toasting forks
roast crown of pork, Florida style
wrapped in a quilt, watching a meteor
    shower

Jeane Dixon, astrologer
surviving an awful Friday the 13th
waterproof mittens
blanket chests
the Beanie and Cecil cartoon
changing a college major
grating cheese
special people
job strategies
the Super Bowl
Tab soda-pop commercials
a butter crock
the fibrous crunch of celery
pocket watches
the art of paper folding
receding chins
second chances
back doors: the ones best friends enter by
Indian pennies
the flimsy paper stretched across the
        examining table at a doctor's office
middy-collared pinafores
sidewalk cafés
a great cat named Sidney
wedding spoons
French mustard
a barometer telling tomorrow's weather
the daily mail
overhead compartments on airplanes
smelling the bakery on your street

Grandma's meat loaf
seed catalogs starting to arrive in the
    mail
the car heater
stereo speakers in the headrests of new
    cars
the 15,000 different kinds of rice
sweatpant drawstrings that retreat
the hiss of a heavy rain
when you went to the appliance store to
    watch the first color TV
steaming teakettle water
where the good times are
the need for imagination
creamed turkey
deep carpeting
the nickname "Bunnykins"
sketchbooks and charcoal
the one leaf that always clings to the end
    of the rake
bees and hives
cleaning rings
poaching fruit for compotes
the silent industry of chlorophyll
the wheezing of an accordion
changing pictures for spring
mint-colored bikes
night crawlers
the softness of kitten's feet, like
    raspberries held in the hand

Log Cabin syrup tins
collecting handbags, supermarket art,
     framed cards, bowls, antique agate
     boxes, art deco, pictures, rugs, hearts,
     wooden eggs, matchbooks, pasta,
     seashells, salt and pepper shakers,
     buttons, printer's type, perfume
     bottles, labels, copper pennies, quilts
vegetable bins
angel-food birthday cake
point d'esprit stockings
using an alias
utility stools
the United States of America
white asters, pale as dry champagne
anisette toast
being a pumpkin, a skeleton, or
     Superman for Halloween
chimney sweeps
exiting a museum via the gift shop
going back to square one
homemade cranberry sauce
making chocolate pudding
taking a snowmobile tour
taking ghost stories to a clambake
biking through the vineyards and
     stopping for a picnic
Halley's Comet
silk broadcloth trousers
gigantic gumdrops

split Portuguese rolls with butter
telephone and television cables attached
     to the house, swinging and creaking
     in the winter wind
Toll House cookie batter
walking suits, blazer, Bermudas, man's
     shirt
wild seascapes
balloon shades
cold feet under blankets
toddlers in firefighter hats
shivering helping to warm you
skipping waves
Dick Tracy
unique designs
sliced oranges
doll carriages
cultivating an open mind
dulcimer music
falling in love with an old friend
pantries
jumping on a pogo stick or walking on
     stilts
lemon butter pats and mint on peas
collecting souvenirs: stones from the
     beach, an antique sewing box from a
     yard sale, a roll of snapshots
journalists with bylines
summer research projects
the elegance of white gloves

homemade soups
the hum of a motor
nonstop snows
a shopping spree
being sensuous
caramel apples
Linde Stars: waltzing, six-rayed star
    rings
ranch dressing: buttermilk, sour cream,
    garlic, spices
run-over pages in newspapers
tiny black-and-white checked tiles
winding alleys
candied spearmint leaves
renting a bike
books of facts
hanging a favorite quilt on the living
    room wall behind the sofa
frosty glasses
cinnabar beads
donating blood
finger bowls and turn-down service
handsome Georgian and Greek Revival
    mansions
loop buttoning
slop
being soothed like a baby
stoves with flat burners
"Tonight" and "Maria" from *West Side
    Story*

wood lathe art
"how-to" books
Goodbye, Columbus (movie)
boogie dancing
an elegant archway
chocolate bark
cloud watching
cooling doughnuts hung on long wooden
     dowels
the drone of a passing plane
food coloring and egg yolk for painting
     food
food that mittened hands can grasp
Evonne Goolagong, tennis player
scruffy skiers
English bone china
a square dance
careful speech
maple syrup on grapefruit, apples, pears,
     grapes, or blueberries
ripening fruit
typing résumés
a plentitude of mixed veggies, prepared
     in a beer batter and deep-fried to a
     golden autumn glow
Arpège cologne
cupcake papers
Esprit clothes
mirrors that distort you
porcelain cups

spray-painting yourself accidentally
strawberry-flavored milk
three-tiered Sandwich glass server
very white tennis shoes and very yellow
    tennis dresses
neighborhood shops
airplane rides
parking lights
New York glass
collecting and arranging seashells,
    pebbles, autumn leaves, dried weeds,
    wheat, flowers, and fruits
baseball terms
cast-iron pots
cereal parties
early evening birdcalls
herbs to use with cheese
post office cubbyholes
the rasp of a file
Puss 'N' Boots

remaining calm when you find out you
    need glasses
new word-a-day calendars
unspoiled beaches, isolated moors, quiet
    country lanes
visiting the grocery store, church, and
    library in your hometown
Wisconsin dairy products
a settle/table
a sweet-spiced wild-mushroom sauce

business sense
watching gardens and children grow
cashmere coats
hospital gowns
kitchens filled with the smell of pungent
    pickles, spicy relishes, fruity jams
    and jellies
lattice checks
matchstick bamboo shades
rainbows
new potatoes steamed in their jackets,
    sweet and moist, with a light spicing
    of salt and herbs
petit déjeuner
sitting on a wooden bridge spanning a
    stream
Saturday shoes
watching rain descend upon an Italian
    garden
a traveler coming upon canyons and
    hidden valleys, waterfalls, and
    freshwater springs
afternoon naps
cattle placidly munching their way
    through the meadows
getting locked in a shed
hot appetizers
artesian wells
an attic's forgotten curios
prune- and apricot-filled kolachy

sounds echoing in the cold: a barking dog,
a slamming storm door

14-inch hanging acrylic arc that makes a
rainbow in a sunny room

squeezing one more brushful out of the
toothpaste tube

South Dakota: Badlands, Black Hills, Mt.
Rushmore, clear days

blue collarism

blueberry soup

couples moving closer and nuzzling

a dhurrie rug of French blue on a white
ground

gourmet gardens tailored to the kind of
cooking you do

never stepping on cracks

Waverly Wafers

a vanilla custard with cake crust and
strawberry sauce

having your gang meet for pictures at a
studio that takes turn-of-the-century
photos

New Mexico: mesas, canyons, caverns,
pueblos

bowling alleys

adytum = any secret place

jazz

"Z'all right!"

10-sided penny-candy jar

a Chinese junk

McDonald's Egg McMuffins

a Parisian tailgate picnic with baskets of
     charcuterie

meals men love

the jingle of a Good Humor wagon

peach daiquiris

staying away from alcoholic drinks

Seals & Crofts

Thanksgiving Day parades

wrapping the evening's mugs or wine
     goblets in cheerful dinner napkins
     tied with plaid ribbons

an attempt by a gumball to sneak out of
     the chute and roll past the buyer

beachside yoga

A Hard Day's Night (movie)

traffic lights

wearing water wings in the bathtub

class reunions

cranberry juice cocktail

an enameled coffeepot filled with dried
     flowers

flannel pants and long, crisp walks

glass-and-wood showcases

the grating of a rusty hinge

lobster pounds and piers

pubs

rubber animals

a beautiful fountain in the town center
     park

baby rings and bracelets
bubble-blowers
crooked cobbled streets
macaroni salad
kiss, kiss, hug, hug
pickly coleslaw and carrot-crunchy
    macaroni
recipes written at night
secret drawers
Rick Springfield, singer/actor
the suck of a pump
ticket windows
doing your job well
diced potatoes
Indiana: basketball, covered bridges,
    steel, yellow poplars, popcorn,
    limestone caverns, Notre Dame's
    Fighting Irish
old, old black-and-white snapshots
Tidewater saltbox homes
wide-brim hats with black velvet
    ribbon trim
body stockings
pushpins
the meaning of existence
ideas about purse design
Indian pudding served warm with a big
    scoop of vanilla ice cream
knee-hi nylons
needlepoint becoming habit-forming

the nicknames "Muffin" and "Midge"
Liège, Belgium
predicting voter turnout
seedless black raspberry preserves
beef brochette
chemistry sets
something sheer as smoke
sleeping in a back field
fairy tales
the peeling of a Polaroid snapshot
sterling-silver tips for the collar of a
    Western shirt
sweetheart pink, pistachio, and peach
    colors
the children's latest school crafts projects
wedding rings
chocolate milk
the glow of street light scattered
the waves on top of a meringue pie
"Vehicle" (song)
peppermint extract
Crenshaw melon
freshman dorms
the 1768 edition of the *Encyclopaedia
    Britannica*
white elephants
chewing the end of a pen
deep-dish pies
Louisiana Cajun potato chips
feeling loved on Valentine's Day

birthstones: garnet, amethyst, bloodstone
     or aquamarine, diamond, emerald,
     pearl or moonstone, ruby, sardonyx or
     peridot, sapphire, opal or tourmaline,
     topaz, turquoise or zircon
freestanding fireplaces
French-Canadian pea soup
ruffled aprons
unfinished coffee tables
figs
Coffee Pot Rapids, Idaho
rags of white clouds rolling in from
     the sea
suggestions for a salad bar: oranges,
     pineapple, raisins, cauliflower,
     apples, asparagus, peaches, grapes,
     avocados, pears, melon, green beans,
     cooked potatoes, corn, celery root,
     fried onion rings, brussels sprouts
The Moonspinners (movie)
onion-shaped glass bowls
pointelle knit
priming a kitchen pump to draw a glass
     of clear, cold well water
spinach, succory, tansy, primrose and
     violet leaves, hyssop, thyme,
     tarragon, marjoram, leeks, a lettuce,
     salad burette, purslane, corn salad,
     cowslip leaves, cress, borage, chervil,
     vine tendrils, and pickled roots

sticks and bars and tubs of butter
a tailgate picnic before the kickoff
Spirographs and Hot Wheels
waitress uniform dresses
white: daisies, milfoil, Queen Anne's lace,
    whitecaps on a windy sea
chili bowls with handles
writing an advertisement
the days of the open range
being surprised at what you learn about
    yourself
cloves = dignity
bright green peas and broccoli in a
    Chinese restaurant
chickens in the dooryard
the swinging of the pendulum
children who behave in restaurants
the word "boo"
chilled pineapple and dairy-fresh cottage
    cheese salad
wrinkle creams
polishing all your shoes
crinkle cotton
the private beaches on the Riviera
glittering ice
going clamming
making and coloring maps
Chicago or country club ice cream:
    vanilla, orange sherbet, and coffee
taking up chess together

piling leaves into huge heaps and
      jumping in
pulling all bedcovers as close as possible
      to keep away ghosts, goblins, and
      burglars
silver doilies
solid farmhouses, whitewashed buildings
      built on downland chalk
all-star games
balcony- and shutter-trimmed houses
collecting jail padlocks
delicious summer Sunday breakfast
      sandwiches
doll strollers
relaxing to the creak of an arthritic
      rocker
falling leaves
golden lockets
kames, kettles, and eskers formed by
      glaciers
no music, no television, no newspaper, no
      distractions
reminiscing while listening to Frank
      Sinatra
tempera paints
bamboo torches
when you start thinking about where
      you'll take your summer vacation
homemade soups served in bucket-shaped
      bowls

hundreds of tones of wool yarns side
    by side
miniature corn
nine
Kentucky mints
homemade cards
pineapple sage
Ping-Pong (or Gnip Gnop)
pints of pork fried rice
rings exchanged at a wedding
running a race
singing groups
tennis jackets
tinkling china
vans
wind waltzing rain across the road
winding canals
Turkish towels
the restaurant pavilion
canaries singing more when they have
    company
finding a hammock and setting out to
    be lazy
generalissimos
snow portraits
gentle grays, juiciest plum colors
hand car washes that you wait hours for
isolated country estate atmosphere
looking at dish patterns
smoked almonds

two tremendous kettles of soup on a
    potbellied stove
homespun goods
a book bag with large ring binder
    (different section for each subject),
    Glamour magazine, Flair pens in five
    colors, a travel pack of Kleenex,
    hairbrush, *Elements of Style*
broad upholstered chairs
browsing through a farmers' museum
cookware racks
flower-sprayed settings
appetizers: canapés, cocktails, dips or
    dunks, hors d'oeuvres, relishes, and
    spreads
the seven virtues: charity, faith, fortitude,
    hope, justice, prudence, temperance
apple wedgers and corers
bathtubs
broil-'n-serve platters
marinara sauce
curtainless French doors
okra
your first Christmas tree together
parking meters
surveying a platoon of jam-filled jars on a
    dark shelf
the six ways a batter can get on base
    without getting a hit
Vermont maple salad bowls

warm pies and spiced whipped cream
aerial mapping
mail-order shopping
burying yourself in a pile of magazines
    you seldom have time for
carrying a bunch of tennis rackets
Christmas chains to count the days
dormer windows
the first kiss of the summer
hors d'oeuvre fork, mini ladle for
    dressings and sauces, nut and berry
    spoon, and olive and pickle fork
rushing brooks and dark, quiet forests
    beside the road
restaurateurs
business suits
horsehead hitching posts
dessert sauces: apple, blackberry,
    blueberry, butterscotch, caramel,
    cherry, cranberry, eggnog, mint,
    orange fluff, peach, fluffy sherry, and
    strawberry
painted wood carousel lions from the late
    19th century
Mikhail Baryshnikov, dancer/actor
yellow stacks of *National Geographic*
letting someone have the last word
outrageous banana splits
unspoiled forests of oak, pine, magnolia,
    and palmetto

the patter of rain
pitting yourself against the wilds
satin slippers
putt-putt toys
votive candles
watching your man shave or shampoo
after the beach, taking an outdoor shower
    à deux
butter curlers
water hyacinths
buttermilk pecan chicken
hot-weather architecture
saving all your wine corks to make a
    kitchen corkboard
catnip mousies
cats not holding grudges
hot apple soup
free concerts in the park
hot zabaglione
mountains flaming with red, orange, and
    purple foliage
nautical knots
sautéed liver with mushrooms, onions,
    and green pepper
a stuffed toy pig with piglets snapped
    on
Brunswick stew
chubby cows chewing contentedly on the
    grass
fruitcake tins

savoring a lake by canoe
advances in science and technology
lowered voices
new potatoes with chives
starting every day a little happier
    because you have the newspaper
    delivered
a woodpile in the garage
toys
buying new pants (the waistband should
    just wrap around your neck if they
    are to fit)
a Chinese red lacquer coffee table
want-to, have-to, ought-to feelings
UFOs
leather floors
Italian ice-cream spoons
peach nut color
NASA
peanut butter and jelly in one jar
playing kazoos backwards
the victory in good work
reading old love letters
roast duck cooked in caraway seeds
shaking a sugar packet vigorously to
    move the contents to the bottom
    before tearing open
Pearl Drops tooth polish
staying away from anyone named
    "Honest John"

an afternoon with friends in a summer
    garden
beach and weekend houses
ordering a car
radio earplugs
brass candlesticks and bayberry candles
    from Williamsburg
chalet-type motel units with their own
    balconies and view of the mountains
blankets: army, baby, crib, horse,
    military, cotton, electric, down,
    thermal, woolen
charitableness
the springy device attached to the back of
    a door that prevents the doorknob
    from marring the wall
coat hooks in schoolrooms
the pile of wrapping paper and ribbon left
    after all the gifts have been opened
cranberry-orange muffins
giant popovers
the joy and contentment of listening to
    favorite music
grating some fresh Parmesan cheese
a beautiful old book crammed with scraps
    of past and present pleasures: dried
    flowers, postcards, fabric samples
the silent wish you make
a brass toasting fork and silver muffin
    dish

babies burping
the polar seas
baby corncobs
picnic areas with campfire circles
rich and ruddy complexions
secret recipes
a chemistry set to experiment with
lollipops
architects of international repute
becoming reacquainted with sunrise
a single flower meaning more than a
    dozen
fuchsia, golden-warm marigolds, coral-
    to-magenta petunias, paper-white
    gardenias
hacienda style
old *Horizons* and *American Heritage*
    magazines
the old cabbage-rose pattern
honesty being the only policy
sidewalk hitching rings for horses
wedge haircuts
bedtime snacks
open restaurant kitchens
avocations
sleeping in one of his old cashmere
    sweaters
the dance boom
old implements hung in restaurants
sweet potatoes ripening in the sun

the 1920s Jazz Age kids
Sierra jackets
the glow of the holidays
apple orchards
buying clothes
the penciled flights of departing geese
   scrawled against the sky
when the computer goofs and gives you a
   bigger paycheck
the "Velveteen Rabbit" story
an eggnog and a slice of fruitcake
American fries = thick potato chips
bleached floors, white fabrics, and
   greenery
cheap lipstick
when the soup du jour at the corner deli
   is your absolute favorite
looking out a bus window
cheese, salads, relishes
crepe de chine
elephant jokes
cheese pumpkins and sugar pumpkins
free road maps
soft-pile rugs
legs
watching the snow from your office
boots for dogs
pears in chocolate sauce
soaking in a scented tub
magazine or newspaper food editors

zigzag weaves

The Flying Nun (TV show)

achieving the "not-decorated" look

ad hoc = for a specific purpose, special
case

painters' hats

collar buttons

the cheering of the crowd

quitting a job

Oriental shops

homemade delicacies brought to the table
beribboned with calico

sling-back espadrilles

snickerdoodles

things that taste, smell, feel, sound, and
look wonderful: the stuff that
romance is made of

Danish swirled pastries

twilight victory parties

white enamel coffee mugs

looking up obscure words in the
Fictionary-Dictionary game

"ringers" on playgrounds

an island frothed with wildflowers

a clipper ship captain's desk with slanted
lift lid and drawers on the sides

edification, enhancement

going back to your hometown: visiting
the schools you attended, bringing
back your childhood

going to an outdoor café
grilled cheese and fries
whirring wings
artists who come to paint a scene and
stay on to open studios and galleries
lukewarm water
making clothes
taking a long walk someplace quiet and
making up lyrics to songs
ankle-tickling sleepwear
Dick-and-Jane books
Alka-Seltzer commercials
baking muffins
Coke and varsity jackets
Holland cheese
tooth fairies
piling tea sandwiches in a pyramid
Milwaukee beer
pull-out-all-stops salad bars
solid-maple lotus tables
yellow: banana squashes, corn, peppers,
sweet potatoes, bananas, lemons,
grapefruit, pineapple
the calendar on soap operas that allows
one day's events to be stretched over a
three-week period
colored gloves
jumping rope to a skip-rope jingle
enjoying sweet, juicy strawberries
unadorned

pom-pom animals
dimpling rains
pumpkin pudding with rum
samba contests and confetti-showered
    parades
almond brittle
dumpling-eating contests
homemade English muffins
punch-and-cookie parties
sunup and sundown colors
sangria or piña colada pitcher-and-
    glass set
tins of cream of coconut
a pushcart lunch
tiny spring peeper frogs
Yankee apple cake with lemon sauce
The Star-Spangled Banner
dancing with a lover to 50s music
tanning lotion
barbecue chips
dinner out and dinner in
fans
short-length ski jackets
dining gardens
snow dinosaurs
those moments that go beyond words
tank swimsuits
wooden puzzles
an old T-pattern quilt
Aromat, a spice by Knorr

blond silk strung with blond beads
phrases from Shakespeare: rotten apple,
   a man of few words, cold comfort,
   mind's eye, one fell swoop, neither
   here nor there, it's Greek to me, it's a
   mad world, haven't slept a wink, seen
   better days
hooks and eyes
seven-minute maple icing
paper quilling
a popcorn cart
happily alone in a crowd
marine biology
purple pansies
serving sliced vegetables and fruits in
   two large wine goblets for dunking
stretching marshmallows like taffy
a raccoon peering out through his
   permanent sunglasses
a robin's 3,000 feathers
air fresheners
Grease (movie)
a riding shirt with gold stickpin on collar
dermatologists
Christmas cookie cutters
early mornings
fireside chats
for purple dye: black cherry bark,
   cocklebur plant, dandelion root,
   grape

garage-cleaning sessions
hardback books
listening to a book tape on your way
to work
mushroom and barley soup
a childhood platform swing
pistachio nuts
snow sculpture
mushroom sauce for pasta
water balloons
Nesselrode pie
pleated lampshades
testing a wine
secondhand compliments
a shore dinner
petrified wood
assorted paper
bus excursions
kitty litter that stays in the box
casino parties
dessert spoons
Easter dinners
lotions, oils, butters for tanning
pottery cruets
bakery boxes tied with string
putting greens
watching bakers at work through a glass
window, pondering over turnovers,
nut breads, doughnuts, and butter
cookies

watercolor ombré stripes
a table with pots of fruit-bearing plants
    placed on it
butterfly lamb
cats sitting in the sun or by heating vents
getting up first, making coffee, and
    delivering it to someone still in bed
hot, hot water
rough-and-tumble clothes
sourwood honey
square-legged redwood plant stands
thumbing the spouts of water fountains
touching someone's rings
your best bib and tucker
chuck = the hole in a pencil sharpener
    into which the pencil goes
country French blue-and-red checks
doughnut glaze
eau de cologne
watching the sun fill the sky with a
    rainbow of colors
fluffy pillows
writing in the sand
fruit peddlers
gourmet provisions for a week-long
    adventure
investing in a few bottles of first-rate
    wine to have with meals
lavender, night-scented stocks, tobacco
    plants, and a vine around the door

moving hurdles
reversible rain slickers
seventh-grade basketball
a vinegary dressing with bits of bacon
    in it
advertisements
giving a party
having the number of a child's birthday
    party guests equal the child's age
jewelry design
walking between the raindrops
New Year's Eve
towel spindles
Ryan's Hope (extinct TV soap opera)
shy beginnings
toys and games
anniversary dinners
trying to answer the phone before the
    answering machine comes on
a young forest in green pinstripes
the intensity of genius
drying flowers
16-ounce beers
the Dr. Zhivago look: tall, furry hat, midi-
    length Cossack coat, and boots
a Brobdingnagian cut of prime rib
Shaker jelly cupboards
meat loaf seasoned with oregano, basil,
    minced garlic, and nutmeg
Rhodes scholarships

snack sessions
sparkling mineral formations in
    brilliantly hued color
The Art Institute, Chicago
Chase and Sanborn coffee
wearing cleats
braised short ribs and apples in cider
    sauce
charity and thrift shops
old-fashioned British ceiling fans
classical music concerts
coaching lamps
wrought-iron fences
diamond tennis bracelets
to take umbrage: to feel offended
a bachelor pad
a band concert
baby bird time
fabric-covered neckroll pillows, scented
    with a soothing blend of potpourri
jacquard-weave place mats
packing a picnic and taking your family
    on a trip to the country
secret gardens glimpsed through tall
    windows
Picardie goblets of tempered glass in
    French restaurants and bistros
taco-flavored corn chips
vacation dates
bicycle paths among the sand dunes

Indian beading
old-fashioned enamel rose pendants
puddle jumpers
Edwardian London
the French custom of making a wish each
time you eat a food for the first time
in the new year
understatement
bedtop servers
the overwhelming desire to pop someone's
bubble-gum bubble
preformed dirt falling off the bottoms of
tennis shoes
prestige activities: hall monitor, honor
committee, yearbook staff, newspaper
editor, athletic advisory board
seeing a red conflagration at dawn
shelves lined with ancient tins and boxes
holding their original contents
Budweiser beer
smells of different gravies crowding
the air
Federal houses
special Swiss pear bread served on a table
set with Waterford crystal, Irish
linen, and Sheffield silver
an October sun peeking into the car
windows
the duck motif
the first kiss

apple pie time
the fuzz on tennis balls
the honest simplicity of breakfast
cheese samples
people who brag that they never watch
  television but somehow know all the
  rules of the game shows
cream biscuits
the joy and spiritual warmth reflected in
  a Currier & Ives print
Spam
the kitchen of a famous restaurant
when the audience smiles and taps
  their feet
age and beauty
Whynot, Mississippi
the pep-rally atmosphere
American humor
beef chop suey
the sloping floor of a movie house
beer, bratwurst, onions, ketchup and
  mustard
bleached fruit
feeling the damp freshness of a Cape Cod
  morning cool on your face
greasy spoon restaurants
Meet the Press (TV show)
curlicues
reflection and reasoning
soft, wet kisses and very big hugs

a gnarled tree buffeted and timeworn
standing in stark silhouette
coffee in a large thermos pitcher for
helping yourself
in-ground pools
"the acid test" = the crucial test
Vogue magazine
digging a hole in mashed potatoes to keep
the gravy in
"Wheaties" nickname for an athlete
rain sounding as though a thousand tiny
flamenco dancers were rehearsing on
the roof
"I love you more than yesterday, less than
tomorrow"
sails against blue water
the miracle of cool sneakers and a straw
hat
slinky dresses
being a men's 9 1/2 shoe size
sticky glazed pecan cinnamon rolls
the "Diver Dan" segment of the Fraser
Thomas TV show
things dear to us around the house
wailing along with Aretha Franklin
the large glacial deposits that form on
the insides of car fenders during
snowstorms
writing letters in an outdoor café
being able to fix your own toaster

the vivid crimson-and-yellow blooms of
the columbines
chicory coffee
the drilling of a woodpecker
making faces at monkeys in the zoo
driving a jeep
Daisy Hill Puppy Farm, where Snoopy
was born
fried dough: puffy, flaky-crusted, steamy
inside, with a gentle, cakey chaw
major kitchen appliances
chicken with orange peel
making sure the water from the shower
hits the back of your neck
local listings of lectures and panel
discussions
taking what seems forever to dress
telling sheep from goats
Waldorf salads
kindergarten drawings on the
refrigerator
the ablative tense
All Fools' Day
bulbs flashing and ribbons popping
color: the least expensive and most
effective decorating touch
Colorforms plastic cut-out toy sets
filling containers with cut green leaves
and air ferns
jam jar drinking glasses

lemonade jelly
pumpkin soup in the fall
North Dakota: Durum wheat, spring
    wheat, wild birds, International
    Peace Garden
comedy records
archaeological digs
complimentary newspapers
ham and Cumberland sauce
homemade French silk pie
manners being the happy ways of doing
    things
Land 'O Lakes butter and margarine
barrettes
monkeypod wood
renting a small airplane
sun worshipers
baking your own pound cake
sunny weddings
tangerine, taupe, tawny, teal blue, terra
    cotta, toast, tobacco, turquoise colors
tanning salons
tins of homemade Christmas cookies
vintage rush-seated English chairs
zinfandel wine
banana or strawberry colada drinks
wanderlust
monogram rings
smoked chicken
benches in between rows of lockers

kids spinning on diner stools
the Candyland game
dancin' in the moonlight
genuine marble desk sets
looking at everything and everybody
    around you as though you're seeing
    them for the first time
your own hammock
slowing down your speech
stone rubbings
a potato pancake, hot chocolate, and
    flannel pjs in bed
stopping to think about how you wish
    it could be and realizing how good
    you've got it
Thompson seedless grapes
whoopie colors
"cocktail" birthday cake
blossom spring
chocolate mint
a lynx on a Rocky Mountain crag
cross-sticking in hockey
crows gathering together
on a train, experiencing a journey of
    endless surprises
good children on a plane
lip pencils, eye crayons
babushkas
poached egg on an English muffin
a popular girl

pie-eating contests
marine paintings and prints
doing something nice for someone
    without letting on that you did it
spring peepers
Pyrex cookware
muscadine wine
bargain prices
carrying a map
Rural, Indiana
throwing a football through a tire
purple sherbet
tortoiseshell or wooden combs
turning off onto back roads, breaking out
    your wine, and doing all the things
    you've dreamed of
barbecued chicken, mashed potatoes,
    and corn
burgundy color
currant bushes hung with clusters of
    berries
derrick trucks
early snows "healing" the landscape: no
    tracks, no muddied slush
massive grain bins awaiting the harvest
    from fields of high corn
burnt-sugar chiffon cake
mustard and soy sauce on a hot dog
mystery novels
oyster color

passing a test

rushing rivers

tasting sweet papaya and pineapple at a
     roadside stand

visualizing an impending occasion and
     considering all the pleasurable
     possibilities

wisps of hair turning up

a sextant used in a race

eating delicious soups, hot puddings
     bathed in cream, and bowls of fresh
     raspberries

a stranded penny in a 5¢ gumball slot

fish

International Morse Code

natural beauty

not underrating your own abilities

settling down in a deep sofa and ordering
     a cup of tea

watching a cook prepare luncheon while
     sitting on the lawn with a view of the
     marina

a tavern table

19th-century magic shows

antique brass weights as doorstops

baths in the dark, with candles lit at the
     last minute

catching the romance of the moment

eating six hot dogs and drinking five
     Cokes at a picnic

hot applesauce
slushy ices made with real peaches,
    watermelon, cantaloupe, etc.
hot days and cool nights
pouring milk into a cereal bowl and
    knowing to stop when the edge starts
    to move
scuff slippers
snuggling into a soft chair with a
    good book
thumbprint art
aquarium light
blue
a stuffed mouse family with unweaned
    "babies" snapped on
cough lozenges
having a heart
favorite aunts
houses clustered like barnacles on
    the hills
plate spinning
scallop shells
monarch butterflies
the crunch of a breaking nut
educational puzzle maps of the United
    States
navy and white
seventh-inning stretches
the Seven Dwarfs: Bashful, Doc, Dopey,
    Grumpy, Happy, Sleepy, Sneezy

envelope sizes

five-year-olds

having breakfast by the window on the
    occasion of a child's first snowfall

New York: Manhattan, the Catskills,
    Niagara Falls, the Statue of Liberty

a warm May day

always growing and thinking up new
    solutions

downtime to reset the mind's clock

boxwood hedges

May's great green canopy spreading
    along every tree-lined street

a "memory box"

Thoroughbred racing

stretch terry cloth

a 17-arm brass candelabra

the NCAA

a European whipped cream dispenser

leaving spaces in your day to do
    something spontaneous

peachy pudding

a quote from a favorite novel

the inn launch

playing penny-ante poker

Blondie and Dagwood

scarlet union undersuits

the sea offering an onmipresent rumble

seasoning salt: a mixture of salt, pepper,
    garlic, onion, and other spices

airmail stamps and stationery
sparkling wine
an apple-ginger preserve
playing Indians-with-tepees
watching baseball five hours in one day
antique trunks
beating your head against the wall
braised sirloin of beef Beaujolais
turnip = charity
coal
nubby-soled tennis shoes
baby-blue eyes
Jack Frost and his magic paint pot
picnic baskets
racing pigeons
burying the hatchet
bicycle shirts
Bach concertos
throwing rice at newlyweds
the dance you perform when a rubber
    band is pointed at you
indoor beachcombing = combing resort
    shops for shells
standing in the lake at sunset, holding
    hands
star sapphires
jade
old Marx Brothers movies
redwood tables
riding a bicycle 25 miles

videocassette recorders ·
Wedgwood blue
the colors of red earth, hemp, wet clay,
    and late-day desert sun
faded leotards
iced porcelain
premoistened towelettes
the fast-falling November twilight
scenic, sandy, salubrious Cape Ann
the best waves
sheets and pillowcases to dream on
the morning room, a quiet center of the
    home
spending a whole night reading,
    sometimes even alternating books
the Rebel Yell
the one you dress up for
a perennial garden, thick with summer
    bloom
the prospect of learning
"There's a sucker born every minute"
the height to which a cat's rear end can
    rise to meet the hand stroking it
a weekend à deux
wreaths of pinecones hanging on heavy
    doors
beef cuts: pot roast, rib roast, brisket,
    chuck steak, club steak, Delmonico
    steak, Porterhouse, filet mignon, top
    sirloin, rib roast, round steak, T-bone

barbecuing, boiling, baking, broiling,
   blanching, braising, browning, deep-
   frying, frying, grilling, heating,
   parboiling, poaching, pressure-
   cooking, roasting, stewing, sautéing,
   simmering, steaming, toasting
bleached-oak salad bowls
creamy tarragon dressing
crêpes stuffed with mushrooms and
   Gruyère cheese in Mornay sauce
breakfast, the most important meal
the teacher you remember
coffee beans and grinder
the tide edging homeward once more
light, silver-dollar-size sour-cream
   hotcakes
side pouches on furniture for magazines
big country dining rooms
digging a moat
"When in doubt—tell the truth" (Mark
   Twain)
cherry-stoners
bread stuffing
lying down on the grass and following a
   cloud across the horizon
sliced London broil with sautéed onions
   and melted cheese on rye
thick, scalded johnnycakes
swimming pools
spice cabinets

chili tomatoes
mellowed red brick walls
pulling out the stoppers
white cotton sailor hats
writing themes
an ice-cream truck with a tinkling bell
and comet's tail of kids
being partners
chic boutiques
British constable's whistle for calling
cabbies and fog-bound boats
chicken with pickles and olives, salt,
pepper, and French mustard
white on white
chipmunk pie, puff pancakes, lemon
twists, hot chocolate, and snowballs
topped with maple syrup
climbing to a lookout point that offers a
sweeping panorama of countryside
drink-of-water requests at bedtime
Chinese-inspired florals
driving past a bakery and smelling the
bread
flip-down airplane trays
Mickey Mouse
going to bed before you get sleepy
Writer's Digest magazine
enjoying the pleasure of discovery
making up songs, both lyric and theme
mukluks: fur-trimmed Eskimo boots

milk
naked maples casting black shadows
bike-decorating contests
oil-and-vinegar dressing
owls
breakfast in a pale pink light
Polish sausage
the tolling of a church bell
bulk groceries
helping with the farm chores: haying,
    milking, grooming the horses
"Mum's the word"
pumpernickel-and-cheese appetizers
remembering when there was no place
    open to buy anything after six
tempura dishes
coin jukeboxes
summer in Franconia, New Hampshire
sailing a dinghy
bones for dogs
making at least a thousand dreams
    come true
armless chairs
dimestore photo machines
home: a quiet and personal space
menu balancing
ornithologists
pinecones for kindling, bought at the
    roadside stand with pumpkins and
    Indian corn in the fall

pink grapefruit with tons of sugar
Monopoly games
"Tennis anyone?"
winning a duel
fireworks
sapodilla
wintertime: waking up in the morning to
    snowstorms or brilliant sunshine
bananas and orange juice
binoculars and notebooks
homemade pea soup with leeks and garlic
candle-dipping
the din of traffic
"honest and simple" the highest
    compliment you can pay
people who act like ultimate experts on a
    topic after having read one article in
    the newspaper
shocks of corn
flowers leaning gently on the rims of
    their vases
short-rooted spearmint and peppermint
    plants
honeymooners wandering the country
    roads, feeding the ducks and swans
    on the pond
spool soldiers
pineapple-coconut flavor
Bunsen burners
sports centers

Troy
an old-fashioned soapstone griddle
a home chock-full of crafts and
     conversation pieces
chocolate chintz ribbons
acres of books
clouds of herbal essence
footsteps in the snow becoming laced
     traceries of purple shadows
frozen chocolate pie and ice cream
Japanese lanterns strung between trees,
     gently lighting the lawn
nipping something in the bud
rippling layers of color
a private end-of-the-road location
Cape Canaveral
dipping soup toward the far edge of
     the bowl
that happy-go-lucky feeling
Hartz Mountain birdseed
marble-topped sideboards
personal branding irons for steaks
teriyaki sauce
tomato spice dressing of zinfandel wine,
     red wine vinegar, tomatoes, soy
     sauce, ginger, and black olives
warm-weather lunch hours
"fresh from the kitchen"
arrangements of corn stalks and colorful
     autumn leaves

driving an old pick-up truck
New York City publishing
barrel jumping
barbecue pizza, made with shredded
barbecued pork in a sugar-and-spice
tomato sauce
foreign stamps
lasagna servers
lush green gardens that roll gently down
to magnificent pink sandy beaches
correspondents
Mazda Miatas
berry-picking excursions
Chris Evert tennis shoes
farmhouse-cum-restaurant
letting the crowd follow
formal gardens
mystery theater on radio
a smile, a sunny day, ice-cold Coca-Cola,
and a best friend to share them with
casual, mobile, outdoor lifestyles
throwing a pot
dusty golden corn for the chickens
fast snowfalls
cushioned tile
laughing when the tennis court lights go
out on people
fish and chips
huts
international road signs

letters with long pauses, reflections, and
    ruminations
lots of books to read in case of bad
    weather
meteor showers
natural beauty, history, botany, geology,
    and sea life
waiting for the team bus
setting things in motion
watching birds
bottle tilters
cats that eat everything
cots
dotted or heart-ed socks
eating a ripe peach and letting the juice
    trickle down your chin
catching wind in a sieve
getting away with things as much as
    possible
hotel and restaurant supply stores
lounging around the pool
true New England chowder: just clams,
    onion, potatoes, and salt pork, served
    with "common" plain, unsalted
    crackers or soda crackers
Azurée cologne
church suppers
country stores
double-decker London buses
fruit basket sewing kits

lavender-scented evenings
love, 15, 30, 40, game, set, match
jewelry pliers
Hawaiian days and Las Vegas nights
New England's "doughnut belt," south of
    muffin country and north of bagels
a widow's walk
medlar = shyness
Boy Scouts making a fire
buying flowers for home on Fridays
crystal chimes
"I'm OK, you're OK"
learning things together
playing the *Nutcracker Suite* at
    Christmas brunch
poachette rings for eggs
roadside tables piled high with fresh eggs
    and produce
sharing "I have always wanted to" stories
plate-size cinnamon buns
spare ribs and egg rolls
whatever you're good at
an ample supply of local postcards
red suspenders
pearl earrings
wrapping gifts
an apple-peeling contest
the beat of a drum
opening a champagne bottle
flat-bottomed paper bags

hearty borscht
library tables
ribs and corn on the cob
umbrella lamps
a beautifully bound book
the first maple leaf drifting down
pecan pralines
Machiavelli, philosopher
tacos and beer
Victorian-style hammocks
bacon broilers
the rope on fancy restaurant menus
cucumber sandwiches sliced like a dream,
 brown boiled eggs, strawberry ice,
 lemonade
foam bath toys
grass-sledding
Halloween smelling of wet, burning
 insides of pumpkins
the old Danish custom of tying a knot at
 a wedding
red-letter days
the season to be jolly: the end of football
 till the beginning of baseball
suds
Tudor-style half-timbers
ice cream for dessert and coffee or
 lemonade
Joe Pepitone, former Chicago Cub
 baseball player

olés
the resident cat on the porch rail
overnight camping on the gym floor
the sensation experienced when an
    elevator stops or takes off too
    suddenly
pregnant women
special children's menus
teeter-totters
the Beach Boys, pop group
branches of trees silvered with crystal or
    flocked with snow
the green shoots of new plants
homemade fudge
feeding birds all winter
old Mickey Mouse records
the pure promise of dawn
country manors
"When there's a will, there's a way"
the tang of autumn fires
whey
the yacht club
fresh fruits arranged with a generous
    scoop of sherbet
chefs' outfits
spring bazaars
Le Creuset cookware
"Jesus Christ Is Risen Today" (hymn)
muffins stuck to the paper holders
coffee carts loose in the building

a rickety wharf, its legs stockinged in
    barnacles
using sugar nippers to break up big
    chunks from a tall, cone-shaped loaf
    of sugar
church bazaars
chocolate charlottes, rich in egg yolk
English muffins served with bacon and
    cheese
"Thankyoufalettinmebemyselfagain" by
    Sly and the Family Stone
schooners and sloops in the harbor
The People's Almanac series
Miss Peach
raisin cookies
Swiss colleges of hotel management
white china drawer pulls
making college education mandatory
white-tailed deer in the clearings
overcoming writer's block
being prankish
chicken salad sandwiches
chipmunks garnering grass seed and
    lining nests with thistledown
editorial mail
going to yard sales early on summer
    mornings
grinding fragrant coffee
taking your time putting on makeup
kiln-dried oak

Halston designer clothes
Lily Tomlin's character Edith Anne
Navajo weaving
salad with oil and vinegar and fresh, hot
    French bread
climbing trees
salmon-orange-pink color
solar-cooked apricot jam
walnut ladder-back chairs
delicate ivory
Coleman stoves
remembering when there were no movie
    ratings
summer theater
taking the time to be appreciative
hunting for natural wood
lunch counters
making up time
buying two Sunday papers
miniature Christmas lights stuffed into
    empty wine or water jugs
a monogrammed cheese chest
piñata parties
miniature golf
pinecones opening early
sanitary socks
Sunday afternoon bowling
tinted windows
winter forcing you to stay home and get
    acquainted with yourself

zingy burritos

Wynken, Blynken, and Nod

bunches of ducks swimming in water

canals with sluice gates

finding out that for years you've
    mispronounced one of your favorite
    words

handle-less Chinese bowls

p.o. = putout in baseball

phone calls from far away

a provincial butter warmer

two-toned sports jackets

"mooshy" beds: feather pillows, soft
    comforters, fresh flowered sheets,
    nearby open windows

"Doonesbury" comic strip

avocado plants

brocaded robes

people who give more of themselves

choosing a car

frosted-glass walls

closet offices

a place of secret magic where nature
    alone quietly renews itself

apple and sweet-potato purée, served
    with pork or chicken or at breakfast
    with sausage or bacon

experimenting with color

happiness coming in three ways:
    anticipation, realization, memory

mirror-sprinkled pillows
script-blue and grass-green colors
straight-backed chairs for working
turtlenecks from Vermont
words pertaining to the nose: sneer,
    sneeze, snicker, sniff, sniffle, snipe,
    snivel, snob, snoop, snoot, snooty,
    snore, snort, snout, snub, snuff,
    snuffle
a room decorated for fall with pumpkins
    and pinecones
spritz cookies
aerosol sprays
burgundy steak
garlic presses
herb tea, the favorite on *General Hospital*
laser printers
lush thickness
garbage plate: baked beans, home-fried
    potatoes, onion, hot dogs, and
    barbecued meat sauce with bread and
    butter on the side
apple pandowdy
haunted houses
muscle sleeves
airing your blankets and quilts on a line
    in the yard, beating your rugs, and
    taking down heavy curtains
postage meters
resting under cool trees

wassail = an early English toast to
   someone's health
a sleepy fishing village
cast-iron and brass beds
a solo drive down unexplored lanes
busy city life
castle-hopping
fish balls and cornbread on a Sunday
   morning
fossiled dinosaur tracks
jute bracelets
kitchen stools

putting on boots and tramping through
   wet fields and woods to remind
   yourself of all the things that were
   buried or forgotten through the
   winter
natural cereal
pinking shears
bonfire colors
consideration for others
nuthatches saying "yank"
oatmeal with maple crumbles on top
funny business
airs
outdoors spilling inside
Little Bo Peep
potato knishes
setting up a breakfast tray the night
   before

not missing a thing
a bed of fress moss
watching model sailboats
a trail of thin mist rising along the
    whispering brook
actions speaking louder than words
Betty Crocker's kitchens
butter-basted fried eggs
eating soup after pig-out weekends
extra-long loaves of bread spread with
    softened butter
gateleg tables
pausing in the damp marsh of a bogland
    among the marsh marigolds
poring over a newspaper
souped-up cars
the thumping of a bass drum
a unique glory
blue waters, white sails, and ruddy
    swimmers
crushed dried juniper berries in stuffing
    for chicken
grungy clothes
house trailers
movable feasts
a veranda with picnic tables and
    expansive windows enabling diners to
    enjoy the wooded scenery
deviled ham toasts crowned with chopped
    fresh parsley

having a marvelous drink in a glamorous
place before going to the theater and
sitting in the cheap seats

antique pine chests

having to wander through a maze of ropes
at an airport or bank even when
you're the only person in line

newsboys' caps

pictures of mixed vegetables

drying racks for clothes

pizza and beer

zarf = a holder for a handleless coffee
cup

Bozo the Clown

rereading old letters, magazines, and
books

a St. Bernard chewing the phone cord in
half

measuring snow

Italian-seasoned chicken

planting seeds

the first day of sandals

the final, hard-fought decision on pizza
toppings

playing in autumn leaves

reading quietly together

Nuance cologne

soap-on-a-rope

stacking cartons to make a dresser

teaching within the home

the exciting moment when you first look
out the window to see what the snow
has done
a basket of soaps and bath goodies
beauty lessons
glass slippers
indulging in an activity that isn't
constructive or goal-oriented
a beach mat that doubles as a tote
gray
the absence of billboards in Vermont
dimples
tubing = floating downriver in an inner
tube
a barbecue bash: wine spritzers, make-
your-own kebabs, pita bread, assorted
ice creams and toppings
ambling through the best boutiques
bubbletop buffet servers
the ballot box
cabins with lobster traps stacked like
cordwood in the backyard
license plates
pickled onions
buckwheat cakes, country-made
sausages, a delicate roll or two, cups
of mocha coffee with cream
cocoa steaming
track lighting
shedding life's little timekeepers

thirsty plants
cucumber sauce
red or white fat jewelry
seeing the biggest evergreen tree of
    your life
red-brown stoneware pots
hidden windows
ice-cold melon
keeping on nodding terms with the
    people we used to be
kneading dough
poetry reading
pretzel sticks
the Snuffleupagus on *Sesame Street*
scented candles and inks
shedding life's little timekeepers
the purest potato taste imaginable
water pressure
entertainers' real names
woodchucks so fat they waddle
trees twinkling with ice
when a hamburger can't take any more
    torture and hurls itself through the
    grill into the coals
special coffee
sweater dryers
the jukebox at the beach
when your temperature is at its 24-hour
    low: the time for your deepest, most
    restorative nap

ages and eras of history
cheese-stuffed green chili peppers dipped
    in egg batter and deep-fried, then
    topped with onions, sauce, and cheese
cleaning the whole house
evening purses
fresh blueberry and peach meringue
clean, crisp sheets, a fluffy duvet and
    mattress cover: ultimate comfort in
    winter
soft red color
gleaming shells in jewel colors, half-
    buried in pearl-white sand
the splash of fish rising to flying insects;
    the crackle of a driftwood campfire
Hefty plastic trash bags
leftover flower children
oxford shirt collars being sexy
fresh croissants and coffee in bed
light switches
white china plates filled with biscuits
    and whipped yams and steaming peas
logs and fires
bags
peg and chalkboard desks
sugar packets
engagement and wedding ring charms
hugs
John Cameron Swayze drowning his
    watch in a commercial

a blanket rack
the smell of popcorn and hot roasted
     peanuts
echoes in a cave
seasonal businesses
whisper-soft, lacy-knit afghans
raising hanging vegetables at home
thick slices of eggplant
things that are part of our dreams and
     hopes
using a shoe to hammer a nail into a wall
white oiled-wool British submarine
     turtleneck sweaters
writing a poem
an icy diamond powdering of stars
white frame houses in tiny hamlets
being able to sample the icing on a new
     cake without leaving a fingerprint
Arizona: winds sending tumbleweeds
     scurrying across the desert floor, red-
     veined copper lodes
briefcase-size computers
the silence and solitude of isolated
     beaches
bringing slippers and wearing
     comfortable clothes to visit someone
     for tea
the click of a closing purse
making a list of things that money
     can't buy

the complete works of Winston Churchill
mallards skimming low over the sea
oil boom towns
taking yourself to lunch
pull-out writing shelves
rolled cookies
a port-of-call
silk screening
velvet Queen Anne chairs
someone all mittened and scarved
taking your time
Colleen Moore's dollhouse, Chicago's
    Science and Industry Museum
folding chairs
a third opinion
helmet-style coal buckets
limbo contests
summer vegetable gardens
tomato baskets
almond extract
bamboo designs
bomber vests and jackets
beating the odds for a change
General Motors
long, stretched-out pop-bottle art
miniature angel food cakes with frosting
    in the middle
owning a house
pens with clocks on them
Pontiac Fieros

a cream-colored wool tennis pullover with
navy and maroon stripes
Sunday afternoon cooking
tiny picturesque harbors
noticing how dirty your windows are and
knowing that winter is almost over
spoon coasters
anniversaries remembered with flowers,
gifts, or cards
candied apples
Central American bananas
dinner service
Concord wagons
handling money
knowing the names of your senators and
representatives
phone-answering services
rooms of looms and spinning wheels
shower benches
when the sky is clear and clean, the air
crisp, the wind free of dust
the sloshing of soft bristles around a
soapy mug
snow bringing a redeeming silence
tropical ferns
wooden book stands for large dictionaries
wrought-iron chandeliers
cookie cutters
croissants and warm Brie
floor-to-ceiling screens

glow
the hoot of an owl
Tennis, Kansas
a carpet of wild strawberries
paper lanterns
popcorn manufacturing plants
tape recorders
a pot of blooming tulips
exploring the twisting passageways of a
    limestone cave
happy children
learning how to play "Mary Had a Little
    Lamb" with push-button telephones
margarine cups
servings of local cheese and honey
surf
surviving strict parents
the many terms common to music and
    baseball
tortoiseshell headbands
Steven Jobs, entrepreneur
an early case of spring fever
Bermuda onions
early woodcuts
inserting change in a vending machine
    according to size or value
errand-running
harbor lights
mushrooms stuffed with pine nuts and
    sausage

rosebuds of ecru organdy
visiting hours
a sharp pencil
a special moment in time
collecting baseball cards
baskets of croissants, brioches, and seed-
capped rolls
designing advertisements
dusk lingering with long light on the
hilltops
the great composers
kitchen timers
optimism leading to happiness and
enthusiasm
putting on records of ocean sounds or bird
songs, leaning back, and imagining
you are outdoors
sit-up pillows
watching the cook prepare luncheon as
you sit on a lawn looking out over the
marina
waterproofing your shoes
the jingle of a pet's ID tags
catfish and hush puppies
eyeteeth
eating all the raw onions you want with
your hamburger
getting up on a 10-foot ladder for theater
scenery work
hot fudge cake

laughing at yourself when you
    mistakenly order beef Wellington
    again
fruit syrup French toast
snuggling up with gentle creatures
spun-apricot, cream-mint, cloud-white
    colors
touring local industries
unusual artichoke plates
abundant wild grapevines
aqua
boudoir stools
church bells chiming as a millstream
    gurgles
a watermelon stabbed with a knife so
    that the rind splits with a crackle and
    the smell comes pouring out
swinging doors to the kitchen
fruit bread with gjëtost
inviting friends over for Monopoly,
    homemade chili, mugs of beer
living a long, long time
a very old mulberry tree
studying self-help books
a volcano-shaped mound of mashed
    potatoes, gravy bubbling out from a
    deep crater formed by a heavy ice-
    cream scoop
governor's palace lights
winning acclaim

a warm mix of vegetables
plastic sandals
a white-fence-enclosed rose garden
"Next window, please" signs
pizza potatoes
a zillion breezy notions
a French dinner
learning to change a tire
leaving the water running
orange-flavored Kool Pops
planning a hot summer midnight supper
    on the beach or near a lake
a willow leaf fully grown: a long, slender
    parcel of chlorophyll
plastic dry-cleaning bags
the quack of a duck
a New England mail basket
sharing clothes
starched linens
a high-placed government source
boiled egg, orange juice, toast, jam, huge
    strawberries, 18th-century hot-milk
    jug, pot of coffee
an art career in New York
Alaska having no state motto
beating boredom
the chapel choir loft, an excellent nook
    for necking
Charleston, flamenco, go-go, and jive
    dancing

crazy and silly and weird times
diaper services
e. e. cummings, poet
fraternity pins as a sign of intended
    future engagement
glass canisters filled with things for
    spring
graph-patterned stoneware
rubber tires in the water
the damask whorls of a napkin
sable watercolor brushes
being looked at
a barbecue sauce poised between
    molasses sweetness and spicy tang
panoramas
a basket of tender, flaky, fresh-from-the-
    oven biscuits
a butcher-paper dispenser
bubbling cauldrons of onion and pea
    soups
commuters
plants on windowsills
brandy snifters
the flag flying
lichens arranged on a piece of wood
pickled peaches
tactful lighting, like apricot-pink
a checkers game set up atop a barrel
cockpit posters
lucky penny in the bottle

sink hand-pumps

cucumber sticks

duck marinated in brandy and port and
wrapped in pastry

encouraging the lost art of reading

kiddy cocktails

odd-shaped mirrors in sinuous mahogany
frames

the most perfect of any music filling
the air

red: beets, radishes, red cabbage,
tomatoes, cherries, red plums,
strawberries, cayenne, cloves

Ted Mack's *Amateur Hour*

wide boulevards

ice-skating on ponds without skates

keeping records and files

meeting in the park for a touch football
game

one of those icy-brittle mornings when
sounds carry far

the exhilaration of pure winter air

oversize balconied rooms looking out on
feathery casuarina trees

ice-cream hugs and kisses

piers

steaks sprinkled with fresh parsley

sterling-silver Christmas charms

Parcel Post's folding/spindling/mutilating
machines

the act of entering a room and
    forgetting why
magnificent, rich colors
forest walking
the seat on the school bus directly over
    the rear wheel
mushroom farms
business cards
the sun bouncing off water
when small miracles occur
acey-deucey: a variety of backgammon
American cheese
Cheshire cheese
the clean, wild, acrid odor of walnut hulls
    and butternut and hickory
cleaning up accumulated dribbles of
    office or housework
deep-sea fishing charters
emerald islands
Goodyear balloons: Bullwinkle, Linus,
    Underdog, Dino the Dinosaur
green
French fry dipper baskets
Oxford, England
the silence of a leafless landscape
defrosting a refrigerator
nighttime outdoor parties
sugar
big beach balls
digging into baked apples

egg-in-the-hole and bacon
Dr. Scholl's exercise sandals
satiny black upholstered banquettes
"when there's no getting over that
 rainbow"
silkworms
taking a refresher course
painting only the ceiling
swirls of butter in a tub
using vine-ripened sweet summer
 tomatoes to make tomato sauce and
 freeze for winter
whims
"like visiting an aunt in the country"
beige corduroys, patchwork pants,
 embroidered corduroys
bright wallpaper and white ceilings
chickadees, weighing as much as a first-
 class letter
making love after a fight
chicken drumettes marinated with spicy
 sauce
drive-in movies
making big root beer floats with long
 spoons and straws
baked pineapple
polished silver
taking a French newspaper to a
 restaurant and ordering a decent
 lunch and decent wine

walking to the beach in the morning
wild carnations
billiard and pool parlors
bylines on the front page
coleus spilling out of a windowbox
delis
falling asleep in the car
colonial patterned floors
talking sweetly
colors against a good tan
full moons and black cats
golf rule books
Home Box Office
summer league baseball and softball
Sambuca for two
handling the first few minutes when
    meeting someone new
sunlamp goggles
armor
combinations of clubs and diamonds in
    gambling sessions
homespun crafts
linen calendars
long toothpicks
manual alphabet
pine footstools
a string of Greek worry beads
Nantucket and New Bedford
ring-toss rings
synchronization of noises

Senator Robert F. Kennedy
vines
taking off in an airplane
venetian blinds between two windows,
    found in Europe
wind-up animals
banana royale made with three flavors of
    ice cream, pineapple, strawberries,
    bananas, pecans, and gobs of hot
    fudge
dropping anchor
bangs
generous dollops of humor
Fanny May candy
handwritten letters that include photos,
    cartoons, dried flowers, or quotes
honey in a tube
knockwurst, bratwurst, frankfurters,
    veal weisswurst
Ivory Snow soap
photographing the changes of season
shower curtains
a stove kettle on a wood-burning stove
bartering
Wyoming: Yellowstone, geysers, bears,
    broncos
clotheslines strung with household goods,
    corsets, long underwear
cooking with a portable TV four feet
    away, enjoying a light, funny movie

floral wallpapers, smoky mirrors, wicker
    chairs, and white-painted woodwork
Sunday supper on the front porch
frostfire color
glowing all day
Japanese pearled unbonium
paper baskets of gumdrops, tiny
    jellybeans, and heart-shaped candy
    wafers printed with words of affection
popular opinion
things as plain as day
"Never complain, never explain"
a quiet, unspoiled island
honeysuckle-covered walls
large sandwiches alternately called
    heroes, wedges, submarines, hoagies,
    grinders, or poor boys
markers from Civil War battlefields
scrub oak woods
strip steak with a tender, charred crust,
    plump and pink, packed with juices
a rag rug, a boot box, a cat to sleep in the
    wash basket
paper-thin plates of bird's-eye maple
a reawakened curiosity about nature
rule of thumb: a homemade recipe for
    making a guess
African violets
birch
European soccer

horns of plenty

museum lectures

hot and sweet mustard, thin slices of rare
steak, Bermuda onion slices, pickles,
smoked bluefish pâté, French bread
and crackers, apple slices, smooth
country meat pâtés, celery stalks,
cream cheese, smoked salmon, lemon
and lime slices, jar of sun tea

nosegays of dried flowers

a set of hats for a child

Miss Chris tennis rackets

roses

visiting a Nativity scene

slow-cooked oatmeal

white and oatmeal colors

a small music system in the kitchen

on Christmas Eve, a stocking on each
guest's chair filled with funny and
special gifts pertaining to each one's
interests

a sunken garden

absence making the heart grow fonder

baskets of eggs

cast-iron floor registers

interesting reproductions

kitchen windows

letting color predominate

nature undefied

a smoking train

not being able to read your own watch
hot-sun yellows
not making any excuses for 24 hours
patchwork mock turtlenecks
sitting on the grass with a child and
    playing
watermelon pickle chunks served in
    diamond-point, cut-glass bowls
anthropology: anatomy, anthropometry,
    ethnology, ontogeny, physiology, and
    psychology
citrus "shells"
cutting down on junk food
getting rid of a headache
"EXCUSE ME!"
hot dog samples
mountain-ledge flowers blooming on sky-
    high rocky peaks
the plunk of a ball in a mitt
rouge
letting your skin breathe
round Band-Aids
shuffling cards
stubby tugboats
mailing five sheets of paper with one
    stamp
adult coffee ice cream: just coffee with
    cream and only a dash of sweetness
blue bath beads
blue-banded white pottery

the countryside bathed in the light of
     autumn sun
double-handled soup bowls
living life spontaneously
love-knot rings
never licking more than three books of
     trading stamps at one time
saving one last treat for the end of
     vacation
rows of mailboxes hungrily awaiting
     their daily feeding
a wheel of Stilton cheese
porcupine quills
a wrist corsage
icy clear water
winding a maypole
thyme
trying on something that is
     too big
McGuffey's six reader-primers
buying a sample jar of imported jam
crystal shakers
"I Get Around" by the Beach Boys
a Saturday morning with cartoons,
     relaxing in pajamas with a bowl of
     cereal
peach paradises
places heavy with history
teaching by example
scarves with snaffle bits

seals
anything you have in mind
swank
baby evergreens
cable car rides
cobbled streets
recalling lines of poetry
backyard dining
crazy hats and sunglasses
drawing tablets

fear of being approached by several dozen
    waiters singing "Happy Birthday"
soapstone boxes
feathery palms and ferns in wicker and
    bamboo
Jack Benny's violin
guarding your private time as your most
    treasured asset
heavenly sights like dreams created
a big glass of wine, jammies, presents to
    wrap, cozy house, and "Rudolph the
    Red-Nosed Reindeer" on at eight
a black lava-strewn coast
bladed grass: a forest of small spears
    of ice
charred hot dogs
the land drawing a white sheet up to
    its chin
the sunny side of an old stone wall
bucolic scenery

cocktail sausages stuffed with cheddar
    cheese
old architectural details
the individual vegetables or tater tots in
    a TV dinner tray that escape over the
    wall into the Salisbury steak zone
Art Deco geometrics
the gravity-defying "Round-Up" ride
cheese in 40-pound wheels
old travel and movie posters
the smell of rainstorms and roses and
    fresh-cut grass
order
adding machines
elderberry wine
the creak and complaint of ice crystals
    shrinking upon themselves
seeing America by bicycle
sterling silver
the Bluebird of Happiness
"the green stuff"
spats
the circling beam from a lighthouse
French dressing
driving defensively
fresh paint
bread factories
Brenda Starr
cream cheese with chives and a slice of
    radish on a Bremner wafer

everyone needing a little self-love
fields bursting with ripening grain
chess sets that invite competition
fresh, golden-hued butter
great elm trees
lofts
muffler scarves
reference books
fresh bread soaked in garlic butter and
    herbs
Bliss, New York
taffy
taking a child to the zoo
daffodils and primroses rising from
    the grass
defrosting in a microwave
chimney corners
grade school
sugary lemonade
togas
Aigner handbags
aches
Thomas Edison inventions: waxed paper,
    mimeograph, electric light, motion-
    picture camera, dictating machine,
    electric vote recorder, storage
    battery, phonograph record,
    electric pen, electric railway car,
    stock ticker, electric railroad signal,
    light socket, light switch, etc.

olive-colored duffel bags
onion-bits barbecue sauce
painting the front door a bright color and
    adding a brass knocker
making love after a party
private rituals
quiet
sailing out of the clouds
brightly striped sweaters
slices of watermelon with small seeds in
    them
Twinkles cereal
using less and less toilet paper as one
    nears the end of the roll
waiters' serving stations
writing old friends about new plans
"Dig it"
being in tune with nature
bright blue and dusty red
a plant supermarket
chili in summer
dainty sandwiches with the crusts
    trimmed off
making words from Alpha-Bits cereal
doing something for money
exercise mats
flickering lights with shimmering
    reflections
grids
taking fried chicken on an airplane

asking yourself if you're really hungry
homecoming mums
baking-soda deodorant and detergent
airtight alibis
melting the ice
July afternoons roaring and rumbling
    with thunderstorms
salt and pepper
taking time off
splendid nature
aglet = shoelace tip
colonial houses
holly
lime marinade for chicken
making special efforts to get to know
    each other better
Homer
the momentary thrill of sitting on a
    washing machine as it goes into spin
    cycle
pumpkin fiestas
the many ways that make a kid feel big
tomatoes and bacon on toast, covered
    with melted cheese
10 most beautiful words: *chimes, dawn,
    golden, hush, lullaby, luminous,
    melody, mist, murmuring, tranquil*
campaign chests
homemade bread and real whipped butter
    for every dinner

men who wear T-shirts: "So many
women, so little time"
non-dairy cream
pineapple juice
Montgomery Ward
sand, sandalwood, sapphire blue,
shocking pink, spring green, sky
blue, slate, Spanish moss, star white,
steel gray, stone gray, strawberry red,
sun orange colors
dots and dashes
the sun coming up over a fog, a warmth of
silver light that seems to come from
everywhere
"Esperanza" (poem)
winter piles drifting over the road
honey
contentment in listening to music and
staring at a fire
hands on a ship
looks
running a dairy
Igor Stravinsky, composer
people who wear sunglasses at night
snow cake with snow icing
produce baskets
scoots = dollars
fine damask linen napkins,
hand-hemmed and graciously
monogrammed

snow ice cream topped with maple syrup
    or concentrated fruit juice
Providence/Fall River, Rhode Island
stock exchanges
two odd friends
something frothy as icing
growing as our love grows
improving your tennis by making it
    sound good
a place where small kittens sit sunning
    themselves on stone walls
jars to collect things in
Hires root beer
remembering when phone exchanges all
    had names
marigold colors
a pond or lake cupped in a hollow among
    the green hills
marinated vegetable salad
strawberry-cream gelatin
merging traffic
narrow snakeskin belts with silver-toned
    buckle, tips, and keeper
scrambled eggs with herbs
appliance carts
streamer-patterned sheets
strict diets and exercise
throwing a towel over a pipe or radiator
    so it's warm as toast when you come
    out of the shower

turkey stuffing

a season for loving and remembering

thirtysomething (TV show)

working concession stands

a reminder of the milkman and his
    delivery wagon laden with fresh cans
    of milk and cream on ice

polliwogs

a romance between a French shop girl
    and a Yale dropout

spring training

three

birds

the aurora borealis

cereal and fruit parfaits

Christmas music

fireflies flashing their taillights

first-aid books

geraniums in earthenware pots vying
    for light

"Hush-a-Bye, Baby"

passion flowers

a shell collection and display case

unsalted butter

a small orchestra playing for a poolside
    buffet at noon

baskets balanced on heads

dessert parties

getting a tailor to make all your
    clothes fit

disaster movies
gaslight era frosted-glass ruffled bell
     lamps
kittens spanking sunbeams
little, round ball candles
not staying home alone on Halloween
a single orchid
puttering about the house
retail terms
$1 Washington, $2 Jefferson, $5 Lincoln,
     $10 Hamilton, $20 Jackson,
     $50 Grant, $100 Franklin,
     $500 McKinley, $1,000 Cleveland,
     $5,000 Madison, $10,000 Chase,
     $100,000 Wilson
watching the ocean change its moods
books about Watergate
antique woodworking tools
bathing beaches
a mishmash
fat burger buns
getting used to computing
hothouse tulips
"Muppet Babies"
sautéed bananas
souvenirs of beach walks
truffles of European chocolate, cocoa
     liqueur, fresh cream, and cocoa butter
your firstborn
adults who talk baby talk

aqua-sand color
cats in between ripples of blankets
blunt-ended Rooster-style knit ties
inviting guests
a living room's litter of unwrappings on
    Christmas or birthdays
chard
revolving doors
seven brass candlesticks in graduated
    heights
leaded-glass kitchen wall cabinets for
    displaying jars of home-canned jams
    and vegetables
a wall TV shelf
bowls of mixed nuts and nutcrackers
The Whole Earth Catalog
foxes
33-inch-tall candlesticks
a 19th-century pioneer fur-trading post
    and gold-mining boom town
Up Periscope (movie)
a New Englander
babies in backpacks
giving presents to yourself
sawed-off trees
upward mobility
a mixed bag
orange segments
roads wide enough for only one car, with
    "meeting" places to wait

Noah Webster's birthplace in West
Hartford, Connecticut
seashells in a glass bowl
starting a show
tearoom food
thank-you notes
Shari Lewis and Lambchop
toasting bagels
veal with honey and lemon
wearing a parachute in the elevator
wrapped candies
abalone hunting
blazing a trail
constantly changing stations on the
car radio
"Kum Bay Yah" Bible camp song
the squish of wet shoes
peanuts and raisins mixed
glassed-in sidewalk cafés
umbrellas and wet streets
a beautiful calfskin leather agenda
baby terrariums
hibachi cooking
a bobbing float
picking a pile of peaches
a bowl of fruit
Crayolas plus imagination
pocket Instamatic cameras
rocks
picnic tables on the pier

a sachet of balsam pine needles, like a
walk in the woods
Rochester lamps
a baby squirrel
heavy green glass jugs with natural
cork tops
tucking a paperback into a friend's purse
or putting a tiny plant on his or her
windowsill
Victorian laces
a can of newer-colored tennis balls
old light bulbs
a carefully arranged mind
a cedar-paneled stateroom
bicycling out to look at the Scotch
heather, wood lilies, and wild roses on
the moors
decorated Christmas trees
judging a bakery on the quality of its
angel food cake
medieval houses
old-fashioned hospitality
the exquisite sweetness of the air
above snow
red velvet bows with long streamers
riding the Colorado River on a raft
soda-pop crates
the gentle mood of a lovely spring
remembered
ice-cream cakes

the grayness of a sky about to snow
keeping the apartment dim
sheepish smiles
opera
taking a flashlight wherever you go
polished stones
the first buttercups beyond the pasture
    fence
sneakers with dress suits
the first frost
steering wheels
stereo speakers
French gendarme's whistle
the calm before the storm
returning overdue books
the company of a mountain
sheep
the silence that pervades a crowded
    elevator when the doors close
thermos jugs of ice water
loving thy neighbor
tie-dyed yellow
cheering up a dreary desk
That Darn Cat (movie)
the scenery along the way, as special as
    the smells and colors of fresh-from-
    the-field produce
cheese served with warm, crusty bread,
    sweet butter, walnuts, and a good
    port wine

"Keep on truckin'"

diets

bread in silvered baskets

a steam explosion of corn kernels

coffee to go for 15¢

the young, restless ocean

evenings: lovely, romantic, home-cooked
    meals served by candlelight, sitting
    by the fireside, snuggling under a
    comforter in an old-fashioned bed

clear blue bays

everyone yelling "bingo" except you

"Desirada" (poem)

coffee desserts

night coming in like a black silk cloak,
    silently folding itself around us

oval picture frames

bags: ethnic, canvas, doggy, saddle,
    and wine

French mushroom omelets

quilted couches

pails

quintessential New England villages

raisin pumpernickel rolls

sailing picnics

slim, crustless sandwiches

animals of intelligence: porpoise, fox, pig,
    chimpanzee, orangutan, elephant,
    gorilla, dog, beaver, horse, sea lion,
    bear, and cat

an iron candle chandelier

being a playground leader

bright white walls and gaily colored
curtains

making spiced apple rings

chicken pot pie

faking your way through unintelligible
lyrics

dried vegetables, hung upside down in
bunches

making a documentary film

taking a shower

island-related music: watered-down
reggae or steel drums

counting the miles

mulling spice balls of orange peel,
cinnamon, allspice, and clove

police and firemen's badges

pulling a rocker close to the stove

salad of deep red sun-ripened tomatoes
tossed with fresh basil and a splash of
vinegar and olive oil

baking tiles for the oven

silk bed jackets

being selective

silver whistles

Rolloplane carnival rides

talkathons and walkathons

Sylvester P. Pussycat's "Thuffering
Thucatash!"

picking your own lobster from the
    restaurant tank
values
velvet cushions
walking to work
gulls
Mr. Magoo
halos
the White Mountains
jumping off the bandwagon
salads mixed at the table
lemon meat loaf
memorizing the penal code
Jimminy Cricket
summer mornings
completely cute = handsome
composing songs
lines from favorite movies or poems
men's woven handkerchiefs
panning a scene
pine and maple banister-back chairs
renting a barge
ringing the bell for doggy's dinner and
    doggy running over to you
singing to the radio when you drive
winning streaks
rustic, weathered boards and planks
music
a street map of your town
pot roast gravy

Winnie-the-Pooh, Christopher Robin,
   Kanga, Baby Roo, Tigger, Eeyore,
   Piglet
candle snuffers
a boy and a boat in a bathtub
dinner for four
finally getting a watermelon baller
ginger pancakes
George Gershwin, composer
looking closely at designs of nature: the
   grain of a cucumber, the patterns of
   leaves
scorched bamboo
PTA potluck dinners
sportswriting assignments
"bowl" haircuts
bloomer panties
Chocks vitamins
enormous bundles of Sunday newspapers
   on street corners
football towers
frogs
frosty chains and pom-poms on a
   Christmas tree
sipping orange juice from a champagne
   glass and toasting yourself
zuppa inglese = rum-soaked cake with
   custard
a placid lake ruffled only by swans and
   other waterfowl

getting a profound sense of well-being
  from a tidy linen closet
apple-glazed beef brisket
coed night at the health club
marketing a fad
Je reviens = I will return
screened porches, unscreened porches,
  glassed porches, unglassed porches,
  with old wicker chairs, pots of
  geraniums, bringing romance to
  summer
shredded toasted coconut
tearing home from work to finish a book
strawberry-flavored cakes
the streetlights of town, like an
  enchanted pearl necklace
  disappearing around a small hill
throwing away 3/4 of the papers in
  your files
Vermont granite
herbal hot pads
musty old books
warm honey buns with whipped butter
a red amaryllis
birds crowding the feeder
cork panels filled with art, ideas, fabric
  scraps, color swatches
curry of turkey
cucumber sandwiches
gardenias and candlelight

garnishes for soups: crispy fried pork
    scraps, bits of crisp bacon, julienne
    strips of ham, grated cheese, sliced
    fried sausage, buttered popcorn,
    salted whipped cream, sour cream,
    lemon slices or wedges, chopped fresh
    herbs (dill, parsley, or chives), or
    sliced or grated hard-boiled eggs
horseback trips
curling your hair
observation and imitation
postcards from friends dear and far
rasping sweaters beginning to feel good
    in the mornings
tossing a salad-bar party
washing out bathing suits
zesty dill dressing of California sauterne,
    garlic, lemon, dill, and fine spices
a semicircular bed with a white eyelet
    canopy
a snap in the air in fall
little girls with their teddy bears
not being too grown up for anything
a spring-flowered leotard
a summer "sleeping" porch
butterscotch sundaes and Pepsi together,
    tasting like banana baby food
a supermarket basket left on a deserted
    beach
baseball lights coming on

a basket of large seashells
designer pizzas
fashion quizzes
Walden by Henry David Thoreau
satin jumpsuits
water fountains = bubblers
a thick mattress pad, soft feather pillows,
    fresh flowered sheets, a cotton
    comforter, and lace bed skirt
a trip to New Hampshire and Vermont to
    see fall foliage
the giving of gifts
buttered new potatoes with skins on
attic sleuthing
automobile running boards
butter crunch and white almond bark
catching peas with a roll
cottage cheese containers
eating utensils
getting snow caked on socks and in jean
    cuffs
hot-water heating systems
mountain vistas
prune ice cream
abandoning all civility and slurping the
    grapefruit juice straight from the
    bowl it's served in
sour-cherry jam
squeezing limes
adust = browned, sunburned

blue chambray work shirts

cluttered rooms

shopping baskets, pie baskets, garden
baskets

love and kisses

the five most consumed food products:
milk, potatoes, beef, sugar, canned
vegetables

jeweled necklines

a waiter presenting the spoken menu

a wall of antique mirrors

luxuriant meadows with wildflowers

paying close attention to everything

pizza served on a large metal tray lined
with white butcher's paper

a cozy chamois flannel jumper with side
buttons

pie-baking contests

no-iron clothes

McDonald's Christmas cups

D-Day

khaki hiking shorts with button-down
shirt and Tretorns

learning to fly

meat carved at your table

peasant scarves

steamboat races

plain doughnuts

Jamestown, Virginia

planning a pond

spring breaks on Martha's Vineyard
shaving a peach
Cabaret (movie)
traditional chants sung at the butter
    churner
an apple barrel
painted turtles
singing in the rain
boats
planting a tree
brandied eggnog
champagne punch
buying new ice-cube trays
clams in festively striped trapezoidal
    boxes
crabmeat with sherried cheese sauce
ships
polished walnut
Clark Cable and Lana Turner or Carole
    Lombard
enameled Play-Doh baskets
framing a favorite recipe
fraternity softball games
toboggan slides
babbling brooks
baby tomatoes that burst
picture-postcard villages
secret messages
chartered buses for wrestling teams
footed bathtubs

Apollo space missions
tucking kids in
lonely French fries at the bottom of a
    fast-food bag
a caring doctor
docks
anchoring just off a sandy crescent down
    the creek and casting for pan fish
coco-fiber rugs
cucumbers-and-apple salad
ducking into the ladies' room for
    10 minutes
madeleines = little French sponge cakes
    in shape of scallop shells
syllables
riding around town on roller skates
ideas
meeting people at parties
predicting rain
Meunster cheese
scented wood: sandalwood, cedar,
    sassafras
apple-pie order
croquet layouts
sneaking to the front of the line
the August college magazine issues and
    major catalogs
lemon strippers
Stonehenge
barns

sugar-cured, hickory-smoked ham, hot
    fried biscuits; hot, sweet funnel
    cakes, fresh hickory nut pie, and old-
    fashioned molasses
the bottom line
French buttercream cookies
muffs
soft, worn jeans
the fullest day of summer
breakfast steak
long-distance calls
serendipitous plans
breathing space
creating a romantic picnic from a local
    farmer's market
beginning a jigsaw puzzle
the loose strand on each forkful of
    spaghetti that beats you on the chin
Chinese flipflop sandals
peppermint schnapps
liking to share
the Golden Rule
making decisions to benefit more than
    just yourself
the muffled clinking of silver from a tree-
    shaded patio
curls
the spot on the shopping-mall map
    marked "You are here"
tweeds, Shetlands, pearls

breads: banana bread, biscuits, bread
 sticks, cinnamon rolls, cloverleaf
 rolls, croissants, crumpets, date
 bread, French bread, French toast,
 hard rolls, honey buns, hot cross
 buns, Italian bread, Jewish rye bread,
 macaroni, Melba toast, muffins,
 onion bread, potato bread,
 pumpernickel, raisin bread, rolls, rye
 bread, scones, toast, white bread,
 whole-wheat bread
broadening someone's horizons
making toast and devouring crumpets
a thought
high jinks and assorted merrymaking
The Scarlet Letter (book)
painting your nails fire-engine red
railroad tracks
shimmering blue lakes bathed in warm
 sunlight, framed by snow-capped Alps
 and lush green hills
curved park benches
dark rooms
a shiny brass bucket full of pinecones
 that have been dipped in wax
Krazy Kat
pregnancy
thin-sliced liver, broiled lightly and
 served with a wine and mushroom
 sauce

"whistlin' Dixie"
being alive with wine, laughter, and love
an in-the-water boat show
being addicted to the systematically
    popping bubbles in packing material
chili over potato patties
making jam and berry pies
feeding kittens
birds' mating calls
making simple wooden toys
oil-free makeup
splurging on a great bottle of wine
Sylvester Stallone, actor
walking a good brisk mile
"cluck cluck" decanters that make
    gurgling sounds to alert the master of
    servants' tippling
a cold arctic wind ripping red and gold
    leaves from the trees
colors of a grocery store
delectably crunchy ginger
holiday cookies
lumps that block the pouring spouts of
    sugar dispensers
snowplows
bumpy learn-to-write pens
cleaning a bike
fumes
homemade pain de chocolat
luncheon orders

mincemeat in peach halves

pints

Nantucket relish, Chappaquiddick and
Cape Cod chutneys and green pepper
jelly, packed in canning jars with
calico lids

Pennsylvania: coal, liberty, midpoint of
13 colonies, laurel, woods, mountains,
steel

wonderful serendipitous experiences

rings

shopping on Christmas Eve

snow-clad peaks

cane and bamboo

stores with lavish displays of chocolate
and marzipan temptations

dance marathons

looking your best

neon depictions

people letting coffee get cold, then having
to get more

room at the inn

sports "picture" trophies

an olive stoner

long, fat yellow ears of sweet corn

two-layer jello

an old bake-kettle, clock-jack, Dutch
oven, and dye tub

flower-sellers arranging their wares in
the town square

an over-the-tub whirlpool
bootee slippers
"Hold the bus!"
brochures on how to buy fruits and
    vegetables
brown thrashers
closing your eyes and thinking "black
    velvet"
banks
Choctaw Indians
flowers basking
gooseneck lamps
a group of long-stemmed goblets filled
    with fresh flowers
Angora rabbits
zippered purses
applying makeup
making apple butter
surprise birthday parties
exploring a new neighborhood
large seashells
meringue pies: foam-white clouds gilded
    with caramelized froth
a more-than-happy feeling
pork chop weather, when dinner had
    better be heavy-duty
studying a menu
corny things
rereading specific passages and chapters
    when seeking inspiration

northern lights
Perry Como-style sweaters
springtime in the Rockies
throwing a cocktail party
turkey buzzards
air travel bags
using a hot tub
eating ice-cream sandwiches by licking
    around the sides
bartending tips
birch trees, flashing and fluttering
carrots sautéed in butter
Christmas celebrated with fireworks in
    Brazil
earth-toned, rustic linens for warmth in
    fall or winter
firing a salute
a truck stop with great spicy ribs and
    sweet-potato pie
Fords
horsehair sofas
kissing games: pass the Life Saver, spin
    the bottle, post office
old iron scales
vases
zesty = spiked with spices
space stations
pears
a spectacular ride over the swirling
    rapids of the Colorado River

a submarine sandwich of roast beef,
shredded lettuce, mayonnaise, and
salt and pepper
dressing casual at night
kitties licking
a post office pen that writes
letting someone make you laugh
sitting in the dorm, philosophizing about
life
water fountains
forts
gyros
antique headboards, tall chiffoniers with
brass handles
auto backgammon
cute feet in blue tennies
apricot soufflé
barbecued beans
buying some lacy underwear and wearing
it for everyday
hot-water method iced tea
sturdy, flat-heeled shoes
an unsupported elliptical staircase
blue light bulbs
church hayrides
four hugs a day
living within your income
Lovenotes dolls
having a different kind of sandwich for
lunch

old-fashioned alphabet blocks
having loved, lost, and loved again
a wall of books
boxes
the sound of roller skates on well-known
    sidewalks
physical education shirts
buying a used textbook at a college
    bookstore
flying midweek
a 28th birthday
cheeks tingling in the winter
77 Sunset Strip (TV show)
a Boston rocker
imagining someone watching and
    admiring or desiring you
leaf fall bringing a crisp scuffling as the
    wind courses the land
the 900-year-old Japanese art of bonsai
peach, brown, pink pearls
placing an order and waiting till your
    number is called
scavenger hunts
luggage racks
a seafarer's knot
the snapping of trodden twigs
training wheels
weaving black-ash baskets
gifts wrapped in tissue paper, tied with
    red ribbon

black raspberry-apple jam
blanket-checked fabric
Crazy Rabbit, who loves Trix cereal
cucumber relish
Diablo printers
heaping sautéed hot red peppers and
    onions on a hot dog
pebbled streets
a barn busy with horses stamping and
    snorting
bran muffins served warm, split, and
    buttered
coaches all dressed alike
a basket of bread cubes to dunk in hot,
    fragrant cheese fondue
fabric rosebuds
jacks
"Dictionary" parlor game
a bevy of eclectic sights
picking strawberries by the pailful
picnics in cars
receiving a fabulous gift from the man
    you love
the polka
society editors
accomplishments
a smiling countenance
cucumbers in garlic sauce
meditating in the bathtub
a pet stuffed frog named Sidney

Wedgwood china
bleached floors
long-stemmed lilies
doing something posthaste
crewel needlework pillows
electric trains
ice-cold cocktail glasses
needle-threading
opening bottles
the first snow falling silently through
    miles and miles of spruce
crib sets
sneaking off to the mountains in the
    middle of the week
the fabrics in a Laura Ashley store
sweet peas on tripods, hollyhocks, pinks,
    columbines, bleeding heart, blue
    geraniums, cranesbill, ladies mantle,
    and the unannounced arrival of some
    self-sown annual
Kentucky Fried Chicken potato salad
the bus arriving on time and with empty
    seats
solidus = slanted line between words
planting tables
colored bottles
the little red wagon under the Christmas
    tree
time-tested friends
the shudder of pipes in the morning

whistling a duet together
black
following your nose
creating a snow sculpture
unity
the strains of the fiddle
when you're in love with the world
avenues of majestic trees
bees filling the air with the hum of
    industry
bad-weather get-togethers
the final four of the NCAA basketball
    tournament
cider made from bruised apples; apple
    juice from undamaged apples
fresh French bread, hot to the touch
green or blue eyes and frosted hair
muffins bought at a bakery while biking
    through Martha's Vineyard
the scent of new-mown hay
soft, summery ivory light
a light-up magnifying glass
regular hedges of fruit trees, covered with
    beautiful flowers early in spring,
    charged with noble fruits in summer
    and autumn
homemade stationery
beginning a journal in a blank book
the Big Countdown on radio stations on
    New Year's Eve

huge ceiling beams inscribed with old
	Dutch proverbs
mahogany bowls from Haiti
chicken ranches
Johnny-jump-ups
school pictures
having good luck on a Friday the 13th
lairs
things not always being what they seem
writing poetry that no one will see
twilight lingering at the end of the day
	like a promise
using mesquite weed in the barbecue for
	a smoked flavor
writing labels recording the jam's fruit
	and birth date
being a showoff
Bridgeport brass products
chicken in brandy, herbs, and cream
gaining control and power over the things
	we can change
long-stemmed compotes for serving
	Chinese food
crisp linen, pink roses, and trays of
	peaches
driving by the house in which you grew up
eminent success
Dairy Queen posters and price lists
going to an oldie-goldie double-feature at
	the drive-in

windowsill planters
rakes
taking a squeaky basket of damp clothes
    to the backyard
baked spaghetti
palm-lined beach T-shirts
walks
yellow colonial glassware
Yale University
calling friends
collecting things for a future home
fellow airline passengers
halters worn with a shirt over
holiday fussing
coming in out of the rain
the yellow-orange blooms of the daisy-like
    black-eyed Susan
computerized dictionaries
ham carved into fine-grained slices
short-legged beach chairs
manicured hands
Kansas City beef barbecue
the Man in the Moon
sensuous scents
Pine Brothers cough drops
sangria and cheeseburgers
10-gallon hats
pine-mint color
tiny leaves drooping on soft stems, too
    young to hold up their heads

a fisherman's sweater
banana muffins with butter and a wedge
    of sharp cheddar
cinnamon sticks
Danish potatoes
scorching edges of paper for effect
finding the perfect illustrator for your
    book
handball courts
Reuters News Agency
lions
moo goo gai pan
moonlight talks
Knorr's vegetable soup mix in the dip,
    instead of onion, and a piece of
    Jarlsberg on a plate with Triscuits
poolside tables
root beer candy
shopping sprees
snow "fluffies"
trout
stoneware tortilla warmers
"Come Touch the Sun" (song)
Smokey the Bear
those moments of life that are utterly
    simple
amour
an orchard that supplies large plastic
    bags and labels which rows of trees
    contain certain varieties

dragging your heels
aromas
blooming tropical flowers
"Hold the pickle, hold the lettuce"
chocolate-striped cookies
chowders: milk, potatoes, onion, salt pork
    or bacon bits
food coloring in snow to make hair and
    eyes for snowmen
good afternoons
group traveling
"Hooey!"
popcorn balls in plastic wrap tied with
    ribbon
ropes of shells
taping your own ankle
rutabagas
happy songbirds
a quaint fishing village of tiny gold-hued
    houses on narrow cobbled streets
perfect couples
four-slice toasters
sprays of true-blue water
Portsmouth, New Hampshire
streamside thickets as red as a stormy
    sunset
three kinds of people in the world: those
    who make things happen, those who
    allow things to happen, and those
    who don't care

Earth Day
world-class photographers
a rabbit's foot
string pictures
a silver jug that holds an equal mixture
    of cream and buttermilk
carpenters' plans
putting food by
slush
Mississippi: antebellum mansions,
    magnolia trees, shrimp boats, pecan
    trees
a riding jacket
"treat her like a lady"
apricot strudel
April: sweet pea or daisy
Bernardo sandals in white
a Carrara marble lazy Susan
ferns
herbs to use with chicken
instant shampoo
mustard and cheese crocks
oyster shucking
pastry crimpers
visiting a formal garden on a sunny
    afternoon
a serious present for a birthday—like a
    desk
baskets for harvesting coffee beans
cashmere gloves

desires made out of nostalgia and
     imagination
not peeking into a cannon
discovering the philosopher's stone
a small flock flying in a precise
     V-formation
country hutches
fashions for every season
ketchup pumps for bottles
kitchens with high wooden ceilings and
     louvered windows
metal pegboards
not taking life that seriously because it's
     here to be enjoyed
paths edged with hibiscus
Youth Fellowship meetings
laboratory research
putting your arm out the car window
setting the table for tea
a tartlet of crumbly meringue and
     amaretto butter crème
watching icy movies: *Dr. Zhivago,*
     Runaway Train, and *Ice Station*
     Zebra
watermelon, Wedgwood blue, West Point
     blue, wet sand, wheat, whiskey,
     willow, wine, wood rose, yellow rose
     colors
a two-generation cookbook
antique-hunting

battery testers

squirting someone with a squirt gun

butterscotch-dipped cones

eating with your fingers; feeding your
lover, your friends, your children,
with your fingers

hot sun cooled by a sea breeze carrying
the heady scents of pine trees and
clam flats

mouthwatering delicacies

babies' name bracelets

sounds, smells, and tastes to extend the
mood of a book

thumb wrestling

touches of gold

"I used to think being more of a woman
meant acting hard to get"
(commercial)

country roadsides sweet with clover

"once in a blue moon"

moving furniture outdoors

ravioli cutters

sic = this

a village street c. 1890, with old bricks,
wrought iron, bay windows, and
antique stained glass at the
entrances of stores

"bunny wunnies"

in winter, snowdrops, early and autumn
crocus under a bare orchard tree

wild plum = independence
jewelry cleaner
newborn puppies with trip-over ears
a waiters' race
"A watched pot never boils"
dawn shimmering with dew; sunrise on
    lawn and meadow
downhill racers
buying a book and getting lost in a new
    topic
crystal candleholders that look like
    snowballs of glistening ice
playing a sport whole-hog
crystallography
"Rain before 7, fine by 11."
trying to work things out on your own
Mr. Freeze Pops
Dr. Seuss books
seasonal cleaning of rugs
a 30th birthday
L.L. Bean jeans
having no TV or radio in the hotel; just
    browsing the books there while
    listening to classical music
meat cross-hatched with grill marks
oranges filled with jello and topped with
    whipped cream
playing hooky to do something you don't
    ordinarily have time for
shades of pink and yellow

sharing popcorn

spaghetti sauce

wrapping up in blankets, hopping a sled
drawn by jingle-belled horses, and
gliding under the stars to a little
cabin

beach umbrellas

beating the weekend blues

a bag of lemons

wall sconces giving off an amber glow

blackberry wine

Beatle haircuts

changing colors

chasing an ice-cream truck and feeling
like a kid again

the clap of thunder

crayons in extremely obscure colors

"rubber baby buggy bumpers" (tongue
twister)

a bowl of meat and potato cubes in rich
gravy

piccata = served with a lemon butter
sauce

classical music

picking cranberries and beach plums

logos, graphics, whimsy, stenciling,
trompe l'oeil, pen-and-ink renderings,
painted primitives, and illustration

secret formulas

suction cups on bath mats

taco salad of mixed greens, kidney beans,
cheese, taco meat, tomato, and green
onions
each inch of a garden revealing some
new life
escaping the winter blahs
individual soufflé dishes
kids with their T-shirts on backwards,
sleepy over toast and jelly
Indian Guides group, YMCA
old dormitories
seedless grapes in sour cream and brown
sugar
pudding recipes
riding bikes in school parking lots
someone understanding enough to hug
you soft and close when you cry, and
kiss away your tears
endless space to fly a kite, play Frisbee,
run, walk, or just sit and think
ice cubes tinkling like wind-chimes
keeping a fire burning as a welcome
open-late shops
overlooking lighted cliffs of a bay
pieces-of-eight
one slice of bread spread with peanut
butter slapped against one spread
with strawberry jam
seeing rainbows
the Hokey-Pokey

knowledge, even in its tiniest increments,
     being one of the few pleasures that
     really endure
smells of baking cookies, cannelloni,
     sauerkraut, hot dogs, and pizza sauce
     filling the warm air
the distance from your elbow to your
     wrist equaling to the length of your
     foot
cobalt-blue bottles
the furling and unfurling of leaves
spending the day looking forward to an
     evening home alone
accolades
big trays
"She sells seashells by the seashore"
     (tongue twister)
keeping your hopes up
the Farrah Fawcett hairdo
cucumber salads
the night breeze gently nudging the
     sailboats
bleached or stenciled floors
the sound of elevator bells, shoppers'
     sighs, and Muzak
kitchen gardens
enduring traditions
the taste of vacuum coffee on a sunlit
     bank or sand bar
Swedish cutlery

the third log for making a campfire
when our children exceed our own
    achievements
theater parties
rainbow sherbet
the munching of golden ears of corn
spearmint, spinach colors
cheeks a chipmunk would be proud of
the hearty shout of labor
chewy brown-sugar muffins
"free for the asking"
shoeshine boxes
the scent of wood fires that fills the mind
    with distant memories
cleaning soft-shell crabs
swimming in a natural brook across the
    road from an inn
deep-dish plum and black cherry pie
electric clothes steamers
the quiet days of Indian summer, quiet
    nights of starlight and leaf scuffle
evergreens, wearing winter's ermine
    gracefully
the shadows of deep water
white
steak and peppers Italiano
feeling really good, alive, aware; filled
    with a tingly sense of well-being
French chocolate custard and cheesecake
    served with whipped cream

"When the team comes marching in"
  (cheer)
angel food cake and cider
sheltered nooks
the trade winds
English farmhouse cookies
"I have seen the future and it works"
mohair sweaters
The New Yorker magazine
"Friday's child is loving and giving"
things that are indispensable
prizewinning playwrights
rainwater on green leaves
sailor collars and shirts
tailoring learning to your life and
  interests
an afternoon nap
Trivial Pursuit
writing letters
Animal Crackers
making a ship-in-a-bottle from a wine
  bottle, piece of pine, thread, glue,
  pins, toothpicks, and ribbons for sails
four-leaf clovers
British English
writing positive inspirational thoughts in
  a quote book
children's eyes
making sure all your friends get home
  safely from holiday parties

oak floorboards
Lakerol candies
poker
"Keep a thing for seven years and you'll
    find a use for it"
asking what the future is
baked squash stuffed with rice and
    flavored with cinnamon, nutmeg,
    allspice, and mint
the minuscule bumps on a strawberry
Orlon
polishing shoes
roll-back cuffs
silky floss, antique lace
waking up naturally (no alarm), pulling
    on a comfortable robe, brewing some
    coffee, picking up the paper, and
    getting right back under the covers
silverware bags
loving forever
valentine myths
calling in sick
ham-filled crêpes and lots of good hot
    coffee
deli roast beef
holster pockets
jam bubbling on the stove
time to think things over
winks
taking a course

homemade cereal
mint milkshakes
hunks of cheese in plastic wrappers
sandwich plates
tents
Alley Oop
kindling in a beer barrel
mandarin oranges and spring flowers
minding your own business
June: rose or honeysuckle
Norman Rockwell art
Mondrian prints
runcible spoons
singing in cars
sun-loving prairie plants
hanging a lamp over the center of the
    dining room table
sunburned faces
tangerine juice
V-neck sweaters
winding country roads, leading past
    rustic farms with weathered barns
    and stone fences
the Banana Splits (Bingo, Drooper,
    Fleagle, and Snorky) in Hocus Pocus
    Park, singing the "Tra-La-La" song
tool kits
bunny-hug coats
genuine Capodimonte porcelain boxes
honeymoon myths

a mother calling to her child
sports banquets
stocking up the larder with jam and
    preserves
wooden ceilings
"How about a little drinky poo?"
    (Ziggy saying)
chocolate mills
shoes
choosing a tennis racket
drowsy mornings
glögg
maple cream-cheese spread
napkins soft to the touch
chopping blocks
papaya, avocado, cucumber, snow peas,
    chives, and green onion salad with
    mint vinegar
pepperoni pizza
Superman dolls
a pudding that makes you feel warm and
    full and at peace
apple orchards wearing their first red
    blush of harvest
liquor stacked along the wall in a
    restaurant
irresistibility
Profiles in Courage by John F. Kennedy
sorrel = parental affection
personalized powder puffs

a screwdriver on a key ring
strong emotions
word processors
working on a bibliography
yarn lampshades
apricot sunsets
rosemary-sage-myrtle herb candles in
    terra-cotta pots
corporate farms
furniture woods
harvest chowder
hiring a baby-sitter who's on a diet
inspiring music
kissing potions
a solid-pine gateleg drop-leaf table
luscious creams
music for ballet practice
"Wash me" instructions found on the
    backs of dirty trucks
Washington, D.C., lobbyists
a spaghetti-spinning fork
absorption of information
basement swings
businessmen's striped oxford shirts
casual partying
hostess dresses
kitchen parties
a spider's web of streets
not trying to do everything at once
outdoor careers

putting a button on the corner of your
    beach towel so you can pull it on as a
    cover-up
Stratton, Stowe, and Mad River Glen in
    Vermont; Sugarloaf in Maine
"To thine own self be true"
scarlet ribbons
vats of salad and cauldrons of soup
an antique spillholder used for long
    fireplace matches or a floral
    arrangement
catching a butterfly
    in the palm of your
    hand and letting it go
getting tickets to a play
hot oatmeal and warm baked apples with
    prunes
nouns
pouring melted butter over potatoes
studying color, design, real estate, or
    public speaking
double features
love that lasts and lasts
beveled mirrors
seashore shirts
envelope purses
five-way Cincinnati chili
unweaving tinsel from tree branches
wall-hung plate racks, a true country
    custom

faucets and their handles
a wienie roast in the woods with
    logs as seats, Seven-Up,
    and barbecue chips
easy-to-read clocks
luxuriating with supplies of fresh towels,
    soaps, body lotions, and powders
buying oceanside property
reading Dickens
etymological dictionaries
porch swings swinging high
jazzing up kids' sneakers
the buzzing of bees
a "homework survival kit"
25¢ posters
a Sunday night salad bowl
"Thousand Lights" full-lead crystal
    pendant
Glade air spray
learning to separate eggs
pull-out trays and fold-out pantries
Italian suits and collarless shirts
the counterculture
making a fall clothes buying list each
    year
plastic orange juice jugs
reading four dictionary pages a day
mother-of-pearl in an abalone shell
rearranging the apartment
snapping towels at people

stained-glass-window coloring books

discovering a new singer, dancer, actress, writer, restaurant, recipe

the soft, new green of a garden pea fresh from its pod

attempting to find and separate the ends of a plastic sandwich or trash bag

sitting on a porch or bench reading *The New York Times*

cracklin' bread

crayons in wicker baskets

drawing energy and vitality from one's surroundings

Crabby Appleton

the sandpaper-like nubs on a cat's tongue

frappes = ice-cream sodas

granny nighties

ribbons to match uniforms

the romance potential of a vacation

a barn of books that cost 25¢ to $3 each

flapped pockets

a blue-and-white pitcher filled with jasmine or daisies

a sense of serenity

embroidering folkloric flowers with picoted icing

lacy valentines

victory over incompetence

sidewalk tables

becoming transfixed by the movement,
    sounds, and rhythm of the surf: waves
    crashing, then gently rolling in and
    edging back
"I can't lose!"
midnight motorcycle rides
the realities of marriage
old white clapboard towns
Modern Library editions of Jane Austen
    and Thomas Wolfe
a broom-swept beach house
red, white, and blueberry ice cream
the police beat
ice cream served in metal stemmed
    dishes that get all frosty on the
    outside
inexpensive lace curtains
Greek fishermen's sandals
leeks
needlepoint eyeglass cases
open rolling fields and stone walls
skewered steak and shrimp
the brake pedal on the passenger side of
    the car that you wish existed when
    you're riding with a lunatic
sleeping naked between crisp sheets
stew made with good-quality beef, fresh
    vegetables, red wine, and herbs,
    served with hot, crusty French bread,
    a dry red wine, and a crisp salad

the spicy fragrance of apples, oranges, or
    peaches filling a room
weekend sailors
even-numbered ages sounding younger
fueling a hot-air balloon
Exeter sundials
life preservers
today
breakfast toast
courage
old teddy bears
muffins made from stone-ground meal
extra effort always making a difference
rafts
tufted cushions
the strange extra digits you find on push-
    button phones
magazine-picture collages
organizing time
huge sandwiches
pairing tennis sneaks, crisp white shorts,
    and pastel argyle socks
Swiss chocolate
Geiger counters
painters' pants
"Silly? Maybe, but that's me and why
    should I change?" (commercial)
sliced tomatoes
Taiwan bamboo chimes
tying shoelaces

a white Christmas
ad infinitum = without end
a bring-your-own-dish party
self-acceptance
taking a sailboat excursion to nearby
    islands
chili casseroles
I-live-on-fresh-air-and-apples glow
Edith Piaf records and café au lait
polishing someone's shoes as a surprise
    gesture of love
sun-ripe peach, sunberry brown, toasted
    pink, ivory peach, sea ivory colors
rejoicing in time alone to catch up
taking advantage of all the opportunities
    to keep your mouth shut
baking a variety of breads and serving
    them hot with a crock of butter
Coke baseball bottle caps
Halloween masks
fringe benefits
melt-away mints
Jell-O cookbooks
nylon
heirloom family pictures on a
    handsome doily
self-sufficiency, self-respect, efficiency,
    and the discipline of hard work
a telephone shelf
tiles

cold lemon soup
fragile, colorful butterflies fluttering
    across the swaying grass
golden trumpets
cults
lemon and tropical spices
removing makeup
someone's silent thoughts
armfuls of spring flowers
Campbell's green pea soup
company picnics
getting a really good haircut
longhorn cheese
a ranch-style wrought-iron triangle for
    announcing dinner
laughing at someone's favorite story—
    again
sunlight streaming through a window
windows with tinted glass
hotel rooms with kitchenettes
wine lists in fat folders
conical evergreens
dandelion, dawn gray, dawn pink, dusty
    pink, ebony, electric blue, emerald,
    and evergreen colors
honeymoon spots
"Nothing Books," blank books for writing
Georgia peaches
poor-boy shirts
"as white as a sheet"

spooky sounds: tree branches scraping
a window; green wood in a house
structure, creaking and groaning;
roofs and walls expanding and
contracting; echoes, air traps; roof
shingles making the wind moan;
thumping water pipes
trompe l'oeil insouciance
men who wear glasses
two glasses of iced tea and a bowl of
cookies on a tray
an original 1958 blond ponytailed Barbie
Doll
Bloom County comic strips
chocolate buttermill cake
snowball lights for a romantic glow
chopping boards
"Looney Tunes" cartoons
inchworms
Japanese green tea brewed with fresh
mint leaves, cooled and iced
paper sailboats
brooms and mops
peppery blue cheese sauce
backstops
esprit de corps
"Happiness is not having what you want,
but wanting what you have"
Herman thrushes
nurturing your own spirit

parks
spreading light
food straight from your grocer's freezer
"ironing" food to heat it
reading lamps that cast the perfect
    amount of light on the page
parfait stripes
a rocking chair in front of a window
    overlooking a lake
birthdays, anniversaries, and red-letter
    days
carved valances
dark brown and light blue
Nevada: alkali flats, yucca, sagebrush,
    Las Vegas
earrings for every outfit
fortune cookies
Psycho-Cybernetics (book)
"As long as we have someone to share our
    dreams, there's nothing we can't do,
    nothing we can't be"
T-shirt legends
a sky the shade of faded blue jeans
missing someone
nests
a smile you wear all over
box seats
Bosco chocolate flavoring
desk accessories in country fabrics
the discreet murmur of voices

intelligence and maturity
blackboards listing specials of the day
giving a speech
kitchen shelves
hutches, highboys, and buffet tables
little luxuries
outdoor chaises
Pete Maravich, basketball player
watching skaters on ponds
a trellised cubbyhole bar
embroidery samplers
nicknames
butter-and-eggs
cutoffs: the first sign of summer
paper tapes of dot candy
getting a puppy
seaside communities
true madras: navy blue, maroon, mustard
    yellow—and it "bleeds"
Wuthering Heights (movie)
brushing out your hair in the soft
    island air
eau de toilette
hour-long telephone calls
love for nature
buying five T-shirts in five colors
Lavalites with gook blobs
giving your least favorite food another
    chance
pewter, faience, or Dutch delftware

rowboats pulled up on a sandy beach
bowling leagues
mixing real flowers and silk leaves
buying things for your new apartment
skating across a lake you swam in last
     summer
the federal payroll
an "everything pot" with six bowls
     mounted on its loops
99¢ paper chefs' hats
charcoal onions
roadside stands
3 1/2-inch computer diskettes
wearing a Shetland sweater as a scarf
loans
planning a trip
reading glasses
smallness
space-dyed yarn
trays glued and shellacked with Audubon
     and Currier & Ives prints
wearing a baby's ring on a necklace
brand-new homes
changing habits
cracker barrels
starting a garden on the windowsill
dial telephones
granola cereals
defying gravity
sunflower ranches

heathery colors
a beautiful state of mind
the gleaming cloud of your own breath,
    white and shimmering
bubble gum cards
licorice sticks
stainless-steel sconces from Sweden
microwave ovens
secret cabinets
escargot, cheese fondue, beef
    bourguignonne fondue with sauces
    and chocolate fondue with fresh fruit
    and angel food cake
hackberry trees
kid's hair curlers
secret herbs and spices in a recipe
pistachio jello
sacks of spices
shabby gentility
old-time crafts and music
radish-and-crabmeat salad
sudden darkness
the electric touching of fingertips
wadded-up pieces of paper
Federalist and Greek Revival houses
tiring yourself out
ice-cream sodas
keeping in step
the cotton makers' symbol
open-mindedness

pie crusts made with lard
sleep
bread, herb butter, and preserves
pretending a Miss America pageant
stencils and snow spray for windows
pleasure being life's major concern
stereoscopic photographs and a special
    viewer
kids riding in shopping carts
teens
"Wherefore art thou, Romeo?"
the Monday wash
singing waiters
the blue lines around jockey shorts
the golden blaze of April forsythia
impoverished students
the room tariff
coats
the widening and lengthening of flower
    petals
tiered pewter chandeliers
"To err is human, to forgive is divine—
    but to forget is altogether humane"
when even your margarine doesn't speak
    to you
the smells of pine and fresh coffee
creamed carrots
"as easy as taking candy from a baby"
evening caftans
flexible straws

greeting-card commercials
lifting your slush-and-snow spirits
your first homemade stuffed mushrooms
soft lagoons by moonlight
pages
tufted-leather banquettes
coffee-flavored parfait served in a tulip-
    shaped cup of icy metal
the songs of summer slowly revealed
regatta stripes
vegetable juice
pillow fights, blanket tents, spooky
    stories, dressing up the cat
"Every minute counts"
hugging a teddy
behind-the-scenes editors
iridescent glass tumblers
onions, carrots, cabbages, lettuces, and
    radishes: fresh vegetables in their
    striped rows, mixing with broad-
    leaved herbs and drifts of flowers
prismed crystal chandeliers
quiet libraries
shirts trimmed with ribbon
suitcases of straw wicker
using canning jars for serving juice
    and milk
children's mittens saved over the years
    and hung on the wall as a collection
    of winter memories

a still-life painting
Chinese cabbage
hair falling on your face
coleslaw and sliced apple or pear on a
    burger
cooperativeness
long hair
the plastic yoke that holds a six-pack of
    beer together
taking Christmas cookies to friends
pelts
baking bread and popovers and having
    time to enjoy them
polished beechwood against the warmth
    of skin
something falling neatly into place
polyester crepe
solacing others
when all you've got is ice cream and
    you're the last one in a long checkout
    line
colorful flower and produce markets
delight at the prospect of a new day, a
    fresh try, one more start
gilt-edged picture frames
wills
half-cartwheels
someone loving the smell of your skin
the commonest words: the, of, and, to, a,
    in, that, is, I, it, for, as

homemade angel-hair pasta
18th-century merchant princes' homes
long, low waves
men's dancewear
Jennifer O'Neill, actress
pancake tossing
doubling the temperature and adding 30
    to convert Celsius to Fahrenheit
having something bright yellow in your
    room at work
Santa's kitchen
the Senate Watergate hearings
windblown hair
celery hearts vinaigrette
wonderfully simple things
benches under olive trees
concentrating on being you
aqueducts
confetti-tossed hair
containers and bottles—a smoked salmon,
    pâté, prawns, chips, fruit, wine—and
    some fine crusty bread
dandelions and buttercups
mechanics' denim jumpsuits
fantod = nervous movements
handwoven Chinese silk wallpaper in
    multicolor pattern
noontime visits
ozone
showing love for children

surprising someone with a special event
bands
snow in October
two ground beef patties, lettuce, cheese,
    special sauce, mayo—on a toasted
    double-deck sesame-seed bun
two-tined forks
Don't Drink the Water (play/movie)
apothecary jars
choosing a Christmas tree
making a birthday special
floral confetti
the double taper of a rolled linen napkin
    emerging from each crystal wineglass
zip codes
good directions
cooking a steak
paper airplanes
Cross or Vermont crackers
spring radishes
a quick drop in temperature and then a
    gradual turn of the leaves
very elegant walk-in bars
words
a rocking horse
carnations with baby's breath
Florence, Italy
listening
topaz = fidelity
large colonial fireplaces

always putting carbon paper in the
    wrong way
perfecting a tennis serve
sorority basketball games
straight razors
Three Dog Night, pop group
varicolored beauty in an old-fashioned
    garden
Vermont scrambled eggs served with
    local cheddar cheese
warm wool socks
a radish cutter
a rainbow seen as a complete circle
carriage clocks
Burger King and Wendy's Fun Meals
curiosity boxes
early spring: violets, whites, pinks, thin
    yellows, light blues
farm-fresh food
garden seeds on display at the hardware
    store
rust-and-cream knits
poses
visions of dark roast coffee beans, crusty
    loaves, peppery garlic sausage, husks
    of aged Romano and Parmesan
    cheese, hot Sicilian pizza
washing your hair
Montpelier and Burlington, Vermont
a strolling trio of musicians

hosting a party
late-day lounging back at the hotel
the little orphan look: prim black
    schoolgirl dress with black tights
optical character readers
potluck recipes
putting on a record by your favorite
    comedian
setting an old chair or wicker rocker out
    in the garden
a tri-screen TV
antique buttons
cutting alfalfa
eating so much spaghetti that you cannot
    move
fortune-telling
patting the cat
scalloped chicken on rice
extra chips of real onion
getting somewhere on time
getting your point across
hot oats cereal
Nurse Nancy Golden Book
a unicorn with a golden horn and
    Borgana flower garland
fruit salad of fresh wild blackberries,
    raspberries, blueberries, peaches, and
    apples
putting the cover over the birdcage at
    night

houses of cards

acts of kindness, no matter how small,
    never being wasted

saving mementos

diving right in

having the windows washed

raw barn siding

Newport, Rhode Island, in a sleeting
    rainstorm

peach and ginger shadings

a waterfall wearing a rainbow tiara

May: lily of the valley or hawthorn

bay leaf flavor

St. Croix, Virgin Islands

a Christmas tree decorated in tiny
    flickering white lights and
    gingham bows

friends coming over

measuring flour

peanut butter so sticky you could mortar
    bricks with it

play being purest relaxation

reading poetry before bed

fuses

toaster waffles

starlit beaches

roasting chestnuts at home in a shallow
    baking pan

seasoning with herbs instead of butter
    or oil

crafts to make, puzzles to solve, tricks to
do, experiments to perform; things to
build, cut out, color, cook, and grow
sparkly pom-poms
cress = stability
practicing dance steps in the middle of
the living room
teaching someone to use a thesaurus
Camelot (movie)
wearing fluffy slippers and making
applesauce
weather brewing
"Walk, don't run, take cover" signs in
Ziggy comics
babies in bootees and snow overalls
Rodgers and Hart
an authentic lobster bake
beamed ceilings
braised leeks vinaigrette
the kitty's annual visit to the vet
an antique railway switching signal
the lilting song of motion that makes the
heart rejoice
examining our consciences
hearing a sound you don't notice until it
stops, e.g., the furnace or refrigerator
shutting off
mobile concepts
the fireside being the tulip bed of a
winter day

baby dandelions

being alone to talk, to dream, to scheme, to take aimless drives to no place special

tubing: bobbing in an old inner tube lazily down a tranquil river

a bay window seat high up around the treetops

babies' silverware

preoccupation

jack-o'-lanterns

the ability to start over

cranberry shrubs

yachts strung with Christmas lights

a charcoal grill right in the middle of the dining area

sweater dresses

charm

arctic hares growing a thicker coat

using the drive-up window

hacking jackets

jade and chocolate colors

old-fashioned gingerbread

red nail polish

video recorders

wading in the water after sleeping in the sun

Valentine, Texas and Nebraska

kneading bread as therapy

omelet-making

the alphabet by code: Alpha, Bravo,
    Charlie, Delta, Echo, Foxtrot, Golf,
    Hotel, India, Juliet, Kilo, Lima,
    Mike, November, Oscar, Papa,
    Quebec, Romeo, Sierra, Tango,
    Uniform, Victor, Whiskey, X-Ray,
    Yankee, Zulu
opening oysters
pretty woodcarvings and stained-glass
    windows
sherbet-striped things
steel-belted radial tires
the best farmhouse butter
making meringue
a cat circling a spot three or four times
    before settling on it
making applesauce and canning it for
    Christmas presents
sleeping soundly when it's snowing
    hard at bedtime; waking full of
    anticipation
breezeless days
the red, gold, and blue-silver leaf of wild
    columbine
the sweet crunch of corn on the cob
writing to lots of people
evening picnics
eyes that never tell lies
beige and black
fresh, crisp air and sparkling light

green-onion dip
soft robes to settle into
trapezoids, pentagons, hexagons,
    octagons
rugby
eight
Athens by night
rainbow-colored swimsuits
stirrup pants or leggings
folding auditorium chairs
gold knot rings
swirled pudding
the Gerber baby
white lightning
writing long messages to out-of-touch
    friends
being misled by the tinted window of a
    toaster oven into thinking something
    is "done"
swimming with a kickboard
cribs
bringing a blanket to sit on outside at
    lunch
British favorites like smoked salmon and
    scrambled eggs
wild-card teams
daily reminders
making the dog taste-test your food
Brie en brioche
taking advantage of walking weather

cake-and-lemonade parties
polished copper
having someone to make you laugh when
    things are tough
polyunsaturates
rolls and honey
Salieri and Brahms, composers
velour hooded sweatshirts
Volkswagen vans
yellow bicycles
the yelp of a puppy
rockers: Presidential, Windsor, Snowshoe,
    Whitley bent-back
Valentine's Day, the oldest holiday
color surprises
cultured pearls
dillweed from California
falling down on bumpy ice
solar energy
golden, succulent chicken with relish
    tray, tasty cottage cheese, and
    crackers
half-cooked sugar cookies
holding your shoulders high
something left over
pumpkin waffles
colored markers
hamburger pizza
something getting "hairy"
times to recall

women who look like they stepped out of
a page in a French fashion magazine
comparing movies to books
a hammered brass ginger jar
striped ribbons
frosted barware
ebony
homemade basil mayonnaise
juniper berries
running a booth at a fair
running around in circles
sending flowers
a tiny teddy bear box by Halcyon Days
Tennis magazine
vanilla wafer crumb crust
"And suddenly nothing is the same"
(commercial)
candy
"red carpet" welcomes
hand-pegged oak furniture
snow swirling on the road
snowbound towns
snowshoe travel
sliding glass doors
Woodhue cologne
"pomander in a pot": apple, cinnamon
stick, cloves, nutmeg, sliced orange
an open fire and the hearth on which
it burns
insightful, thought-provoking books

premoistened towelettes
swings made from old tires
sloshing around in waders
chocolate mints
cookbooks with small type
homemade chokeberry syrup
floor-to-ceiling cabinets
goosing
growing midget vegetables
Florida oranges
improving eating patterns
strange, unintelligible symbols for
washing instructions on clothing
labels
paper-bag lamps
popcorn parties
browned turkey hash served with
mustard sauce
ripe cantaloupe
appearing on TV
a quiet area in the office building
dress codes and getting into trouble
wearing pants on a cold day
perilous cliffs
the scratch of a slate pencil
serving flaming bananas for dessert
strengthening your skills
teriyaki steaks
popsicle sticks
working with a new client

"Worryin' is like rocking in a rocking
    chair: it gives you something to do
    but it doesn't get you anywhere"
a rubber stamp printed with a favorite
    slogan
apricot refrigerator cake
Bermuda bags with button-on cloth
    covers and monogramming
chrome on bikes
a child's sandbox
farewell kisses
hats: Derringer, drifter, longhorn,
    panama, safari, plantation
European cheese
a refuge from the city with fine, flat
    beaches
horehound candy
responding with a jump of the heart
Christmas gifts
a walk downtown
rose-red mornings to begin each day
washing the car
a barrel-shaped cornflower blue
    stoneware urn for cider, ale, iced or
    hot tea
the piping of a piccolo
a stack of baseball mitts
best done alone: eating all the pound
    cake, especially right out of the box
Casper the Friendly Ghost

fishing with bamboo poles
high school yearbooks
late fall when men move indoors like
    bears to doze before the TV
little boys with froggies
no-turning-back situations
oatmeal apple bar cookies
petting a horse
corridor fights
potatoes and onions fried with barbecue
    spice
vitamin cereals
a terry face mitt for the bath
antique violins
getting married on safari
exploring the intricate possibilities of
    idleness
mountain crafts
plunger = the disconnect button on a
    telephone
sculpture in papier-mâché
slumber parties
carrying things
bluegrass fairs
clumps of blackberry brambles heavy
    with ripening fruit
sash-wrapped waists
love: reaching, touching, caring, sharing
    sunshine, showers and flowers, happy
    hours together

airing the quilts, thinking about the
gardens, taking off the storm
windows, going for long walks,
buying a new hat
brooms made of long birch saplings
(Indian broom)
caves
daisies and black-eyed Susans
mowing the lawn in your swimsuit and
sneakers
sewing scissors
"Away in the Manger" (carol)
1-2-3-BUZZ game
a Coach handbag
planning a hike
the "Pass-Out" game
leafing through boxes of unsorted
photographs
playing while someone mows the lawn
the roar of a crowd
roasting chestnuts in the fireplace
starting a pogo stick fad
travel journals
wraparound corner windows
an antique two-seater school desk with
cast-iron legs, inkwell
wrapping hair with thread
years from now, remembering everything:
the light, the words he said, the
magic mood

adapting a novel for film
classic baklava
sharing a dream
whale oil lamps
a beer tent at a festival
classy uniforms
secretly planting tulip bulbs all over the
    neighborhood
coal and shovel
flashing lights
dodgeball
nubby wools in solids and tweeds,
    abundant flannels, gabardines,
    camel's hair, cashmere, alpaca
rubber stampers
subdued pastels
a beauty shop appointment
noises at night
a bowl of shrimp on a bed of ice with a
    delicious sauce
cobalt blue bromo bottles
mock road signs
orchestra seats
packing a two-week wardrobe in a carry-
    on bag
a brace-back Windsor fancy oak desk
social climbing
uncovering an unexpected patch of
    wildflowers
creamy coleslaw

backward letters used only on clubhouse
   doors
cocker spaniels
individual cartoon frames
Lucy Angle and Barbara Minty, models
red sweatpants
iced tea loaded with slices of lemon, lime,
   and oranges
a Greek picnic: bread, feta cheese, and
   retsina
meeting friends
open-air beauty
the summer song of mowers
overnight trips
seeds changing to flowers
steep-walled, water-filled quarries
Shetland sweaters in ice blue, sawdust,
   Oxford gray, hunter green
the delicate hieroglyphics of raccoons and
   deer down by the creek
progressive jazz
the pong of a tennis ball
making the freshest juice
wedding invitation charms
teeth
weeping willows
"penny" valentines, secret love notes,
   and candy hearts
cherry tomatoes
feeling changes

taking a "constitutional"
fresh-laid eggs
geese flying in formation
Great-grandmother's cameo
chevron stripes
quaking green aspen trees
regimental ties
English-American décor with a dash
     of seaside resort and women's
     handicraft
john = bathroom
The Absent-Minded Professor (movie)
unhurried hours away from pressures
drinking from the garden hose
knit bedspreads
paisley, plaid, cabbage-rose chintz
     wallpaper
quick postcards
writing "Happy Birthday" on a pizza
rainbow bridges
shining indoor plants' leaves with
     mayonnaise
Philadelphia cheese steak
Swiss steak burgundy, smothered in
     vegetables
Twinkie "fixes"
"sipping" fun down to the last drop
an inflated glitzy metallic balloon
making concrete
being realistic

bright sun causing an afternoon nap
good news
cricket matches
driving to the beach with the windows
    wide open and radio blaring
griddle-breads: soda-leavened batters
    based on flour, eggs, and milk, cooked
    on a greased griddle, skillet, or waffle
    iron
climbing up on some hill at sunrise
the button at the top of a baseball cap
making friends with a dog
homemade soup: bubbling softly,
    warming the house with delicious
    aromas and comforting your tummy
    on chilly nights
taking the time to plump your dog's
    L.L. Bean doggy bed
baked pears in sour cream
kilns
complimentary wine and cheese
relaxation and a chance to let down
rolls in a basket with a napkin covering
    them
seltzer bottles
wall stenciling
children hurling rubber cows from
    their cribs
bells on baskets you pass at dinner
cold peach soup

falling in love
hills
taking an art appreciation course at a
museum
short-sleeved camp shirts
a polar ice cap
flowers in crannied walls
names
summer camps: learning how to make
belts, ashtrays, gimp lanyards
yam and postal blue colors
short necklaces
menus
Lanny Wadkins, pro golfer
pinball-lit pizza emporia
singing on the school bus
pineapple color
sunken treasure
piñon- and juniper-covered foothills
ring-toss games
running around in the sun
sending glints of firelight all over the
room
sun-tawny color
window-shopping
banana puddings
cinnamon butter puffs: muffins rolled in
spiced sugar
fine-print maps
rearranging the entire house in one day

hand-rolled and -cut pasta
chocolate-butterscotch pie with whipped
    cream
handcuff-size onion rings
candle lighting
honesty being so delightfully, pink-
    cheekedly seductive
scouting shirts
sports trophies
the toot of a train
being booted, mufflered, and storm-
    coated
choosing, at whim, quiet back roads
broiled tenderloin breakfast steaks
brown
apples and bananas in caramel sauce
Broadway flips, double cherry Cokes, and
    licorice-whip garnished black cows
chocolate 'n cream color
cloudy-day gray
dropping a pound cake on your big toe
flower arrangements scenting a room
watching kids dive into a swimming pool
sap-bucket rocking chairs
apple crisp pie
Scandinavian glögg or Austrian
    Gluhwein
requesting a song and dedication from
    the radio station
a quiet day with the kids

cool, gray days
purse atomizers
strawberry, plum, pear, cherry, crab-
    apple, elderberry, apricot, cranberry,
    whortleberry, quince, blackberry,
    cape gooseberry, almond, orange,
    grape, medlar, cowberry, nectarine,
    loganberry, hope, and sloe
tartan blankets
lavender = mist color
sleeping on a train
warm applesauce
a roll-arm sofa
Christmas hobby stockings
downspouts after the rain
airmail routes
bare trees spreading mantillas of black
    lace against the pale sky
Barnes & Noble bookstores
a steak for two
whittling
carving chicken
coral-to-magenta petunias
direct sunlight
warm-windowed houses and frosted-
    roofed barns
first the margarine, then the cereal not
    speaking to you!
eating breakfast on your front stoop
misty tan color

visiting WLS Radio Station, Chicago

a showery afternoon with great rolling
   clouds

elevators

a stack of buttered toast

cushions of brushed denim
   disguising cottage cheese

getting less wet walking in the rain and
   least wet standing still

intricate bronze garlands linking
   chandeliers

literary guilds

a sea horse in an aquarium

no two fingerprints being alike

sitting beside a fire and hearing wind
   tides suck at the chimney, swish
   against the corner of the house, and
   quiver the panes

Totes umbrellas and overshoes

asking advice from a youngster

great shadows lengthening in the fields

the way peanut butter spreads

antique oak lapidary tubs

eating everyone's discarded pickles

getting back to the time when you
   couldn't think of anything but each
   other

hot chocolate and big marshmallows at a
   hamburger joint

sturdy chowders

blueberry pails
light, fluffy ladyfingers
seven
having a menu of reading with enough
    variety to ensure there is always
    something new to work on
Iowa City, Iowa
sewing your own place mats
a walk in the country with a friend
cows with bells
thinking "Maybe I'll write a letter"
trying licorice ice cream
anything yellow
sitting up straight
eating the cookie batter before it makes it
    to the oven
antique crock-eye marbles
playing "spy" in the woods
hazelnut waffles with whipped cream
"Dr. Livingstone, I presume"
Thousand Island salad dressing
an October owl in the dusk
measuring things
orange
pea-planting day
pearl-blue color
a staircase of huge boulders
starting a relationship with a feeling of
    wonder at the uniqueness of the other
    person

tea cakes and honey butter
tranquil bubbles
veal parmigiana
whales
academic freedom
beaches you're sure no one else has
    discovered
chairs of bent bamboo and floors of cool
    tiles
Brazilian coffee
practicing speaking French
flaming-bright maple trees
flats of pansies
hearty soups straight from the stove
public relations
robins
letting someone in line get in front of you
tabletop mirrors
heart pacemakers
zebras
notebooks with blank pages to be filled
a bucket filled with little bunches of
    flowers that perfectly combine all of
    nature's colors
embellishing with brilliant camellia and
    oleander blossoms
wet suits
incomprehensible good luck
machine-washable things
recalling childhood warmth

secrets of magic
a camp breakfast
ascots
bachelor's buttons
bicycling around an island
the last day of school
having your talents used but not abused
old-fashioned bridal gowns
oodles
padded shoulders
red clover, sugar maples, hermit
    thrushes, and honeybees
riding on the crossbar of a bike late
    at night
side-slit shorts
soda-pop bubbles
andirons and bellows bought at an
    antique show
hide-a-bed sofas
ice-cream table and chairs
Count Basie records
keeping a sketch pad next to the bed
open-air cinemas
that over-the-rainbow feeling
poetry that doesn't rhyme
seeing 200 sails of different colors
the Yale libraries, especially Sterling
working at home
inexpensive cafeteria lunches
having a favorite book bound in leather

"Your guess is as good as mine"
soft-shell clams and crabs
the origin of the hamburger: broiling
    hamburger patties with a thin slice of
    onion and placing them on a plate
    with home fries
rust-color silk
the perfect spot
eating the chocolate Easter bunny's head
    off first
the thrill of fresh starts and unimagined
    adventures you feel when you buy a
    new diary or agenda
warm, dry socks
the whistle of the ferries
thermal underwear to wear under your
    nightgown
a won't-leave-you-hungry meal
Sharper Image catalogs
trees whispering
the head on a freshly made egg cream
when the cat makes friends
pigeonholes for stationery and supplies
when the hot dogs come in an eight-pack
    and the buns in a six-pack
beer-cheese soup
checking out a foreign grocery store
brainstorming
the last pickle in the jar that resists
    being captured

elegant pewter swirl bowls

fresh, free, and sensitive people

being able to say "I made it myself"

fresh-sand color

great compotes of honey and tubs of fresh
country butter

French lollipops

inflatable boats

muffled clinking of silver

the smell of rain when the first drops
come down and sink into the hot
earth

soft breezes, longer days, lightning bugs,
and fireworks

the soft splat of snow falling

finding the perfect hairstyle

pegboards

cigar boxes for stationery

high, sexy heels

blue eyes

"the mountaintops of love"

rainbows apologizing for angry skies

smiling your smile

making cozy provision against winter

spiral notebooks

thin slices of pink ham and dark red beef,
garnished with a mound of gherkins
and pickled onions

being houseproud

bringing a cookout down to the beach

chimes
the clinking of ice in a glass
self-instruction
tall booths in restaurants
well-aged brandy
Chiquita bananas
simplicity and sophistication
taking something off the grocery shelf,
deciding you don't want it, and then
putting it in another section
the Brooklyn Bridge
bricks
island exploring
a milkshake served on a glass plate with
doily, vanilla cookie, straw, spoon,
and metal container of more
pale peach color
pilots
calligraphy pens
silk sleepthings
Children's Digest magazine
talcum
California honey
thinking for yourself
colorful markets
enlarging a favorite photo
Hamburger U. for McDonald's trainees
simple vanilla coffeecake
summer cardigans
atmospheric haze

camels
camp-style meals
gumbos
the art of conversation
the junk page in the newspaper
pencil asparagus
chocolate cups with strawberry cream
penny valentines
penthouse cocktail lounges
any sign that takes on a new meaning
    when a magnetic letter falls off
vending machines
Winnie Winkle
bon voyage gifts
bundling up for a long walk while the
    turkey is roasting
ice-cream makers
Conestoga wagons
ginger-jar lamps
ivory-mist color
looking forward to the mail each day
"Something's Burnin'" (song)
progressive dinner parties
stonewall-lined cow lanes
wood burning with a special flame and
    fragrance of its own, whether pine,
    birch, maple, oak, apple, or cherry
convention weeks
Woody Woodpecker
chop and fowl paper frills

provolone cheese
shopping arcades
a silk pocket handkerchief
croissants in, doughnuts out
frothiness
improving yourself
a riot of colors
Christmas lights
ripe grass in need of comb and brush
prognostications
Tupperware locked-food ads
pinot blanc, pinot noir, pinot chardonnay
    wine
putting together a swing set for children
    and seeing the look in their eyes
dapperness
exploring your unconscious
a roaring fire scenting the air with
    woodsmoke
mirrored objects
park-league basketball championships
purses
rural remoteness
visiting museums
three-piece menswear suits
Turk's-head nautical knot
unread textbooks
warm cookies and cold milk
carving pumpkins
dozens of places to curl up with a book

ABOUT THE AUTHOR

Barbara Ann Kipfer received her Ph.D. in Linguistics from the University of Exeter in England. A lexicographer, she works on research projects involving dictionary use in artificial intelligence. She lives in Milford, Connecticut.